FREE VIDEO  FREE VIDEO

Essential Test Tips Video from Trivium Test Prep

Dear Customer,

Thank you for purchasing from Trivium Test Prep! We're honored to help you prepare for your TExES exam.

To show our appreciation, we're offering a **FREE *TExES Reading Specialist Essential Test Tips* Video by Trivium Test Prep.*** Our video includes 35 test preparation strategies that will make you successful on the TExES exam. All we ask is that you email us your feedback and describe your experience with our product. Amazing, awful, or just so-so: we want to hear what you have to say!

To receive your **FREE *TExES Reading Specialist Essential Test Tips* Video**, please email us at 5star@triviumtestprep.com. Include "Free 5 Star" in the subject line and the following information in your email:

1. The title of the product you purchased.
2. Your rating from 1 – 5 (with 5 being the best).
3. Your feedback about the product, including how our materials helped you meet your goals and ways in which we can improve our products.
4. Your full name and shipping address so we can send your **FREE *TExES Reading Specialist Essential Test Tips* Video**.

If you have any questions or concerns please feel free to contact us directly at 5star@triviumtestprep.com.

Thank you!

– Trivium Test Prep Team

*To get access to the free video please email us at 5star@triviumtestprep.com, and please follow the instructions above.

TExES Reading Specialist (151) Study Guide:

Exam Prep with 2 Full-Length Practice Tests for the Texas Examinations of Educator Standards [3rd Edition]

J.G. Cox

Table of Contents

Online Resources

To help you fully prepare for your TExES Reading Specialist (151) exam, Cirrus includes online resources with the purchase of this study guide.

PRACTICE TEST

In addition to the practice test included in this book, we also offer an online exam. Since many exams today are computer based, getting to practice your test-taking skills on the computer is a great way to prepare.

FLASH CARDS

A convenient supplement to this study guide, Cirrus's flash cards enable you to review important terms easily on your computer or smartphone.

CHEAT SHEETS

Review the core skills you need to master the exam with easy-to-read Cheat Sheets.

FROM STRESS TO SUCCESS

Watch "From Stress to Success," a brief but insightful YouTube video that offers the tips, tricks, and secrets experts use to score higher on the exam.

REVIEWS

Leave a review, send us helpful feedback, or sign up for Cirrus promotions—including free books!

Access these materials at:

www.cirrustestprep.com/texes-reading-online-resources

Introduction

Congratulations on choosing to take the Texas Examinations of Educator Standards (TExES) Reading Specialist (151) exam! By purchasing this book, you've taken the first step toward becoming a reading specialist.

This guide will provide you with a detailed overview of the TExES Reading Specialist (151) exam, so you will know exactly what to expect on test day. We'll take you through all the concepts covered on the exam and give you the opportunity to test your knowledge with practice questions. Even if it's been a while since you last took a major test, don't worry; we'll make sure you're more than ready!

WHAT IS THE TExES?

TExES tests are a part of teaching certification in Texas. In conjunction with completion of an educator preparation program, TExES exam scores are used to complete a state application for teacher certification. The Reading Specialist (151) exam ensures that the educator candidate has the skills and knowledge necessary to become a reading teacher in Texas public schools.

WHAT'S ON THE TExES READING SPECIALIST EXAM?

The exam consists of one hundred multiple-choice questions that measure your knowledge of literacy concepts in instruction, development, and learning. Major content areas covered on the test include language development, methods of assessment and instruction, and strategies for designing an effective curriculum. You will have to demonstrate a full knowledge and understanding of reading and language skills. See the table below for all the competencies included on the exam.

What's on the TExES Reading Specialist (151) Exam?

Domain	Domain Title	Approximate Percentage of Exam
I.	Instruction and Assessment: Components of Literacy	57%
II.	Instruction and Assessment: Resources and Procedures	14%
III.	Meeting the Needs of Individual Students	14%
IV.	Professional Knowledge and Leadership	14%
Total		***100 questions; 5 hours**

Due to rounding, percentages do not add up to 100.

Instruction and Assessment: Components of Literacy questions ask about oral language development, its role in literacy development, and instructional strategies to promote speaking and reading skills at every grade level. Important developmental concepts to know include phonological and phonemic awareness, concepts of print, word identification, fluency, comprehension, and vocabulary acquisition. You should also know appropriate methods of assessment and progress-monitoring.

The Instruction and Assessment: Resources and Procedures questions test your knowledge of assessment tools and procedures and their role in instruction planning. Be aware of the features of different types of assessments (e.g., strengths, limitations, reliability), understand how to analyze assessment data, and know how to adjust instruction to promote growth. You should also know how to choose diverse, appropriate instructional materials for different grade levels.

Meeting the Needs of Individual Students questions measure your understanding of effective, needs-based literacy instruction. You should know teaching techniques to promote development in English language learners and students with reading difficulties or disabilities. Understand how to apply your knowledge of assessment and intervention to support students with special needs.

Finally, Professional Knowledge and Leadership questions require knowledge of theories, foundations, and research concerning literacy and reading programs. You should know theories of language acquisition, environmental influence, and technology integration. These questions cover a range of professional development topics, including communication strategies, ethical standards, program implementation, and family and community involvement.

How is the TExES Reading Specialist Exam Scored?

The multiple-choice questions on the exam are equally weighted; the number of questions you answer correctly is calculated to determine your raw score. Your raw score is then converted to a scaled score. Scores are scaled on a range of 100 – 300; the minimum passing score is 240. There is no penalty for guessing on TExES tests, so try to answer every question to the best of your ability.

Your score report will be available online on the score report date associated with your testing window. You can also select to have the report emailed to you when you register. Scores will be automatically sent to TEA and SBEC, so you do not have to manually report your scores.

How is the TExES Reading Specialist Exam Administered?

The Reading Specialist exam is a computerized test administered by Pearson Education, Inc. at testing centers across the nation. Check https://home.pearson-vue.com/tea to find a testing center near you and register for your exam. The $116 testing fee is due at the time of registration.

On test day, arrive at least thirty minutes before your exam appointment and bring valid photo identification. You are allowed no personal effects in the testing area. You will review a fifteen-minute tutorial before the exam. You will then have four hours and forty-five minutes to complete the test. For details on what to expect at your testing center, refer to the Pearson Vue website.

About Cirrus Test Prep

Cirrus Test Prep study guides are designed by current and former educators and are tailored to meet your needs as an incoming educator. Our guides offer all the resources necessary to help you pass teacher certification tests across the nation.

Cirrus clouds are graceful, wispy clouds characterized by their high altitude. Just like cirrus clouds, Cirrus Test Prep's goal is to help educators "aim high" when it comes to obtaining their teacher certification and entering the classroom.

About This Guide

This guide will help you master the most important test topics and develop critical test-taking skills. We have built features into our books to prepare you for your exam and increase your scores. Along with a detailed summary of the test's format, content, and scoring, we offer an in-depth overview of the content knowledge required to pass the test. Our sidebars provide interesting information, highlight key ideas, and review content so that you can solidify your understanding of the exam's concepts. Test your knowledge with sample questions and detailed answer explanations in the text that help you think through the problems on the exam and practice questions that reflect the content and format of the TExES. We're pleased you've chosen Cirrus to be a part of your professional journey!

Phonetics and Word Analysis

PRINT AWARENESS

Print awareness involves a basic understanding of the nature of reading: we read from left to right and top to bottom, and we are reading words on a page. Very young children without solid print awareness may believe that meaning is gleaned from pictures on a page rather than words. Some younger children may understand that books convey meaning but may not quite know how. Teachers may see these children modeling reading a book upside down.

Concepts of print are the principles that must be mastered before learning to read and are key to print awareness. These principles include knowledge and identification of a word, letter, and sentence; knowledge of the many uses of print; and knowledge of the overarching structure of a book or story (title, beginning, middle, end).

Many young students have some print awareness through environmental print. **Environmental print** describes the words children see regularly in their environment, like product names, street signs, business names, and menus at restaurants. Teachers can use popular environmental print, like the names and logos of popular children's products, stores, and restaurants, to encourage pre-readers to "read" these words.

Teachers should also consider using environmental print in each of their students' home languages in the classroom. For example, a teacher might label the door in English, Spanish, Thai, and Vietnamese. This builds confidence and familiarity and reinforces the idea that these words in languages other than English also have meaning.

Teachers should have young students point to words on a page and also point to words (rather than pictures) themselves during storybook reading. This will reinforce concepts of print and help students develop print awareness. Such practice will help even very young students begin to understand that while both the pictures and words on the page contribute to the overall meaning, the part being read is the words, not the pictures.

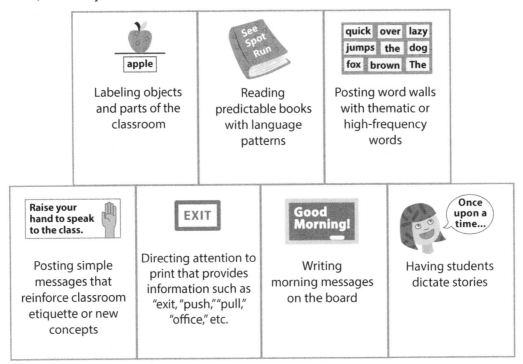

Figure 2.1. Concepts of Print Classroom Strategies

1) Which activity will help gauge a student's print awareness?

    A.   asking him to recount story events

    B.   asking him to point to a sentence

    C.   asking him to write the letter *p*

    D.   asking him what sound *p* makes

ALPHABETIC PRINCIPLE

The **alphabetic principle** presumes an understanding that words are made up of written letters that represent spoken sounds. Students should be given many opportunities to develop **letter-sound correspondence**, or the recognition and association of a letter with its sound.

There is no firm rule on the pace at which the letter sounds should be mastered. Most experts agree that high-frequency letters should be introduced first, as well as those that allow children to sound out short words quickly. It is sometimes easier for children to master simple sounds like /t/ and /s/ before more challenging or confusing sounds like /b/, /d/, and /i/.

Regardless of how teachers practice the alphabetic principle (e.g., a letter of the week or teaching the letters in succession), they should recognize that repetition is key. Students should have many opportunities to practice each letter and sound. Letter sounds should be taught explicitly and in isolation from one another first. Then students can practice saying the sounds of letters and sounding out simple words in context.

Strategies for teaching the alphabetic principle and letter-sound correspondence include:

> **DID YOU KNOW?**
>
> Most strategies for introducing students to the letter sounds draw on **high-frequency letter-sound correspondence**, whereby the most frequent and useful letter sounds are taught first. This allows students to begin reading as soon as possible without having to wait for mastery of each letter sound.

- ▶ Begin instruction with lowercase letters, as these are the primary letters used in forming words.

- ▶ Avoid overemphasis of letter *names* and focus primarily on letter *sounds*. Students do not need to know letter names to learn to read, and some may be confused by the distinction between the letter name and letter sound.

- ▶ Teach easy consonants first, followed by easy vowel sounds, introducing a new sound every two or three days.

- ▶ Teach the most common sound a letter makes first. For example, the letter *g* should be associated with the sound it makes in *grass* before associating it with the sound it makes in *rage*.

> **DID YOU KNOW?**
>
> The "alphabet song" was copyrighted in 1835 but is actually an adaptation of a Mozart melody.

- ▶ Teach letters that look similar and/or have somewhat similar sounds (e.g., /b/ and /d/ or /m/ and /n/) separately and to limit confusion.

- ▶ Model the correct pronunciation when teaching letter sounds, introducing continuous sounds (*f, l, m, n, r, s, v, w, y,* and *z*) before stop sounds (*b, c, d, g, j, k, p, q, t*). Stop sounds require control to pronounce correctly (/b/ for *b* vs. "buh" for *b*).

- ▶ Teach short vowel sounds before long vowel sounds. This is practical and allows for young readers to begin to sound out short consonant-vowel-consonant (CVC) words like *dig* and *run*.

Some activities that promote letter-sound correspondence include:

- ▶ Using letter-sound charts or letter-sound flashcards with or without picture cues with individual students, small groups, or the entire class. The "I say, you say, we say" method can be used effectively with these tools.

- ▶ Creating alphabet boards or even a computer keyboard with lowercase letters taped over the appropriate keys for instructional or assessment activities. As the teacher says a sound, students can point to the letter, type it, or move a tile over it.

▶ Having students trace or form lowercase letters with pens or pencils or in sand or shaving cream while saying the sound the letter makes. This can develop fine motor skills and reinforce letter-sound correspondence.

▶ Having students sort items into groups or piles based on initial letter sound. For example, students could place all the toy animals or pictures of animals with a /c/ sound in one group or pile.

▶ Using alphabet picture books for guided storybook reading, stopping to reinforce and practice letter sounds. *Chicka Chicka Boom Boom* by Bill Martin, Jr. and John Archambault and *Eating the Alphabet* by Lois Ehlert are popular choices.

▶ Having students draw a line around, color in, or circle all items on the page that begin with a given letter sound.

SAMPLE QUESTION

2) **Which activity is MOST appropriate for students to practice onsets and the alphabetic principle?**

    A.   having them sort toy animals into tubs based on the initial letter sound of the animal's name

    B.   asking them to help clap out the syllables in a student's name

    C.   asking them to point to a sentence on a page

    D.   having them remove a sound from a word and say the new word

PHONEMES

Phonemes are distinct units of sound and are the basic units of language. There are twenty-six letters in the alphabet, and most researchers agree that there are at least forty-four phonemes in English. Some letters represent different phonemes, and some phonemes are made up of more than one letter. There are eighteen consonant phonemes, such as /r/ and /t/, and fifteen vowel phonemes, such as /Ā/ and /oi/. There are six *r*-controlled vowels, such as /Ä/, and five digraphs, such as /ch/ and /sh/. **Phonetics** is the study and classification of phonemes or sounds and is part of explicit, systematic phonics instruction.

HELPFUL HINT

Phoneme blending involves blending sounds together, like putting them in a blender, to make a word. Phoneme segmentation involves unblending, or segmenting, each sound, like the segments of a worm.

Table 2.1. Phoneme Chart

Phoneme Consonants	Example	Phoneme Vowels	Example	Phoneme *R*-Controlled Vowels	Example
/b/	bat	/a/	lap	/ã/	hair
/d/	dog	/ā/	late	/ä/	art
/f/	fish	/e/	bet	/û/	dirt
/g/	goat	/ē/	see	/ô/	draw
/h/	hat	/i/	hit	/ēə/	rear
/j/	jump	/ī/	ride	/üə/	sure
/k/	kick	/o/	hop	**Digraphs**	
/l/	laugh	/ō/	rope	/zh/	measure
/m/	milk	/oo/	look	/ch/	chick
/n/	no	/u/	cut	/sh/	shout
/p/	pot	/ū/	cute	/th/	think
/r/	rat	/y//ü/	you	/ng/	bring
/s/	sit	/oi/	oil		
/t/	toss	/ow/	how		
/v/	vote	/ə/ (schwa)	syringe		
/w/	walk				
/y/	yak				
/z/	zoo				

Phonemic awareness refers to the knowledge of and ability to use phonemes. Because this awareness does not come naturally, students need explicit instruction to master it. It is often best to work with students in small groups because proficiency levels of phonemic awareness may vary substantially.

Phoneme blending involves putting sounds together to make words. To work on phoneme blending, teachers can say sounds and ask students what word is made: "I like /ch/ /ee/ /z/. What do I like? That's right, I like cheese." Teachers can also ask students to repeat the sounds in words during circle time or storybook reading: "The car went vvvvv-rrrrr-oooo-m!"

Phoneme segmentation is the inverse of phoneme blending and involves sounding out a word. The use of **Elkonin boxes**, or the placement of tiles or letters that correspond with each phoneme, is a helpful activity for phoneme segmentation.

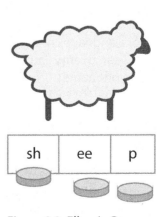

Figure 2.2. Elkonin Box

Phoneme segmentation is important both for reading and spelling a word. More advanced phonemic awareness activities include **phoneme deletion**, in which a phoneme is removed to make a new word (e.g., ramp – /p/ = ram) and **phoneme substitution**, in which one phoneme is changed to make a new word (e.g., fla/t/ to fla/p/).

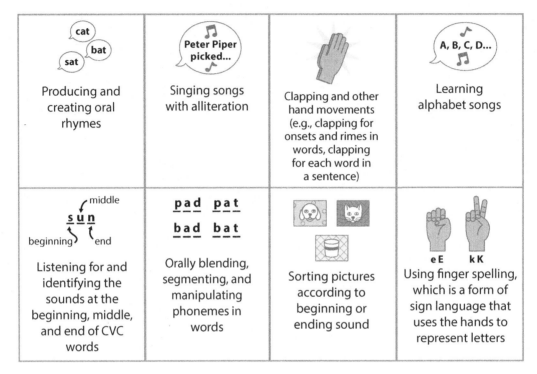

Figure 2.3. Phonological Awareness Classroom Strategies

Early childhood teachers should work on phonemic awareness with students in a variety of contexts. For example, teachers can ask students questions like "What word could I make if I took away the first letter of *cow*?" Alphabet boards, letter cards, and alphabet sorters provide fun and effective practice for phonemic awareness.

Educators should remember that students will have varying backgrounds, skill levels, English language proficiencies, and possibly speech and language delays and hearing loss. When planning inclusive activities, teachers may need to modify activities for some students. Also, phonemes are not the same in all languages. Students from non-English-speaking households will need additional practice in English phonemes.

Phonemic awareness activities usually occur in a sequence from simplest to most difficult.

1. Students usually understand the concepts of rhyme and alliteration first. These skills can be practiced by listening to and singing rhyming and alliterative songs and stories. Rhyme is often taught explicitly as

well: students think of words that rhyme, or they listen to and repeat favorite nursery rhymes or stories.

2. The recognition of syllables in words is usually the next step. Students can clap out syllables in multisyllable words or stomp feet while saying each syllable.

3. Identification of **onsets**, or the first sound of a word (*cat*), and **rime**, or the remaining letters of the word (*cat*) is next. Scrambled onset/rime word cards or word families (*tug, bug, lug, rug*) are two of the many strategies for developing recognition of these concepts.

4. Once students are familiar with onset and rime, they can usually "hear" and understand individual letter sounds within words. Students should have plenty of practice with the more basic concepts and easier skills before practicing blending (adding sounds together) or segmenting (pulling sounds apart).

SAMPLE QUESTION

3) Mark, a kindergartner, has mastered his letter sounds. He is sitting at the oral reading table with Ms. Hayes, trying to read a short sentence. He gets stuck on the word *glad* and stops reading. Which strategy might Ms. Hayes have Mark use?

    A. phoneme substitution
    B. phoneme blending
    C. phoneme segmentation
    D. thinking of a rhyming word

PHONICS

Phonics is an age-old strategy for helping students read by connecting written language to spoken language or by correlating certain sounds with certain letters or groups of letters. Essential to phonics instruction is a subset of the alphabetic principle—**letter-sound correspondence**. As discussed above, this correspondence is simply the knowledge of a phoneme associated with a given letter. Letter-sound correspondence is a foundational skill for effective phonics instruction, as most phonics strategies require students to draw from this memory bank of letter sounds.

DECODING

Phonics instruction draws on the strategy of **decoding**, or the ability to pronounce the sounds of written words orally and understand their meaning. Because of its focus on the specific sound structures of words, phonics instruction tends to involve more explicit, direct instruction. Some critics, however, believe it overemphasizes the mechanics of reading while sacrificing the enjoyment. Most classrooms today use an approach that balances inquiry-based student learning. This allows for the open exploration of high-interest literacy games and activities, with more direct instruction when necessary.

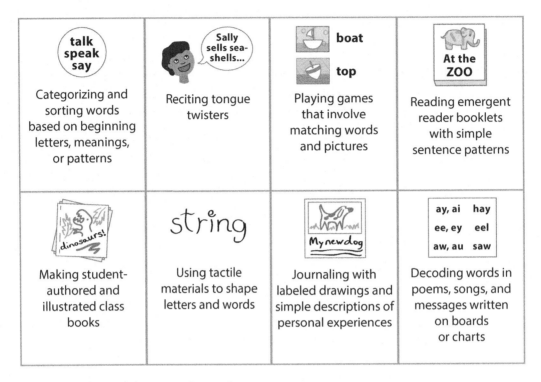

Figure 2.4. Phonics Classroom Strategies

There are a number of structures for teaching decoding, such as a teacher-directed table or a mandatory computer-based phonics drill segment. But whatever the curriculum, it is highly likely that it will contain some phonics component. This approach is proven to work for most students and is adaptable to a variety of student skill levels and special learning needs. Further, explicit, systematic phonics instruction has been proven to be one of the most effective intervention strategies for students at risk of not meeting reading fluency goals.

Many words are **decodable**, meaning they follow basic principles of phonics. Students should be able to sound these words out once they master basic structural deviations, like long vowel sounds with a word ending in –*e*, and various digraphs, where two letters make a single sound such as /th/ and /ay/.

Other words are **non-decodable**, meaning they deviate from the standard rules of phonics. Typically, these words must simply be memorized through frequent exposure.

There are many types of phonics-based instruction, each with its pros and cons and each with its advocates and opponents. Some methods may work better with particular students or particular instructional scenarios. However, the main goal of any phonics approach is to aid students in decoding words they encounter while reading.

SAMPLE QUESTION

4)   Which word is MOST likely a non-decodable word?

   A.   atlas

   B.   flute

   C.   sign

   D.   save

SYNTHETIC PHONICS

Synthetic phonics is one of the most common and effective types of phonics instruction. Students are explicitly taught to break down words into their component phonemes and sound them out. For example, a student would sound out the word *sheep* based on its three distinct phonemes, /sh/ /ee/ /p/. Synthetic phonics at its most basic level is associated with students "sounding out" unknown words as part of the decoding or meaning-making process. As students do this, they synthesize the sounds in the words to make meaning, hence the term *synthetic*.

Synthetic phonics discourages the practice of guessing at words based on initial letter sound (a common habit among many early readers) or other context or picture cues. It also teaches spelling and reading in tandem, with students sounding out or segmenting words before spelling them.

Synthetic phonics provides an explicit framework for decoding and allows students to tackle most words reliably. However, it is not without disadvantages. Some students rely on the strategy of sounding out far too long, and this can slow down reading rate and fluency and thus overall comprehension.

SAMPLE QUESTION

5)   A reading specialist is helping a kindergarten teacher implement a new synthetic phonics curriculum. The specialist observes a student working with the teaching assistant to read a short sentence: "He ran to the woods." The student becomes stuck on *woods*. Which question should the teaching assistant ask to stay aligned with synthetic phonics instruction?

   A.   "What do the pictures tell you this word might be?"

   B.   "What sound do the letters in the word make?"

   C.   "Where would someone run?"

   D.   "What other words do you know that rhyme with *wood*?"

ANALYTIC PHONICS

Analytic phonics, or implicit phonics, does not sound out each phoneme in a word. Instead, students identify an initial sound (onset) and rime and recognize word families. They do this by applying knowledge from previously learned words or phonograms (symbols representing sounds like /th/ as a representation of the sound it makes). Further, whole words are introduced first, and then they are broken into their component parts to determine similarities (e.g., *pin, pig, play, pride* all have the same initial sound).

Analytic phonics has its shortcomings. Students are encouraged to guess at words (based on initial letter sound/known structures/context clues), so accuracy may be diminished. Further, this method relies on students drawing connections themselves and is less explicit, making it challenging for some learners to pick up as quickly as synthetic phonics.

SAMPLE QUESTION

6)   **Compared with synthetic phonics, analytic phonics relies more on**

    A.   letter-sound correspondence.

    B.   phoneme blending.

    C.   knowledge of syllables.

    D.   context clues.

ANALOGY-BASED PHONICS

Analogy-based phonics, or **analogy phonics**, teaches students to decode new words based on known words. It is used as part of an analytic phonics approach and also sometimes used in isolation.

Analogy phonics often relies on student familiarity with rimes in words. For example, if a student knows the word *think*, he can use this knowledge to decode similar words like *drink*, *wink*, and *sink*. Like analytic phonics, analogy-based phonics is often criticized for encouraging guessing and relying on student recall or memorization that may not be applicable in all situations.

SAMPLE QUESTION

7)   **Which instructional aid is MOST likely to be used in an analogy-based phonics lesson?**

    A.   a letter-sound chart

    B.   a high-frequency word list

    C.   a word-families chart

    D.   a picture dictionary

EMBEDDED PHONICS

Embedded phonics, or phonics through context, is an approach to phonics instruction that relies on incidental learning. In this method, whole texts are the primary curricular resources. Explicit phonics instruction is only used when students have trouble reading a particular word. Once that word is decoded, explicit instruction ceases. This approach is often used with the "whole-language" or "whole-word" method of reading instruction, in which reading is considered a natural process that is an outgrowth of presenting children with appropriate texts.

Embedded phonics is also somewhat controversial, as it is neither systematic nor linear. Because specific phonics structures are only taught as needed, more complex structures might appear first. Other structures, often certain less-used vowel sounds, may never be explicitly taught at all.

SAMPLE QUESTION

8)   A preschool has an emergent curriculum that supports reading as a process that students must come to naturally. This preschool would most likely use embedded phonics instruction because it

   A.   relies on an unpredictable sequence.

   B.   encourages the use of hands-on learning.

   C.   works better for advanced learners.

   D.   can adapt to any text learners choose.

PHONICS THROUGH SPELLING

Phonics through spelling is a combined approach whereby reading and spelling are taught in tandem. Students are taught to spell words phonetically by sounding them out or breaking them into their individual phonemes. The practice is based on the interconnectedness between the sounds of words and their spellings. This interconnectedness is what allows for **invented spelling**, whereby children learn to spell by spelling all words phonetically. For example, they might spell *different* as *difrint*.

The advantage of this approach is that spelling is taught early and alongside reading. Many educators believe invented spelling is a natural part of the learning to write process. However, some critics argue that a total phonetic spelling approach fails to account for all the nuances of the English language. For example, a student using this approach exclusively might spell *phone* as *fone*.

SAMPLE QUESTION

9)   At some point in their academic career, students will need to deviate from the exclusive use of a phonics through spelling model because

   A.   not all words are spelled phonetically.

   B.   it is only applicable to single-syllable words.

   C.   the method does not address reading skills.

   D.   it requires students to work in collaborative groups.

Best Practices for Teaching Phonics

Research indicates that a synthetic phonics approach is the most universal method of phonics instruction that can meet the needs of the most learners. Research also indicates that **systematic phonics instruction** that occurs in a particularly designed sequence is most effective. Typical approaches to explicit, systematic synthetic phonics instruction involve:

▸ teaching individual letter sounds

▸ teaching consonant blends

▸ teaching consonant digraphs

▸ teaching irregular/challenging vowel sounds like *r*-controlled vowels

When learning more advanced phonics structures, like blends and digraphs, students will need explicit instruction, as these are multiple letters that make a single sound. This is done through a combination of modeling and then guided and independent practice. At the early childhood levels (typically preschool to grade two or three), educators use small-group instruction to work with students more closely and provide more targeted oral feedback.

DID YOU KNOW?

Research draws a correlation between a teacher's knowledge of phonics and their effectiveness in teaching it. Reading specialists are often called on to increase teacher knowledge of phonics, particularly those in early childhood classrooms.

Research also shows that phonics instruction is most effective when it also includes **connected texts**, or words in sentences and paragraphs instead of only in isolation or lists. These texts can be chosen for practice and reinforcement with a particular skill or phonics structure and can allow students to practice new skills in an authentic context.

Practicing phonics skills in connected texts is different from an embedded phonics approach. In embedded phonics, phonics is only taught explicitly when understanding of connected texts breaks down. In a systematic, explicit phonics approach, phonetic structures are first introduced in isolation through direct instruction and practice. Only after this are connected texts introduced.

Phonics word patterns are introduced in sequence based on degree of difficulty:

1. VC or CVC words with simple (continuous) initial sounds (e.g., *man, pat, fin, at, on*)

2. VCC or CVCC words with initial continuous sounds (e.g., *ask, mash*)

3. CVC words with initial stop sounds (e.g., *cab, hit*)

4. CCVC words (easier blends with continuous sounds are generally taught before more challenging blends with stop sounds) (e.g., *flat, slap, stop, crab*)

5.   CCVCC, CCCVC, or CCCVCC words with various levels of complexity are then introduced, including consonant digraphs (e.g., /sh/ /ch/) and vowel combinations (e.g., *ee, ea, oo*) as well as *r*-controlled vowels like *butter, wither, firm, germ,* and so on.

While it is unlikely to find an entire text that contains only VC or CVC words or even only decodable words, shared/paired/choral reading strategies can help make texts accessible to all learners. Further, explicit practice with high-frequency sight words alongside phonics instruction is recommended. Instant recognition of common words will make decoding connected texts easier, faster, and more enjoyable for young readers. Above all, explicit and systematic phonics instruction should be calibrated for each student but should always aim at giving students the most useful and widely needed skills first. In this way, even young children can begin reading independently early, building confidence and possibly a life-long love of reading.

SAMPLE QUESTION

10) **Which word is the most difficult for students to decode and would thus be introduced toward the end of the phonics continuum?**

   A.   dirt

   B.   stop

   C.   call

   D.   flat

SIGHT WORDS

Some words deviate from basic sound structures and cannot be sounded out. These words should be presented to students frequently so they can simply be memorized. These words must become **sight words**, or words that require no decoding because they are instantly recognized and read automatically. Some high-frequency decodable words, such as *get, and,* and *as* should also be memorized by sight to increase reading rate and fluency.

There are many lists of sight words. The most popular is the **Dolch Word List**, which contains 315 words determined to be the most frequently used in English. Early childhood teachers might post some of these high-frequency words around the classroom or encourage students to play games with sight word flashcards. Repetition will lead to mastery of these words and will help students read more quickly, fluently, and easily. Many state and national standards require students to recognize and read from a "research-based list." Some states and districts provide such lists to parents and students for practice at home.

DID YOU KNOW?

Fifty percent of all written material is made up of only one hundred of the most used words.

The balance between phonics and sight words is important. Students whose only reading strategy is sounding out may continue this even when they come across a word they know. This prevents automaticity and slows reading rate and, subsequently, comprehension. As students become more proficient readers, they should be encouraged to say words they know by sight or memory automatically without having to sound them out.

Educators should provide plenty of opportunities for students to be exposed to and read high-frequency words. Students can practice targeted activities aimed at memorization (such as paired drills or group activities) and read a variety of texts with these words. When students get stuck on high-frequency sight words, teachers can practice the "I say, you say, we say" method for immediate reinforcement.

SAMPLE QUESTION

11) **Sight words are unlike other words that early readers encounter because they**

    A.   lack typical structures that allow for sounding out.

    B.   appear infrequently and only in certain genres.

    C.   have multiple meanings based on context.

    D.   should be memorized and recognized instantly.

WORD ANALYSIS

The human brain uses three cuing systems to determine the meaning of words: semantic, syntactic, and grapho-phonetic. Together, these systems form word-analysis strategies or **word-attack strategies**, methods of decoding unfamiliar words.

SEMANTIC (MEANING) CUES

Semantic cues are cues to a word's meaning drawn from background knowledge or prior experience. Semantic cues are the brain's most efficient cuing system, since words are immediately retrieved from memory and processed. Semantic cues rely on students to activate knowledge and make reasonable predictions and inferences regarding a word's meaning. For example, in an informational text on fishing, the word *bobber* might come up. A reader familiar with fishing could activate this knowledge and recognize that "bobber" refers to a float used on a fishing line.

Semantic cuing is used in **cloze exercises**, in which words are removed from the text and students must supply them. To activate students' background knowledge to allow for maximum semantic cuing, some strategies include:

▶   Using metacognitive strategies and questions like "What type of word would make sense here?" "Does this meaning make sense in a text about _____?" "What qualities do _____ have that might lead to a clue of this word's meaning?"

> ► Having students make a list of words they predict might be used in the text after previewing its title, illustrations, and headings.

> ► Engaging students in scripted exercises in which they confirm predictions such as "The word _____ must mean _____ because I know that _____."

Semantic cues can also be based on the text itself. These are called **context clues** and do not necessarily have to be integrated with existing background knowledge. Context clues are any cues that help readers to determine word meaning in connected texts. They can be other words in the text or graphics. Students should be explicitly taught to identify other words in a sentence, paragraph, or passage that provide possible clues to the meaning of an unknown word. Students of all ages can also look to illustrations or charts to understand new words. This is particularly helpful with subject-specific vocabulary, such as terminology associated with organelles within plant cells.

Other words in the text are also essential in decoding **homographs** (words that are spelled the same but have different meanings) and **homonyms** (words that sound the same and may or may not be spelled the same but have different meanings). Educators often teach decoding homonyms and homographs explicitly. Teachers should direct students to the most commonly used homonyms to prepare them for encountering them in texts.

Context is usually the only way to determine the meaning of a homograph or multiple-meaning word. Homonyms can, at times, be decoded based on spelling alone, presuming the spelling differs, but this method should always be confirmed based on context to ensure correct decoding and understanding. Students can be asked to circle, underline, or highlight the other words in the text that "back up" their interpretations of multiple-meaning words.

SAMPLE QUESTION

12) **Which activity would MOST likely help students develop the knowledge to use semantic cues effectively?**

    A. reading books that provide information on a variety of places and cultures

    B. underlining confusing sentences and diagramming them

    C. reading a text aloud twice, once to oneself and once to a partner

    D. encouraging students to increase their reading rate to retain more information

SYNTACTIC (STRUCTURAL) CUES

Syntactic cues are based on the structure of language and are regarded as the brain's second-most efficient cuing system while reading. They include sentence structure and word order, structural clues within words, and structural analysis of the word.

A word's meaning can sometimes be clued or determined by its placement in a sentence. For example, figuring out whether a word is used as an adjective, noun, or verb can help with determining its meaning.

Structural clues within words such as affixes (prefixes and suffixes) and roots (base words with no affixes) can give clues to a word's meaning. This is sometimes referred to as **morphemic analysis**, or the analysis of morphemes (the smallest units of meaning within words).

Students should be taught common Greek and Latin roots and their meanings as well as the meanings of common prefixes and suffixes. Students can practice roots and affixes by creating words with a single prefix like *geo* (e.g., *geography, geology, geopolitical, geoscience*) or with a single suffix like *–ly* (e.g., *friendly, happily, angrily*). Students can then determine what all the words they have created have in common. Students can also be given roots and asked to create as many new words with affixes as possible. Students should then be encouraged to transfer this knowledge when they encounter new words in texts by using known roots or affixes as clues to the word's meaning.

Structural analysis of the word can also be a useful strategy. Students can decode compound words, for example, by breaking the word into its two component parts.

SAMPLE QUESTION

13) **A student is stuck on the word *Istanbul* in the sentence "My father took a trip to Istanbul." She asks, "What is an Istanbul?" How best can the teacher encourage her to use syntactic cues to aid in determining the word's meaning?**

   A.   Have her break the word into its three syllables and sound out each syllable individually.

   B.   Ask her if she has ever been to Turkey and, if so, what cities she visited.

   C.   Cover up *Istanbul* and ask her what kind of word would most likely go in the blank.

   D.   Ask her if she thinks the sentence "makes sense" as written or if the word "Istanbul" should be moved.

GRAPHOPHONIC CUES

The **graphophonic cuing** system is based on applying sound (phoneme)-symbol (grapheme or letter) knowledge while reading. It is the most basic level of decoding and tends to be the least efficient since its focus is on individual units (e.g., letters and letter patterns) instead of larger chunks of text like words and ideas.

One common word-attack strategy based on graphophonics is knowledge of syllabication and syllable patterns. Students can be taught to break words into syllables and then identify the six syllable patterns to aid in decoding.

1. **Closed syllables** are the most common. They end in a consonant that causes the vowel to make a short sound. *Stretch*, *com*-puter, *bat*, and *backing* are all words with closed syllables and short vowel sounds.

2. **Open syllables** end in vowels and make long vowel sounds. *Ri*-val, *mi*-*cro*-phone, and *to*-tal are all examples of open syllables.

3. **Vowel-consonant-e syllables**, or VCE syllables, end in –*e*, which makes the final vowel sound long. De-*code*, *rude*, *bake* all have VCE syllables.

4. **Vowel teams** are two vowels next to each other that make a single sound. Some vowel teams are digraphs (only two letters), and others consist of three or four letters. L*augh*, h*igh*, and h*ay* are examples of vowel teams.

5. **Consonant–le syllables**, or C–le syllables, are also sometimes called final syllables or final stable syllables. When these endings are joined with an open syllable, there is a long vowel sound and no double consonant. When they are joined with a closed syllable, there is a short vowel sound and double consonant. There are eleven –*le* patterns in English: –*ble* (*trouble*), –*gle* (*struggle*), –*zle* (*dazzle*), –*fle* (*trifle*), –*tle* (*battle*), –*dle* (*idle*), –*stle* (*whistle*), –*ckle* (*buckle*), –*ple* (*triple*), –*cle* (*recycle*), and –*kle* (*wrinkle*).

6. *R*-controlled syllables, also called vowel-*r* syllables, are often the most challenging. A vowel is followed by the letter *r*, which changes the way the vowel is pronounced. For example, in the word *water*, the final syllable is not pronounced as a purely short *e* because it is an *r*-controlled vowel. Research suggests that explicit instruction and practice with *r*-controlled vowel forms (*er, ir, ur, ar, or*) and frequent repetition and review is essential to help students master these types of sounds to aid in decoding.

For graphophonic cuing to be most effective, readers must have some knowledge of the word they sound out to make meaning. For example, a first-grade student might be able to apply graphophonic cuing to successfully sound out the word *telepathy* and might figure out the correct pronunciation of this word while reading orally or even silently. However, this word is not truly decoded, or taken meaning from, unless the student can apply the graphophonic cues to existing knowledge of oral language vocabulary.

For this reason, many educators employ the **language experience approach (LEA)**. (See chapter 4 for more discussion of LEA.) In this approach to literacy instruction, word recognition is thought to come not from graphophonic cues but rather from words that have been experienced and written about by the students and teacher. This and other similar approaches are called **whole-language** instruction, which does not use any cuing system smaller than the word level. This is the antithesis of phonics and graphophonic cuing. In a whole-language approach, students must use semantic and syntactic cues as the only method for decoding new words.

14) **Which word contains both an open syllable and an *r*-controlled vowel?**

    A.   rigorous

    B.   related

    C.   hunger

    D.   miser

Vocabulary Development

Vocabulary can and should also be broadened through a variety of strategies. Vocabulary knowledge makes reading more expedient and fluent, as readers can simply decode a word semantically without having to resort to other cuing systems. Vocabulary is developed through one of two ways. **Incidental vocabulary learning** occurs while reading, either independently or through teacher-guided oral reading activities. **Intentional vocabulary teaching** requires educators to more explicitly direct vocabulary acquisition. There are two methodologies to intentional vocabulary teaching: specific word instruction and word-learning strategies.

Specific Word Instruction

Specific word instruction involves activities that help learners acquire knowledge of new words. Some strategies for specific word instruction are:

    Predict-o-gram: Students are given a list of words. They then predict how these words will be used in a text. This strategy can be used effectively for both fiction

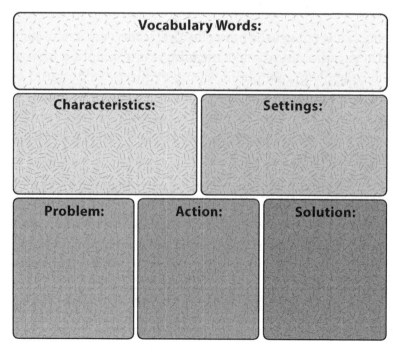

Figure 2.5. Predict-o-gram

and nonfiction texts, though it is most often used with fiction, as it can easily be integrated into existing knowledge about plot structure.

Semantic impressions: Students are given a list of words in the order they appear in the text. The definition of each word is then briefly discussed by the teacher. Students write their own story using the words in the same order, using each word only once. They then read the text and compare their finished story to the original.

Semantic feature analysis, also called a semantic grid, is a graphic organizer that helps students think deeply about the features or properties of each vocabulary word.

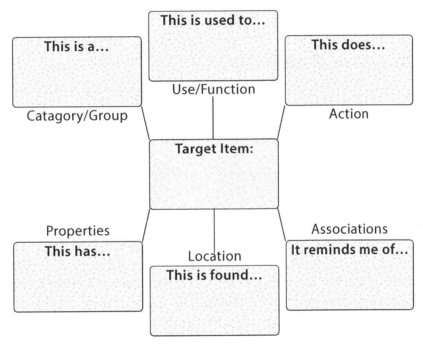

Figure 2.6. Semantic Feature Analysis

List-group-label is a semantic mapping strategy in which students brainstorm all the words they can think of that relate to a particular topic. They then divide the list of words into subcategories based on common features. For example, words like *dorsal fin*, *gills*, and *teeth* might be placed in the category of "parts of a fish's body."

Possible sentences: Students are given a list of vocabulary words from the text they will read. They then write a "possible" sentence for each word, illustrating the word's possible meaning. After reading the text, students return to their possible sentences to see if they were accurate or if the sentences need to be changed based on the word's actual meaning as revealed in the text.

OPIN (short for *Opinion*) is similar to a cloze exercise in which students fill in the blank with a word they think belongs in a sentence. Then, students break into groups to "defend" their word choice to other members of the group. This strategy helps reinforce other skills as students use context clues and background knowledge to justify their answers.

15) **A reading specialist is planning a professional development event on ways to incorporate creative writing into daily reading instruction. Which vocabulary-building activity is he MOST likely to discuss?**

A.   list-group-label

B.   OPIN

C.   semantic impressions

D.   semantic grids

WORD-LEARNING STRATEGIES

In addition to specific word instruction, educators must use various strategies to help students learn new words they encounter.

Using a dictionary, glossary, and thesaurus: In today's digital age, there are many opportunities for students to practice using resources to find the meaning of unfamiliar words. **Dictionary** skills are typically introduced around third grade and require explicit instruction on how to locate the word's pronunciation, etymology, parts of speech, and definition. Students should be taught to use both print and digital dictionaries. Many state standards require this knowledge, which is tested on annual accountability tests.

There are, of course, some limitations to dictionaries. They tend to focus only on a word's **denotation**, or literal meaning, when each word also has a **connotation**, or subtle or implied meaning. Readers must be taught to use context clues to determine connotation.

Thesauruses should also be used in reading and English classrooms. Students can learn when a thesaurus is the resource of choice and when a dictionary is more appropriate. Use of the **glossary** should also be explicitly taught, and students should be encouraged to apply this skill across the content areas, as many of their texts for other courses will likely contain glossaries.

Morphemic analysis breaks apart the morphemes within words and analyzes them for meaning. Morphemic analysis should be taught explicitly as a unit of study and referred to frequently throughout reading instruction. Students should be asked to think about unfamiliar words in the context of their morphemes to help with decoding: "Are there roots or affixes I already know from other words?" "What does the word ending tell me?" "Is it a clue to the part of speech or singularity or plurality?"

Contextual analysis applies context clues to infer the meaning of unknown words. As mentioned above, contextual analysis can involve semantic or syntactic cues that aid in meaning. Some educators find strategies in annotating the text (see chapter 3) very helpful in teaching context clues. For example, students can put a question mark next to unknown words and then circle other words in the text that might provide clues to the word's meaning.

English language learners will need additional vocabulary-building practice, as vocabulary knowledge is one of the key foundations that leads to reading success for students with little background in English vocabulary. Specific strategies include picture dictionaries, teaching cognates, and teaching idioms, in addition to explicit and direct vocabulary instruction.

SAMPLE QUESTION

16) Which vocabulary term would MOST likely be included in a lesson on dictionary skills in a fourth-grade classroom?

A. noun

B. phonogram

C. context

D. origin

REVIEW

Read the question, and then choose the most correct answer.

1

One disadvantage of an analytic phonics approach is that it

A.   may diminish decoding accuracy.

B.   does not allow students to transfer knowledge.

C.   does not build on instruction in onset and rime.

D.   may require intensive one-on-one instruction.

2

Research shows the MOST effective phonics approach for the largest number of learners to be which of the following?

A.   analogy-based phonics

B.   embedded phonics

C.   analytic phonics

D.   synthetic phonics

3

Which of the following is an advantage of a phonics through spelling approach?

A.   Students read a variety of connected texts.

B.   Students spell words only at their independent reading level.

C.   Handwriting instruction is embedded within phonics and spelling instruction.

D.   Spelling instruction is embedded within reading instruction and is begun early.

4

The main goal of providing students with an arsenal of word attack strategies is to

A.   increase oral fluency and prosody.

B.   develop automaticity through sight word awareness.

C.   improve decoding of unfamiliar words.

D.   decrease reliance on context clues.

5

A teacher encourages students to activate background knowledge as they read and come across unknown words. Which of the following cuing strategies is the teacher using?

A.   semantic cuing

B.   syntactic cuing

C.   structural cuing

D.   graphophonic cuing

6

An elementary school teacher might teach a lesson on open syllables in order to do which of the following?

A.   provide students with vocabulary-building practice

B.   encourage students to read texts at their frustrational reading level

C.   help students determine if a vowel makes a long or short sound

D.   help students develop a Standard English dialect

7

The word "bread" contains a vowel team because it has

A.   two vowels in sequence.

B.   both a long and a short vowel sound.

C.   a consonant blend in the onset.

D.   two vowels that make one sound.

8

A student who reads the word "cute" as /cut/ might benefit from instruction in which of the following?

A.   closed syllables

B.   open syllables

C.   graphophonic cuing

D.   syntactic cuing

9

Which of the following is the BEST definition of the term "morpheme"?

A.   an individual sound within a word

B.   the smallest unit of meaning within a word

C.   an established orthographic pattern of a word

D.   a pattern by which a word is articulated

10

A teacher hears a student read the following sentence: *I blow bubbles with my brother.*

The student sounds out the words "blow" and "brother" as:

/b/ /l/ /ow/ and /b/ /r/ /o/ /th/ /er/

Which of the following skills should the teacher emphasize?

A.   phoneme deletion

B.   syllabication

C.   *r*-controlled vowels

D.   consonant blends

ANSWER KEY

SAMPLE QUESTIONS

1) A. Incorrect. Asking a student to recount story events is a recall and comprehension gauging question. It is not related to print awareness.

    B. Correct. Knowing the difference between a letter, a word, and a sentence is an important component of print awareness.

    C. Incorrect. Having a student write a letter is a motor skills and alphabet knowledge exercise.

    D. Incorrect. Asking a student what sound a letter makes is a letter-sound correspondence question.

2) **A. Correct.** This sorting exercise helps students identify both letter sounds and the initial sounds of words.

    B. Incorrect. Clapping out syllables would help students master overall phonological awareness but not the alphabetic principle or onsets.

    C. Incorrect. Having students point to a sentence on a page addresses concepts of print.

    D. Incorrect. Removing a sound from a word and saying the new word is phoneme deletion, a strategy to work on phonemic awareness, not onsets and the alphabetic principle.

3) A. Incorrect. Phoneme substitution would make a new word, not the word the student is struggling to read.

    B. Incorrect. In phoneme blending, the student is given the sounds and must then say the word.

    C. Correct. Phoneme segmentation is the strategy of "sounding out." Mark could be encouraged to sound out both phonemes "gl-ad."

    D. Incorrect. Coming up with a rhyming word will help promote phonological awareness but will not help Mark read the word.

4) A. Incorrect. The word *atlas* is easily decodable and does not even contain any blends or long vowel sounds.

    B. Incorrect. The word *flute* contains both a blend and a long vowel sound but is easily decodable once those types of phonics structures are mastered.

    C. Correct. The word *sign* deviates from standard phonics structures. The fact that the /g/ is not pronounced and the /i/ is a long vowel sound must simply be memorized.

    D. Incorrect. The word *save* follows a long vowel, silent –e structure and is decodable once this concept has been introduced.

5) A. Incorrect. Asking about the pictures would encourage guessing at the word based on the picture cues, not by sounding out.

B.   **Correct.** Asking about the sounds the letters make will help the student decode the word *woods* by sounding it out.

C.   Incorrect. This question is a syntactic clue and would also encourage guessing, not sounding out.

D.   Incorrect. Asking about other words could be used as a follow-up question after the word is decoded, but thinking of rhyming words is not part of synthetic phonics instruction.

6) A.   Incorrect. This describes synthetic phonics.

B.   Incorrect. This also describes synthetic phonics.

C.   Incorrect. Syllabication is used more in synthetic phonics.

D.   **Correct.** Analytic phonics encourages readers to guess at words by using context without sounding out each phoneme.

7) A.   Incorrect. A letter-sound chart is more likely to be used in synthetic phonics instruction.

B.   Incorrect. A high-frequency word list is used as an adjunct in many types of phonics instruction but is not specific to analogy-based phonics.

C.   **Correct.** In an analogy-based phonics lesson, students use knowledge of word families to aid in decoding. For example, a student who knows *lug, bug,* and *tug* can build on this knowledge to decode *shrug*.

D.   Incorrect. A picture dictionary is likely to be used with English language learners, not in an analogy-based phonics lesson.

8) A.   Incorrect. Embedded phonics does rely on an unpredictable sequence, but this alone is not a good reason to use this method.

B.   Incorrect. Embedded phonics is not any more or less hands-on than other phonics approaches.

C.   Incorrect. Embedded phonics might work better for advanced learners, but there is no indication that the preschool is for advanced students.

D.   **Correct.** In an emergent curriculum, students determine the course of the curriculum and would likely choose their own reading materials. This means that whatever utilitarian phonics skills they need to decode a text could be taught as needed with an embedded phonics approach.

9) A.   **Correct.** One of the disadvantages of this method is that more complex words cannot be spelled phonetically.

B.   Incorrect. Phonics through spelling can be used with any word that has a phonetic spelling (*Nintendo*, for example).

C.   Incorrect. The idea of phonics through spelling is that reading and writing are interconnected processes and that any word that can be written can also be read.

D.   Incorrect. This method does not require students to work in collaborative groups.

10) **A.   Correct.** The word *dirt* contains an *r*-controlled vowel, which is one of the most challenging structures.

B.   Incorrect. The word *stop* is merely a consonant blend and a short vowel sound, which is easier for most students than an *r*-controlled vowel.

C.   Incorrect. *Call* is a simple CVCC word with a short vowel sound that would likely be introduced early.

D.   Incorrect. The word *flat* is also only a consonant blend with a short vowel sound that is generally easier than an *r*-controlled vowel.

11) A.   Incorrect. Many sight words *can* be sounded out; it is just easier or preferable to recognize them instantly.

B.   Incorrect. Sight words appear in all types of texts.

C.   Incorrect. Only some sight words have multiple meanings. Most of them do not.

D.   Correct. Sight words should be memorized for instant recognition to aid in automaticity.

12) **A.   Correct.** Reading a broad array of books builds background knowledge, which can then be applied and retrieved.

B.   Incorrect. Diagramming sentences might provide syntactic cues, but it is more an exercise in grammar.

C.   Incorrect. Multiple readings of a text might help students develop fluency but will not necessarily help them use semantic cues.

D.   Incorrect. An increased reading rate will not necessarily increase comprehension; it depends on how balanced the increased rate is in terms of accuracy. However, this is not related to semantic cues.

13) A.   Incorrect. Breaking up the word into syllables is related to phonetic decoding, not to syntax.

B.   Incorrect. Asking about the country of Turkey is more semantic cuing based on background knowledge.

C.   Correct. This exercise helps the student to use the sentence's structure to determine that the word *Istanbul* must be a place.

D.   Incorrect. This exercise is syntactic analysis, but it does not directly help the student determine the meaning of the word.

14) A.   Incorrect. *Rigorous* has neither an open syllable nor an *r*-controlled vowel.

B.   Incorrect. *Related* has an open syllable but not an *r*-controlled vowel.

C.   Incorrect. *Hunger* has an *r*-controlled vowel but not an open syllable.

D. **Correct.** *Miser* contains both an open syllable and an *r*-controlled vowel: *Mi* (open syllable) *ser* (*r*-controlled vowel).

15) A. Incorrect. List-group-label does not promote creative writing but rather categorization of words.

B. Incorrect. OPIN helps students develop oral language skills but not creative writing skills.

C. **Correct.** In semantic impressions, students write a story with the words from the text.

D. Incorrect. Semantic grids help students think more deeply about certain vocabulary words but do not necessarily promote creative writing.

16) A. Incorrect. A fourth-grade student should already know the word *noun*, though the abbreviation *n.* might be taught.

B. Incorrect. The word *phonogram* is unrelated to dictionary skills.

C. Incorrect. Use of context clues should already have been taught by fourth grade, so students would be familiar with the word. Also, *context* is not a term directly related to dictionary use.

D. **Correct.** Most dictionaries include an entry for the word *origin* that students should be taught to use.

REVIEW

1) **A.** **Correct.** When students are encouraged to guess at words, this can lead to inaccurate decoding.

    B. Incorrect. An analytic phonics approach does allow students to transfer knowledge of previously learned sounds and structures to new words.

    C. Incorrect. An analytic phonics approach does build on instruction in onset and rime.

    D. Incorrect. Any phonics approach will involve some one-on-one instructional time, but explicit or synthetic phonics instruction typically involves the most. Analytic phonics is often based on implicit learning.

2) **D.** **Correct.** Synthetic phonics, whereby students synthesize sounds in words, is highly effective for the largest number of students.

3) A. Incorrect. Reading connected texts is an advantage of an embedded phonics approach.

    B. Incorrect. Students likely will spell words at a variety of degrees of difficulty using this approach.

    C. Incorrect. Handwriting instruction is not necessarily part of phonics through spelling.

    D. **Correct.** Students see the interconnectedness between spelling and reading and begin spelling very early.

4) A. Incorrect. Word attack strategies may increase oral fluency and prosody since they increase decoding skills. However, this is not the main goal.

    B. Incorrect. Word attack strategies usually involve cuing systems beyond just memorized sight words.

    C. **Correct.** The main purpose of helping students develop a variety of word attack strategies is to improve decoding of unfamiliar words.

    D. Incorrect. Using context clues is an excellent word attack strategy.

5) **A.** **Correct.** Semantic cuing systems allow students to make meaning of unknown words based on other knowledge such as context clues or activating background knowledge.

    B. Incorrect. Syntactic cuing is based on the structure of the word.

    C. Incorrect. Structural cuing is another term for syntactic cuing.

    D. Incorrect. Graphophonic cuing is a system of applying phonemic knowledge as one reads to decode.

6) A. Incorrect. Open and closed syllables aid in decoding, not vocabulary development.

B.   Incorrect. Students should not be encouraged to read texts at their frustrational reading level.

C.   Correct. Open syllables make long vowel sounds, and closed syllables make short vowel sounds.

D.   Incorrect. Open and closed syllable instruction is associated with decoding, not oral language production.

7)   A.   Incorrect. Some words have two vowels in sequence, but they make two distinct sounds. Vowel teams contain two vowels in sequence that make a single sound.

B.   Incorrect. There is only one vowel sound in "bread."

C.   Incorrect. A consonant blend at the onset of a word does not mean there will be a vowel team in the word.

D.   Correct. The definition of a vowel team is two vowels that make one sound.

8)   A.   Incorrect. "Cute" has only one syllable.

B.   Incorrect. "Cute" has only one syllable.

C.   Correct. If the student used graphophonic cuing to understand the pattern of vowel + consonant + *e* = long vowel, that would help the student decode this word.

D.   Incorrect. Syntactic cuing is based on the structure of the word or how it is used in a sentence.

9)   A.   Incorrect. An individual sound within a word is a phoneme.

B.   Correct. A morpheme is the smallest unit of meaning in a word.

C.   Incorrect. Orthography is more about structure/spelling, and morphemes are related to units of meaning.

D.   Incorrect. Morphemes are units of meaning; they are not related to how words are articulated.

10)   A.   Incorrect. Instruction in phoneme deletion can help with overall phonemic awareness, but it is not directly related to the way the student sounded out each letter individually instead of each sound.

B.   Incorrect. "Blow" has only one syllable, so instruction in syllabication would not be helpful.

C.   Incorrect. The issue is not mispronunciation or misidentification of vowel sounds, so instruction in r-controlled vowels would not be helpful.

D.   Correct. /bl/ and /br/ are consonant blends and should be pronounced as single sounds.

Reading Fluency and Comprehension

FLUENCY

Fluency refers to the rate, accuracy, and expression of a text when read. It is an important measure of a student's reading development because it affects comprehension and enjoyment of reading. **Reading rate** is a measure of speed, generally calculated in words per minute. **Accuracy**, or the correct decoding of words, is entwined with rate when measuring fluency, since reading quickly but incorrectly is not desirable.

Fluency is not limited to oral reading, although it is virtually impossible to assess it during silent reading. Most educators rely on frequent oral reading assessments to determine student progress. (See chapter 5, "Assessment and Diagnostic Teaching," for more discussion on how to assess reading fluency.)

Prosody, or the overall liveliness and expressiveness of reading, is another skill to nurture in students. Prosody includes appropriate pauses and changes in pitch and intonation based on punctuation and the overall meaning of the piece. Teachers should model prosody as they read stories, passages, and even directions aloud. They should also give students plenty of opportunities for oral reading practice.

> **DID YOU KNOW?**
>
> All students will develop fluency at a different rate. Accurate assessments of fluency are developmentally appropriate and are NOT presented as high-stakes testing situations.

Another component of fluency is automaticity. **Automaticity** is the ability to easily recognize words automatically. Students who read with automaticity do not need to sound out or break down each word. They are able to read rapidly with little effort at the most basic levels of decoding. Automaticity only comes with automatic word recognition, which must be taught along with explicit phonics instruction aimed at decoding unfamiliar words.

Fluency is linked with comprehension because students who struggle to read and decode individual words will have difficulty comprehending entire sentences and paragraphs. Also, students who read at a slow rate may have trouble recalling what they have read. It is worth taking the time to listen to students read aloud as much as possible.

There are many strategies for developing oral fluency in the classroom.

▶ **Timed repeated readings** are repeated readings of familiar texts at the independent reading level. Students read a text three or four times as the teacher records time and words correct per minute (WCPM).

▶ **Shared reading** occurs when teachers model oral fluency and students share the experience. They can do this by turning the pages and showing illustrations while asking students basic comprehension questions and to make predictions or inferences. Shared reading is also referred to as shared storybook reading, particularly in the early childhood setting.

▶ **Choral reading** involves the entire class or group reading a text aloud in unison. First, the teacher models the passage with appropriate rate and prosody. Students then read aloud, using their finger to follow the text. Choral reading helps develop confidence, prosody, and automaticity and can assist in sight word acquisition.

▶ In **paired reading** pairs of students take turns reading to each other. Often more fluent readers are paired with readers still developing fluency.

▶ **Reader's theater** uses drama or other texts with different roles or parts for students to read aloud with appropriate dramatic expression.

▶ **Audio-assisted reading** is a common strategy for students who lack fluency. Students follow along in a written text as they listen to a fluent reader read it aloud, usually on an audiobook.

▶ **Neurological impress** is a twist on choral reading whereby teacher and student read the same text at the same time while both following along with their fingers. This method is thought to "etch" the words in students' minds and help them develop automatic word recognition.

SAMPLE QUESTION

1) **A second-grade teacher notices that his students often read in monotone during oral reading practice. Which strategy can the reading specialist recommend to help students develop prosody?**

    A.   setting aside timed oral reading each day

    B.   modeling an appropriate reading rate

    C.   using ability grouping for silent reading

    D.   having students act out a play from a script

READING COMPREHENSION STRATEGIES

FOUNDATIONS

Reading comprehension does not happen in a vacuum. It exists in combination with other processes. Reading comprehension is built on three foundations:

▶ **Linguistic foundations** describe the ways written and oral language are involved in the reading process. Students with a strong background in the basics of the English language will generally have much stronger comprehension of texts.

▶ **Sociological or cultural foundations** describe the ways readers approach the reading task based on their unique environment and cultural constructs. Readers come from different backgrounds that will guide their approach. Teachers should respect and facilitate this with a variety of approaches.

▶ **Psychological or cognitive foundations** describe how the brain works during the reading process. Examples include how the eye and brain work together to make meaning of texts, and how the brain processes and stores such information for recall.

These processes inform how each student will experience the process of learning to read and how the process must be differentiated for all readers. For example, a student with few oral language skills will find reading more challenging than a student with many oral language skills. A student from an environment that does not value reading as a worthwhile leisure activity may not be interested in learning to read at first. A student with a cognitive disability such as Down syndrome may need extra help to recall what has been read.

Reading is also a very connected process. **Transactional reading** or transactional reader-response theory was first developed by Louise Rosenblatt. This theory states that text on a page is nothing until it becomes a performance of meaning in the reader's mind. This theory relies on an individual's interpretation of a text to give it meaning.

> **QUICK REVIEW**
>
> What are some assessment tools or techniques that could help a teacher determine a child's current linguistic foundation?

Teachers should understand the transactional nature of reading a text and provide students with ongoing, systematic instruction in a variety of reading strategies to equip their students to become active readers. **Active readers** get involved with a text by making connections between their **background knowledge** (what they already know) and what they are learning or experiencing. They seek meaning in what they read in order to solve a problem, to gain new knowledge, or to answer a question about something that matters to them. Teachers can instill active reading skills in their students throughout the reading process—before, during, and after reading.

2)   **Which strategy can be employed to help students activate background knowledge before they read a text?**

    A.   reciprocal teaching

    B.   the Frayer Model

    C.   OPIN

    D.   K-W-L Chart

STRATEGIES FOR COMPREHENSION

Teachers should model and practice pre-reading strategies throughout reading instruction, before beginning each new text. One such strategy is **previewing** a text, which involves identifying the author, the genre, and the general subject matter before reading the text. It also includes reading headings and chapter titles, examining related graphics, researching the author and the context of the work (as age-appropriate), and anticipating the author's purpose.

Previewing general information about a text allows an active reader to use another pre-reading strategy: **setting a purpose**. A teacher might introduce each new text with a guiding question (What does it mean to be evil?) or a hypothetical situation that pushes students to examine their own value systems (Imagine you are a business owner. Should you be required to hire a certain number of individuals with disabilities?).

After facilitating a discussion about the question or scenario, the teacher directs students to a particular text to examine how the author or characters would respond. By setting a purpose for students' reading, the teacher is guiding them toward the thematic elements of the text. Students are encouraged to draw connections between the author's choices and the overall message.

Before reading a new text, and throughout the reading process, students should also make predictions about what they are reading. A **prediction** is a kind of inference that is concerned with what is going to happen next in a text. Making predictions is a valuable active reading skill because it requires readers to be constantly aware of what is going on in the text and what the author may be foreshadowing through their specific choices.

In addition to making predictions as they read, students should be thinking about their own level of understanding, also known as metacognition. In **metacognition**, readers think about what they are thinking as they read. This helps to immediately identify any confusion or uncertainty. Readers who are aware of their thought processes are able to recognize and react when understanding breaks down.

Part of metacognition in reading is using **fix-up** or **fix-it-up strategies**. Active readers apply these strategies when they realize they do not understand what they are reading. Common fix-up strategies include:

- ▶ slowing down the reading pace
- ▶ rereading the section in question
- ▶ reading beyond the text in question to see if confusion is cleared up
- ▶ using text clues
- ▶ illustrations/graphic elements
- ▶ text features (bold words, italics, headings, relevant punctuation)
- ▶ figuring out the meaning of unfamiliar words
  - ▷ using context clues/words around the confusing word
  - ▷ using picture clues
  - ▷ using a resource to look up the word or words
- ▶ asking a peer or teacher for assistance

Annotating is another important strategy that takes place during reading. To provide effective instruction in annotation and ensure that students are mastering the skill, teachers should set clear guidelines and expectations. For example, a teacher might ask students to make VISA annotations. **VISA annotations** involve noting interesting or new **v**ocabulary, important **i**nferences, helpful **s**ummaries, and brief **a**nalyses.

Other annotating strategies include:

- ▶ underlining or highlighting main ideas or important information
- ▶ circling key words
- ▶ placing question marks next to confusing parts that might need further attention
- ▶ writing notes in the margins

Questioning is another way students can develop overall comprehension of a text. The reader asks and then answers questions about what has been read. Questioning occurs on three levels.

1. **Literal questions** are based on explicit information in the text and require only recall or identification of information from the text.

    "On what day did Mark send the letter?"

2. **Inferential questions** are based on implicit information in the text. These questions require students to make an inference or prediction or to draw a conclusion.

    "What will Mark most likely do after he sends the letter?"

3. **Evaluative questions** require readers to form an opinion on the text. Students will need to understand explicit information and then consider how they feel about this information.

    "What do I think about Mark's action in sending the letter?"

Summarization is a reading strategy to help readers determine what is important in the text. Using their own words, readers reduce a text or section of text to its main points or central ideas. Students do this by skipping insignificant details and redundancies and looking for general ideas rather than specific facts and examples.

Student-produced summaries can provide valuable insight into comprehension levels. Students who actively comprehend what they read will produce accurate summaries. Those who struggle with comprehension may leave out important ideas or leave in unnecessary information. Summaries should be used throughout the study of a text and in the post-reading process to gauge how well students understood the basic ideas of the work.

Teachers can encourage students to engage with the text using other post-reading strategies, such as having them **reflect** on their experience of the text and write formal or informal responses. They may also ask students to return to the guiding question, synthesizing their understanding of the text and its thematic and cultural relevance. Students can also **make connections** between the text, themselves (text-to-self), the world (text-to-world), and other literature (text-to-text).

Students should be encouraged to use **text evidence** in any post-reading exercise, even in their personal responses. It is important that their conclusions and understandings are fully informed and truly based in the text itself. In fact, as readers consider textual evidence, they may change or expand their original interpretations. Examination of textual evidence is an essential part of the process of constructing meaning.

SAMPLE QUESTION

3)   A reading specialist is working with a small group of fourth-grade students receiving Tier 2 interventions aimed at improving comprehension. Which technique is the reading specialist MOST likely to recommend to students?

   A.   using graphophonic cues

   B.   applying fix-up strategies

   C.   coarticulation of phonemes

   D.   moving tiles in Elkonin boxes

INDEPENDENT READING STRATEGIES

While teachers and reading specialists will be explicitly teaching various comprehension strategies, it is vital that students **read independently** without scaffolding. Research shows that students who read independently have better educational outcomes in almost every area. When students read independently, they must apply all the active reading strategies they learn in the classroom in an authentic context.

Unfortunately, research also shows that many children neither engage in nor enjoy independent reading. These students will need extra encouragement from educators to read independently. Following are some strategies to promote independent reading in various settings and grade levels.

▶ **Daily reading logs** can be used in or outside of school. Many elementary and middle schools require at least fifteen minutes per day.

▶ Formal independent reading programs like **Sustained Silent Reading (SSR)** or **Drop Everything and Read (DEAR)** can be used on a school or classroom level.

▶ Classrooms can be stocked with **lending libraries** full of books that teachers enthusiastically recommend to students.

▶ Educators can recommend books based on student interests. Resources like annotated bibliographies organized by topic and Lexile/grade level as well as digital applications that match books to interests and reading level can be very helpful.

▶ Frequent use of the school library can promote student desire for independent reading. Educators can help scaffold book selection by guiding students to relevant material.

▶ **Book clubs** and **book discussion groups** can be particularly effective, especially among older students. The accountability factor of reading the book before the meeting can be a strong motivation to read independently.

▶ Independent reading can be promoted across the school's digital community. School social media sites might encourage a #nowreading hashtag or encourage students and parents to post book recommendations. School or teacher websites can include curated booklists or summer reading lists.

SAMPLE QUESTION

4) After conducting a survey, a reading specialist discovers that only 12 percent of students are reading independently at home outside of reading for homework assignments. How might the reading specialist MOST effectively address this situation?

A. encourage teachers to assign more self-directed reading comprehension exercises

B. conduct additional research to find out why students do not enjoy reading for pleasure

C. start a program that rewards students for completing independent reading logs each week

D. send home literature with students that describes current research in the importance of independent reading

TEXT COMPLEXITY

Finding a balance between the complexity of a text and a student's level of literacy development can be challenging. Many programs recognize this challenge and structure goal-setting and student assessments in a growth-over-time approach. Regardless of the milestones laid out by a school or district, teachers should encourage students to tackle ever-more sophisticated texts as they develop the foundational skills they need to take on new challenges. However, this does not mean pushing students beyond what they can decode. Giving students developmentally inappropriate texts may lead to a lack of confidence and less interest in and enthusiasm for reading.

Many factors contribute to a text's complexity. In determining appropriateness, educators should evaluate texts based on both qualitative and quantitative measures and their match to the reader. **Quantitative measurements** include anything for which a number can be calculated, such as word frequency, length of words and sentence length, average syllables per word, and so on.

Quantitative measurements can calculate a range or score that is assigned to a text. For example, **MetaMetrics** is a company that uses word frequency and sentence length in an equation to yield a score. Scores are assigned to both readers and texts. Those assigned to readers typically come from standardized tests and measure current level of reading ability; these are called **reader measures**.

DID YOU KNOW?

MetaMetrics also offers Lexile measures for Spanish-language texts.

MetaMetrics also assigns **Lexile ranges** to texts called Lexile text measures or Lexile measures. While these ranges do not have a direct correlation to grade level, educators can use charts created by MetaMetrics and/or a state or district to find the typical Lexile ranges for a given grade. The company states that the best results come from a reader measure that falls within a "sweet spot" range per the text measure.

HELPFUL HINT

Lexile measures are only effective for texts that follow a typical structure. They are not effective for poetry and drama—these types of texts must be measured for complexity using other methods.

Most of what students read (textbooks, passages in software programs, published children's literature) has already been assigned a Lexile text measure. Teachers can raise students' chances of enjoyment and comprehension of texts by ensuring that the Lexile text measure fits within the average range for the grade level and, more importantly, for each student's reader measure.

Table 3.1. Lexile Reader and Text Measures for Grades 1 – 12

Grade	Reader Measures, Midyear: 25th to 75th Percentile*	Text Measures**
1	BR120L to 295L	190L to 530L
2	170L to 545L	420L to 650L
3	415L to 760L	520L to 820L
4	635L to 950L	740L to 940L
5	770L to 1080L	830L to 1010L
6	855L to 1165L	925L to 1070L
7	925L to 1235L	970L to 1120L
8	985L to 1295L	1010L to 1185L
9	1040L to 1350L	1050L to 1260L
10	1085L to 1400L	1080L to 1335L
11 and 12	1130L to 1440L	1185L to 1385L

* This is the typical range of reading ability for students in each grade. These measures are designed to help compare a student's level to a typical range; they are not intended to be standards.

** These text measures have been revised from previous measures to better align with the Common Core State Standards for English Language Arts to ensure that students will meet these standards and be "college and career ready" by the end of high school.

Other metrics for measuring the readability of a text include scales such as the **Flesch–Kincaid Grade Level**, the **Gunning fog index**, and the **SMOG index**. A specific program or school may also use another proprietary tool such as Accelerated Reader Bookfinder or Scholastic Book Levels.

Beyond the quantitative measures determined by Lexile and others are qualitative measures, such as:

▶ the layout of the text: illustrations, text size

▶ the overall text structure: simple narrative chronology, more advanced argumentative essay

▶ sentence structure: prevalence of simple or more complex sentences

▶ levels of meaning: whether ideas are explicitly or implicitly communicated

▶ knowledge demand: the cultural knowledge or other ideas that the reader must already know

The overall language and vocabulary of the text also generally fall under qualitative measures, although some quantitative scales measure the frequency of vocabulary that students of a particular age or grade are not likely to be familiar with.

SAMPLE QUESTION

5) **What is the BEST way to differentiate instruction in a first-grade reading classroom?**

A.   practice oral reading with only the more advanced students so those struggling will not feel uncomfortable

B.   use only texts on the lower end of the first-grade Lexile range to ensure they are accessible to all students

C.   set aside time for students to engage in silent reading with a teacher-selected book based on student ability and interests

D.   conduct additional phonics drills with students who need help with decoding while the other students do a science experiment

SELECTING TEXTS

No single measure of any text can determine appropriateness for all students. For example, Lexile ranges do not account for mature subject matter. Teachers also need to differentiate literacy instruction in the classroom. While literacy development requires reading more and more complex texts, students do not benefit from inaccessible reading material. In fact, this can lead to bad habits such as guessing at or skipping unfamiliar words instead of trying to decode and asking for help before figuring out an unfamiliar word or text.

Whatever strategy a program uses to address individualization of reading instruction (pull-out, push-in, small groups, intervention teacher, etc.), teachers must find a just-right level of text complexity where students are challenged but not frustrated. Text complexity is highly individualized and should be matched to the instructional task:

▶   Texts at the **independent reading level** (for independent reading) require students to read with 99 percent accuracy and 90 percent comprehension. These are generally texts just "below" a student's reading level.

▶   **Instructional reading level** texts are used for teacher-guided instruction and are typically read at 85 percent accuracy with over 75 percent comprehension. These texts are usually "at" the student's reading level.

▶   **Frustration level** texts are those read at less than 85 percent accuracy and less than 50 percent comprehension. These texts are generally "above" a student's reading level and are not recommended. New research, however, suggests such texts might be effective in paired reading activities with proficient readers.

In addition to selecting texts based on text measures, educators should consider other factors that depend on age. These are good questions to ask when selecting appropriate texts for early-childhood classroom instruction:

- Does the text introduce or reinforce concepts introduced in the curriculum (sight word acquisition, phonemic awareness, letter sounds, etc.)?
- Does the text have picture/text correlation that will hold readers' attention and provide comprehension clues?
- Does the text teach an important lesson or moral?
- Are the characters and situations diverse and engaging?

The following questions should guide the selection of texts for students:

- Are texts aligned to instructional goals?
- Are texts at the appropriate level (instructional or independent) for the planned activity?
- Are texts relevant and aligned to student interests?
- Do texts promote deep comprehension or analysis?
- Do texts contain highly specialized or nuanced vocabulary that students may not be familiar with?
- Do texts offer **multimodal elements** (appealing to different modes of communication such as written text, spoken language, and visual images) that might be relevant for instructional objectives?

When students are **self-selecting texts** or choosing something to read based on their own interests, they may still need scaffolding from educators. Knowing a student's personality, interests, and independent reading level can be helpful in this regard. However, even independent reading levels can evolve. Some students may seek out and enjoy more challenging texts, while others become frustrated at that level. Knowledge of the individual student should guide suggestions.

SAMPLE QUESTION

6) One disadvantage of relying on Lexile level as the sole indicator of text appropriateness is that
   A. it is only applicable to students whose first language is English.
   B. it fails to account for qualitative text features.
   C. it does not encourage the reading of rigorous texts.
   D. it can only be used to measure fiction texts.

BUILDING COMPREHENSION OF FICTION

Readers of all ages usually enjoy fiction texts, thanks to relatable characters and well-developed plots. Teachers often use familiar stories as a springboard to more in-depth comprehension because students are familiar with the literal meaning of the text. For this reason, many readings of the same story in an early childhood classroom are not uncommon.

Reading several interpretations of a familiar story such as *Cinderella* from different cultural perspectives can allow students to apply background knowledge of a familiar tale in new contexts. While there are many specific strategies to aid students in comprehension of literary texts, some of the most common include:

USING GRAPHIC OR SEMANTIC ORGANIZERS

- ▶ storyboards or event sequence frames or timelines
- ▶ story maps (beginning, middle, end) or plot diagrams (rising action, climax, falling action, resolution)
- ▶ character maps (actions, feelings, appearance, dialogue)
- ▶ character trait identification charts

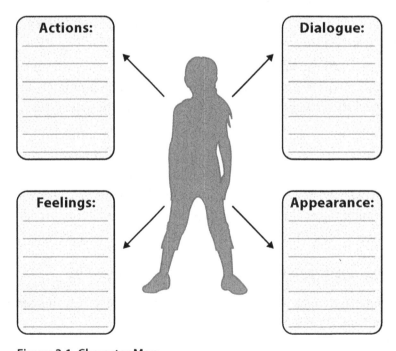

Figure 3.1. Character Map

GUIDED COMPREHENSION QUESTIONS

- ▶ those requiring students to underline, highlight, and locate the answer in the text

▶ those requiring a constructed response

▶ cloze exercises in which a portion of the text is removed and readers must fill in the blanks

SUMMARIZATION AND MAIN IDEA EXERCISES

▶ written retellings that ask students to recall and write down important parts of the story in their own words

▶ exercises that ask students to create an outline of the story

▶ asking students to identify main or central ideas in the story

▶ asking students to identify themes or messages within the story

SPECIFIC TARGETED STRATEGIES

▶ **Directed Reading-Thinking Activity (DR-TA):** Students make predictions and read up to a preselected stopping point. They then evaluate and refine predictions based on text evidence.

▶ The **QAR Strategy** encourages students to identify the type of question and to think about *how* to find the answer.

  ▷ "Right There" questions are literal questions that require only the location of the relevant part.

  ▷ "Think and Search" questions require synthesis from multiple parts of the text.

  ▷ "Author and You" questions require the text to have been read, but the answer is not directly in the text. They are typically inference and depth of knowledge (DOK) 2 and 3 questions.

  ▷ "On My Own" questions require background knowledge and do not rely on text evidence directly.

▶ The **SQ3R strategy** was developed for reading textbooks, but it is useful for many different reading materials.

  ▷ **Survey:** previewing the text and taking note of graphics, headings, etc.

  ▷ **Question:** generating questions about the text after previewing

  ▷ **Read:** reading and looking for answers for the questions

  ▷ **Recite:** rehearsing or saying the answers to the questions

  ▷ **Review:** reviewing text and answering or responding to any other questions

QUICK REVIEW

Practice using the SQ3R strategy for the next chapter of this text. Did you find it useful? Which grade levels and types of texts do you think it would be most useful for in your current or future practice?

GROUP OR PAIRED STRATEGIES

▶ **Reciprocal teaching** assigns roles to groups of four students who together work to read and comprehend a text.

▶ **Think-pair-share** pairs students to answer comprehension questions about a text. First, students think about their own answer, activating background knowledge. They then pair with another student or a small group. Then they share their answer with their group or partner and then the entire class.

▶ **Peer-Assisted Learning Strategies (PALS)**, in which a student partners with a classmate. They take turns providing each other assistance and feedback in reading comprehension.

SAMPLE QUESTION

7) **A sixth-grade reading teacher asks the reading specialist for advice on how to structure independent practice in a classroom with students of various skill levels. What recommendation should the reading specialist make?**

   A. focus instruction on pragmatics so that students see the connections in what they are learning

   B. switch to an analogy-based phonics method of instruction to engage all students

   C. use running records to keep track of student progress and current skill level

   D. implement Peer-Assisted Learning Strategies (PALS) as appropriate to provide scaffolding

LITERARY GENRES

Literature can be classified into **genres** and subgenres, categories of works that are similar in format, content, tone, or length. Most works fall into one of four broad genres: nonfiction, fiction, drama, and poetry.

As students experience each genre throughout a school year, they should receive instruction that integrates all aspects of literacy. That is, students should not only experience reading practice in each genre, they should also have plenty of writing and discussion practice to deepen their knowledge of the genre they are studying.

FICTION

Fiction is a prose genre. Texts are made up of narratives created by the author. Fiction is typically written in the form of novels and short stories. Many subgenres fall under the category of fiction. Students can be guided to determine whether a text is fiction or nonfiction by asking whether the text is a "true" or "real" story.

Folklore is a set of beliefs and stories of a particular people, which are passed down through the generations. Folklore comes in many forms, including:

▶ fables: short stories intended to teach moral lessons

▶ fairy tales: stories that involve magical creatures such as elves and fairies

▶ myths: stories, often involving gods or demigods, that attempt to explain certain practices or phenomena

▶ legends: unverifiable stories that seem to have a degree of realism about them

▶ tall tales: stories that are set in realistic settings but include characters with wildly exaggerated capabilities

Students can be guided to identify folklore by asking certain questions about texts:

▶ Are there supernatural elements, such as magic, dragons, or fairies?

▶ Does the story teach a lesson?

▶ Do the characters in the stories have exaggerated abilities?

▶ Is the story from a particular cultural tradition?

Science fiction is a category of fiction in which writers tell imaginative stories that are grounded in scientific and technological theories or realities. Science fiction writing often explores ideas involving the future of humanity and its relationship with the universe or with technology. A subcategory of science fiction is dystopian fiction, in which authors explore social, cultural, and political structures in the context of a futuristic world.

Horror fiction is intended to frighten, startle, or disgust the reader. Often, horror fiction involves paranormal or psychological content. Mysteries and thrillers, which may also arouse fear or paranoia, tend to be fast-paced and outcome-driven; they also tend to focus on human behaviors or relationships and not on paranormal activity.

Realistic fiction is meant to be relatable for readers. Authors of realistic fiction try to create a degree of verisimilitude in their writing, especially in the dialogue between characters. **Historical fiction** relies on realistic settings and characters from an earlier time to tell new stories. Often the setting is central to the motivations and actions of characters. Students might need to explore the background of a historical era before they can comprehend a historical fiction text at the highest level.

Satire is a literary text that uses critical humor to reveal vice and foolishness in individuals and institutions. The purpose of satire is to somehow improve the object of ridicule. The literary or rhetorical devices that create satire include sarcasm, irony, mockery, exaggeration, understatement, as well as an honest narrative/speaking voice that is dismayed or appalled by the object of the satire.

Because satire is a complex literary device that requires comprehension well beyond a literal or even basic inferential level, it is regarded as a more challenging type of text reserved for older students and more advanced readers.

SAMPLE QUESTION

8) **A reading interventionist is working with a second-grade student receiving Tier 3 interventions in fluency and decoding. Before the day's activity, which will involve reading from a leveled reader, the interventionist asks the student to preview the booklet's title and illustrations and make a prediction about the type of book it is. This helps the student to**

   A.   develop metacognition.
   B.   apply fix-up strategies.
   C.   determine genre.
   D.   analyze plot.

Drama

Drama is expressive writing that tells a story to an audience through the actions and dialogue of characters, which are brought to life by actors who play the roles onstage. Dramatic works, called **plays**, are written in poetic or lyrical verse or in regular prose. Along with the dialogue between the characters, authors rely on **stage directions** to describe the sets and to give directions to the actors about what they are to do.

In some plays, actors perform long speeches in which the characters explain their thinking about philosophical ideas or social issues. These **monologues** can be directed toward another character. A monologue delivered as if nobody were listening is called a **soliloquy** (as in Shakespeare's famous "To be or not to be" soliloquy from *Hamlet*). Sometimes characters in drama (or fiction) have very unique attributes such as a manner of speech, dress, or a catchphrase. Such devices make characters memorable to readers and are known as **character tags**.

Using drama in the classroom is a great way to get students interested in different types of texts. A simple stage in a kindergarten or elementary classroom is a natural outgrowth of a dramatic play center sometimes found in preschool classrooms. Building on students' innate curiosity and imagination, the possibilities are endless. Acting out dramas not only helps students work on expressive reading (prosody), it also reinforces social and emotional learning as students analyze the emotions and actions of characters.

It is important to have older students think about how both the stage directions and the dialogue contribute to the play's meaning. To jog student interest, especially in linguistically complex dramas like those of Shakespeare, teachers might have students watch video clips of actual performances. Comparing specific scenes performed by different actors stimulates interest and can be used to discuss the different ways a scene can be interpreted.

Students may also benefit from acting out scenes or giving speeches, allowing them to express their own interpretations of the characters or action. To engage students in writing activities, a teacher may have them write their own scripts or write a research report on the play's context, author, characters, or subject matter.

SAMPLE QUESTION

9)   **Drama is a genre well suited for helping students develop**

  A.   phonemic awareness.

  B.   prosody.

  C.   alliteration.

  D.   concepts of print.

POETRY

Poetry is imaginative, expressive verse writing that uses rhythm, unified and concentrated thought, concrete images, specialized language, and patterns. Different poetic forms use techniques and structures in unique ways.

A **line** is a unit of poetry. The lines of a poem can be separated by punctuation, meter, and/or rhyme. Although a line may be a unit of attention, it is usually not a unit of meaning.

A **stanza** is a group of lines followed by a space. Each stanza of a poem may have a specific number of lines; the lines are sometimes arranged in a pattern created by meter and/or a rhyme scheme. The pattern is often repeated in each stanza, although it can be varied for effect. A stanza with two lines is a **couplet**; three lines, a **tercet**; four lines, a **quatrain**; five lines, a **cinquain**; and so on. Modern poems may have stanzas with varying lengths or no stanzas at all. Some modern poems are written entirely in **free verse**, without any fixed form.

Teachers can introduce several common types of poems to students during reading instruction:

▸   A **ballad** is a short narrative song about an event that is considered important. Ballads are intended to be recited. They are characterized by a dramatic immediacy, focusing on one crucial situation or action that often leads to a catastrophe.

▸   A **sonnet** is a lyrical poem with fourteen lines, usually written in **iambic pentameter**. This pattern alternates stressed and unstressed syllables in a line of verse with ten syllables per line.

▸   A **haiku** is a short poem format that originated in Japan. It has three lines of five, seven, and five syllables.

▶ A **villanelle** is usually nineteen lines long. It has five stanzas, each with three lines, and a final stanza of four lines. It includes a refrain—two lines that repeat throughout the poem following a specific pattern.

Teachers can use poetry lessons as ways for students to respond both to the effect the poem had on them personally and to the aesthetics of the poem itself. To introduce poetry and build interest for a poetry unit, a teacher might select an especially forceful poem, read it dramatically, and invite students to discuss their responses.

When students are analyzing a poem, it is important to read it more than once. The teacher can model with a **think-aloud**, the process of modeling one's thinking during a reading. Students should have copies of poems to annotate and have a routine for collaborative and independent poetry reading, such as:

1. an initial reading to experience the mood of the poem and the musicality of the language

2. a second reading to focus on the pauses and thought units and to identify the **speaker**, who may not be the same person as the poet

3. a third close reading to take marginal notes on the structure of the poem, the denotation (literal meaning) and connotations (subtle meanings) of unfamiliar words, the impact of imagery and figurative language, and the meaning of confusing lines or phrases

4. a final reading to come up with some thematic ideas, drawn from the details

Along with analyzing poems, students can present their original poetry in classroom "coffee houses" or "poetry slams." Depending on the age and grade, students might learn different poetic forms, like sonnets and ballads. They might also learn about the characteristics of the different types of poetry, including metaphysical poetry or Romantic poetry.

While poetry analysis may be associated with older children, even young students can appreciate and recognize rhyme. Poetry with **rhyme** can help reinforce phonological awareness and is a natural outgrowth of many young children's love of song. **Meter**—the rhythm, or beat, of the poem—can also engage young students with different texts. A beat can be clapped to, stomped to, or even danced to. Many timeless books for children—such as *One Fish, Two Fish, Red Fish, Blue Fish* and *Each Peach Pear Plum*—have both rhyme and meter and expose young children to poetry in a fun way.

QUICK REVIEW

Lexile text measures are not used for poetry. Create a list of qualitative text features that could determine the appropriateness of a poem for a grade level or group of students.

Young writers may even begin to write simple poems with one or two stanzas, or groups of lines similar to paragraphs. Students should be encouraged to recognize and create their own rhyming words as an additional outgrowth of phonological awareness. Asking students to name all the words they can think of that rhyme with *dog*, for example, will allow for continued practice with rhymes.

Poetry often uses **figurative language**, or phrases not meant to be interpreted literally. A simile compares two things of a different type ("brave like a lion"). A metaphor applies a characteristic or meaning to an object or action that is not literally applicable ("the anger of the rose stung us with its sharp fury"). Poems may also use **sensory imagery**, or descriptive language that appeals to one of the five senses ("the shrill cry of the alarm"). **Alliteration** is the repetition of the same sound in nearby words ("the rotund rhinoceros roared").

SAMPLE QUESTION

10) **A reading specialist is helping the special education teacher plan a lesson on rhyme and meter in poetry for students with reading disabilities. Which assistive technology might she recommend?**

 A. an e-reader or digital copy of the poem

 B. an audio recording of the poem

 C. a large-print version of the poem

 D. a version of the poem adapted at a lower Lexile level

LITERARY RESPONSE AND ANALYSIS

The **structural elements** of literature such as setting, characters, conflict, tone, point of view, main idea, and organization can be introduced with other literacy activities, even with students who are pre-readers.

SETTING AND CHARACTER

Setting is the time and place of events in a story. When considering setting, students should look at how characters interact with their surroundings, how they are influenced by the societal expectations of that time and place, and how the location and time period impact the development of the story. Students might have trouble understanding the difference between setting and plot. Teachers can ask, "How would this story change if it were set in a different time or place?" to help students understand setting.

An author uses **character development** to create characters that are complex and, to some degree, believable. Authors might develop their characters directly by telling the reader explicitly what the character is like by describing traits and values. Sometimes, authors include the thoughts and feelings of the characters themselves, offering readers even more insight. Authors also develop their characters indirectly by revealing their actions and interactions with others. They might do this by including what one character says or thinks about another and allowing readers to draw their own conclusions. Most authors combine direct and indirect characterization. This ensures that readers know what they need to know and provides opportunities for reflection and interpretation.

SAMPLE QUESTION

11) A reading specialist suggests that the eighth-grade English teacher invite a guest speaker to present a lecture on the historical background and setting of *Johnny Tremain* before the class reads a portion of the text. Which is the MOST appropriate strategy to use with the guest speaker?

   A.   listen-read-discuss

   B.   predict-o-gram

   C.   peer tutoring

   D.   reader's theater

TONE

The **tone** of a literary work is created by the author's attitude toward the reader and the subject of the text. In a sense, it is the tone of voice the author uses to speak to the reader. Depending on word choice, an author's tone can range from playful, familiar, or sincere to detached, sarcastic, or indifferent. It can be alarmed and forceful or philosophical and serious. It might be concerned or careless, saddened or overjoyed, triumphant or defeated.

Whatever the case, students should be encouraged to consider how the author uses language to convey tone. Students can think about what the author is suggesting through language choice. This process will reveal the author's attitude and, ultimately, the theme of the work.

Students should also be able to distinguish the author's tone from **mood**. Mood is the emotional atmosphere of a literary work that shapes the reader's experience of the text. Mood is created through an interplay of the literary elements of plot, character, setting, point of view, tone, and figurative language. By examining the emotional effect of the author's choices, readers can further develop their understanding of the text's larger meaning.

SAMPLE QUESTION

12) Which of the following strategies would BEST help a student identify the tone of a literary work?

   A.   implementing pre-reading strategies like previewing, scanning, and predicting

   B.   using a list-group-label process to dig deeper into key concepts from the work

   C.   focusing on the morphology and orthography of words found in the text

   D.   identifying specific words in the text that evoke feelings or emotions

POINT OF VIEW

Point of view is the perspective from which the action in a story is told. By carefully selecting a particular point of view, writers are able to control what their readers know. Most literature is written in first-person or third-person point of view. In the **first-person** or "I" point of view, the action is narrated by a character within the story. This can make the story feel more believable and authentic to the reader. However, the reader's knowledge and understanding are limited to what the narrator notices and are influenced by what the narrator thinks and values.

A **third-person** narrator is a voice outside the action of the story, an observer who shares what he or she knows, sees, or hears with the reader. A third-person narrator might be fully omniscient (able to see into the minds of the characters and share what they are thinking and feeling), partially omniscient (able to see into the minds of just one or a few characters), or limited (unable to see into the minds of any of the characters and only able to share what can be seen and heard).

The **second-person** point of view uses "you" and can be read as the narrator speaking directly to the reader. It is used mainly in nonfiction texts, particularly in introductory and concluding paragraphs in which the writer might make a direct appeal to the reader to reflect on the points about to be made or already made.

Students can learn to associate certain pronouns with certain points of view if such an exercise is developmentally appropriate. For example, teachers might ask very young students questions like "Who told the story?" and "What was (character name) like?" to introduce these concepts.

Although point of view may be harder for very young students to grasp, teachers can begin introducing the basic concept by reading the narrator's part in one voice and each different character in a different voice and encouraging students to do the same. Older students can practice second-person point of view by reading and writing letters to other students, the teacher, or administrators or other school personnel.

SAMPLE QUESTION

13) A high school English teacher is working on an integrated reading and writing unit on point of view. He wants to expose students to multiple perspectives in texts but discourage them from using the pronoun "you" in formal academic writing. The teacher would most likely NOT assign which writing task?

   A. personal narrative

   B. research report

   C. formal letter

   D. compare/contrast essay

Main Idea and Theme

As students progress in their literacy and are able to consistently decode longer passages, their focus will shift to the comprehension of many different types of passages. This usually happens around the second and third grade, but even students still practicing decoding and very young pre-readers can learn to explore the **main idea** of a story and make predictions. Questions like "What was this book about?" and "What do you think character X will do next?" will help students make predictions and **summarize** or condense the main elements of a story.

As the stories read to students become more complex and as students begin reading their own stories, teachers can introduce other literary elements. Students of all ages generally enjoy stories with **themes**, or topics, that they can relate to or are already exploring. (Of course, *theme* can also mean the moral, lesson, or general statement about life a literary work conveys.) Integrated curricula, or those that structure several cross-curricular units around a central theme, are popular in many early childhood and some lower-elementary settings.

Even without a formal daily or weekly theme in the classroom, teachers can help students make connections by integrating texts from other areas like science and social studies into literacy activities. For example, a unit on conservation might feature a story that includes a moral, or lesson, about the importance of conserving natural resources. Teachers might even encourage students to further explore their own interests and create their own integrated literary experiences by selecting and reading different works centered on a theme of their choosing.

> **DID YOU KNOW?**
>
> The Supreme Court ruled in *Island Trees School District v. Pico* (1982) that a local school board may not remove books from junior high and high school libraries just because they dislike the ideas contained in them. However, controversy over student access to certain titles remains. Does your school or district have policies regarding the adoption of titles for the school library or classroom use?

SAMPLE QUESTION

14) John, a second-grade student, is assigned to read a paragraph from his social studies textbook and write a sentence stating the central idea. What can a reading interventionist do to help him with this task if he gets stuck?

   A.   ask him what he liked about what he read

   B.   ask him to list all the details from the paragraph

   C.   go over key vocabulary with him

   D.   ask him what he thought was most important

Plot Diagrams

To facilitate deep comprehension of literary texts, teachers can help students understand key elements through a **plot diagram**. This graphic organizer helps students identify the **exposition**, or beginning, of the story, which sets the stage by describing the time, place, and main characters. Students can then pinpoint the **conflict** of the story, or the main struggle that drives the action. Next is the **rising action**, or sequence of events leading to the eventual climax, or turning point, which is the apex of the diagram.

The curve slopes sharply downward as the **falling action**, or results of the climax, unfolds. The diagram closes with the final resolution, or ending of the story. Depending on student age and grade level, teachers may introduce the idea that the resolution might not be happy, but all stories do have one.

Introducing the plot diagram is easiest when students already have some background with a story. Teachers may draw on a popular children's movie or fairy tale to introduce these elements. Students struggling to comprehend a new text will have trouble understanding these elements. Timeless stories with plots that students know by heart are ideal for an initial exploration of the plot diagram.

QUICK REVIEW

Practice filling out a plot diagram for a fiction text you are familiar with. Think about what texts you would recommend to teachers to introduce this concept.

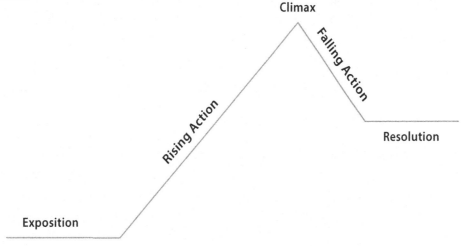

Figure 3.2. Plot Diagram

SAMPLE QUESTION

15) A teacher wants to introduce her first-grade students to the idea of conflict in stories. Which technique is MOST appropriate?

   A.   ask students to go to the library and select a storybook with lots of conflict

   B.   project-based learning asking students to solve a major global problem

   C.   have students compare and contrast problems in their lives they consider major and minor

   D.   guided storybook reading in which the emphasis is on the problem the characters resolve

NONFICTION

Nonfiction is a genre of prose writing that is based in fact. Its information is, to the best of the author's knowledge, true and accurate. This does not mean, however, that nonfiction is dry or uninspiring. Nonfiction writing comes in many forms, most of which display creativity and originality in how factual information is presented. **Literary nonfiction**, or **creative nonfiction**, for example, is a mix of expressive and informative writing that tells a true, verifiable, or documented story in a compelling, artistic way.

AUTHOR'S PURPOSE

Nonfiction texts are written to persuade, inform, explain, entertain, or describe. Authors who write to **persuade** try to convince the reader to act or think a certain way. They may use specific reasons and supporting evidence to do this. Persuasive writers also use **rhetoric**, language chosen specifically for its particular effect, to influence readers.

Writing to **inform** is as straightforward as the term suggests: the author sets out simply to communicate information to the reader. Purely informative writing is found in many textbooks and news articles. Some informational writing may also **instruct** the reader. This type of writing includes items such as lists, steps to be followed, and a sequential order.

Similar to informing, some writing **explains**. It might explain how things are similar or different, it might define a term, or it might explain a problem and its solution.

Nonfiction may also entertain. Typically, this type of writing will **narrate**, or tell a (true) story. Like fiction, narrative nonfiction (sometimes referred to as literary nonfiction) will include a setting, characters, and a plot. The writer may also use figurative language and other devices to entertain the reader.

Finally, nonfiction texts may **describe** something: a detailed description of an event, person, place, or even inanimate object.

The acronym **PIEED** helps students think about the author's purpose. It is accompanied by a picture of a pie with various slices to illustrate each of these purposes.

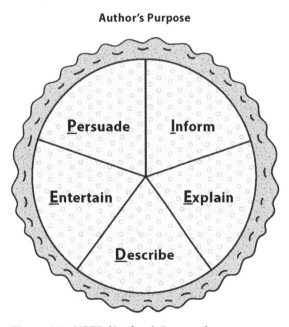

Author's Purpose

Persuade   **I**nform

Entertain   **E**xplain

Describe

Figure 3.3. PIEED (Author's Purpose)

- ▶ Persuade
- ▶ Inform
- ▶ Explain
- ▶ Entertain
- ▶ Describe

Nonfiction takes many forms, which are often related to the author's purpose:

- ▶ an essay is a short work about a particular topic or idea
- ▶ a speech is a short work with a specific purpose, intended to be presented orally in front of an audience
- ▶ a news article is a short recounting of a particular story
- ▶ a biography is a detailed, creative textual representation of a person's life
- ▶ an autobiography is an account of an individual's life, told by the individual

The author's purpose is sometimes further revealed by the text structure. For example, a problem-solution text structure is most likely to be used in a persuasive text. A compare and contrast structure is used to describe two like or unlike things. Transitional expressions that are part of the organizational pattern of the text can be used as clues for overall comprehension and in determining the author's purpose. Phrases like "most importantly" and "in contrast" are hints to the author's goal in writing.

Many educators use this step-by-step process to identify the purpose of a text.

1. While reading the text, think of the question "Why did the author write this?"

2. After reading, complete the statement "The author wrote this mainly to _____."

3. Find important details in the text that support the statement. If no such details exist, the purpose statement might need to be modified.

SAMPLE QUESTION

16) A high school teacher is working with students to identify the purpose of a science article in preparation for similar questions on the SAT/ACT. Which advice should he give students to help them answer the question "What is the author's purpose?"?

   A.   Always ask whether the author achieved their purpose for writing the text.

   B.   Look for specific text evidence that supports an assertion about the author's purpose.

   C.   The purpose will generally be revealed explicitly in the introductory paragraph.

   D.   A "call to action" never gives possible clues to the author's purpose.

Text Structure

Authors organize nonfiction texts with a text structure that suits their purpose. This structure may be a **sequence** of events, such as a news story about the days leading up to an important event. It might also be a thorough **description** of something, as in the opening paragraph of an essay describing a person or place in detail.

Many historical texts use a **cause-and-effect** pattern in which the cause is presented first, and the result is discussed next. A chapter in a social studies text about the Industrial Revolution, for example, might follow this pattern, citing the Industrial Revolution as the cause for a change in working and living conditions in many cities.

Other works are organized in a **problem-solution** structure, in which a problem is presented and then a possible solution discussed. Teachers might introduce this structure through a collaborative activity in which students identify a problem in the classroom, school, or community. They can then write a letter to a decision-maker about the issue and a possible solution. Finally, students can read other problem-solution texts to see how other authors structure their arguments.

Students can use a **compare and contrast** structure to explain how two things from their everyday experience are similar and different. Charts and other graphic organizers can help them organize their thoughts and understand this structure. A teacher might ask students, for example, to use a **Venn diagram** to determine the similarities and differences presented in a text.

It is helpful to integrate reading and writing nonfiction/expository texts that use the same text structure. This approach is used in many textbooks and curricular resources based on the Common Core State Standards.

SAMPLE QUESTION

17) A reading specialist is helping an interdepartmental team plan a cross-curricular lesson for a tenth-grade world history course and a tenth-grade English II course. One of the objectives is based on the following Literacy in History/Social Studies standard:

Compare the point of view of two or more authors for how they treat the same or similar topics, including which details they include and emphasize in their respective accounts (CCSS.ELA-Literacy. RH 9-10.6).

Which activity is MOST appropriate?

A.   Students watch two recorded lectures by famous historians with two different perspectives on the fall of the Roman Empire.

B.   Students read Shakespeare's *Julius Caesar* and then compare it to the information about Caesar in their history text.

C.   Students read Shakespeare's *Richard III* and compare and contrast it with *Julius Caesar*.

D.   Students watch a film about some aspect of Roman history and compare it with the information in their history text.

IDENTIFYING CENTRAL IDEAS

Nonfiction texts contain a central or main idea. Identifying this idea is an important though sometimes challenging skill for students. This step is part of a process in which students master simpler skills before moving on to more advanced ones.

1. Students practice identifying the **topic** of the text. For example, the topic of a text might be "horses."

2. Students ask themselves a question such as "What is the author saying about horses?"

3. The answer to that question is the central idea of the text. "Horses are animals that have helped humans throughout history."

When using this method, students should not confuse topic with main idea. They should use the identification of the topic to determine the main or central idea.

The main idea of the text is stated explicitly or implicitly. When stated explicitly, the main idea is referred to as a **thesis** or thesis statement. Students can practice identifying the thesis of a short text before studying text with an implicitly stated main idea.

An implicit main idea is more difficult to identify. Students must **synthesize** or put together information and details from many parts of the text. The following process can help students identify the main idea.

1. Identify the main idea of each paragraph first. It might be stated explicitly as a topic sentence, or it might be implicit. If the idea is implicit, students will need to summarize the paragraph in a single sentence in their own words.

2. After determining the main idea of each paragraph, students can think about what these main ideas have in common or make a "summary of summaries."

3. Students should check their main idea statements to make sure they have no specific details or examples and that they encapsulate only the most important points.

Because identification of the central idea and summarization are similar thought processes, these skills are often taught together. Teachers might also introduce the central idea as the most important idea within the summary.

Students can use text organization and text features like headings and bolded terms to help them distinguish between central ideas and supporting details. Finally, students should understand that identifying the main idea of the text overall (and often of each paragraph) is not a skill to be used in isolation. Rather, it is a critical part of actively reading any nonfiction text.

18) A reading interventionist is working with a small group of third-grade students to identify the main idea. When asked, "What is the main idea of the article?" students say, "Jupiter." What question should the interventionist ask next to guide students to identify the main idea?

    A.   "What did you already know about Jupiter before reading?"

    B.   "What are some new things you learned about Jupiter after reading?"

    C.   "What is the author trying to teach us about Jupiter?"

    D   "What did you think was most interesting about Jupiter?"

Nonfiction Texts Across the Curriculum

Students encounter nonfiction texts throughout their coursework, so the reading specialist's role is not limited to working with ELA/reading teachers or ELA curricular resources. Reading specialists are asked to help teachers across the content areas to select and use nonfiction texts. This might include any or all of the following recommendations:

- **Leveled nonfiction texts** can be used in multiple settings. Content area teachers can use texts on the same topic divided by complexity. Sites like the Smithsonian's *TweenTribune* and *Newsela* offer a variety of science and social studies texts for readers of all levels.

- Persuasive or argumentative texts that cover both sides of an issue can be used across the content areas to spark discussion and encourage higher-level analysis. When using such texts for instruction, teachers should ask students to analyze the author's rhetoric and use of **hyperbole**, or exaggerated language. Students should also determine whether a piece of persuasive writing has used any **logical fallacies—** errors in reasoning that weaken the argument.

- Nonfiction texts that are highly descriptive or that seek to describe a real-life work of art in words can be used as a springboard for creative expression in an art, music, or theater class.

- Students should be given explicit instruction in reading their textbooks or other resources in each course. For example, a science teacher might say, "As you read, underline or highlight the main idea in each paragraph and circle any words you do not know." This type of direction encourages active reading and makes any reading assignment more meaningful.

- Nonfiction texts should be carefully selected based on readability and appropriateness as well as alignment to standards. Reading specialists might be asked to review resources and make curricular recommendations for resources across content areas.

19) **A seventh-grade science teacher asks the reading specialist for help in meeting the needs of English language learners in a unit on parts of a cell, since the textbook chapter is not wholly accessible to some students. What should the reading specialist recommend?**

    A.   use graphic aids like diagrams and images in the text as much as possible to promote understanding

    B.   assign each student a peer tutor to read the textbook chapter aloud to ensure correct pronunciation

    C.   provide English language learners with an audio recording of the textbook chapter to listen to multiple times

    D.   avoid using the textbook chapter and focus instruction on lectures and note-taking to meet the needs of all learners

NONFICTION INSTRUCTIONAL STRATEGIES

Comprehension strategies for nonfiction texts are similar to those for fiction texts, though nonfiction texts might be less predictable in purpose and structure. In expository texts, the writer wants to teach something to the reader. That means that students are learning something new from a factual perspective while also analyzing rhetorical techniques. Many of the strategies previously mentioned for literary texts can also be used for nonfiction texts, but there are additional considerations.

Students will encounter nonfiction texts more often than fiction texts both across the curriculum and in their everyday lives. They should be given plenty of strategies for overall comprehension of nonfiction texts.

Tap into or activate background knowledge by helping students draw connections between what they already know:

- Use a **brainstorm web**. Write the subject of the text in the center and encourage students to fill in the rest of the web with information they already know about the topic.

- **ABC brainstorm** in small groups or as a class. Students write one word or phrase they already know about the topic for each letter of the alphabet.

- **Free brainstorm** by asking students to freely write down (or draw) what they already know about a topic.

Students might be unfamiliar with certain terms they need to know to fully understand a nonfiction text. Help them by introducing subject-specific or challenging vocabulary before and during the reading. Strategies to introduce vocabulary include:

- **Word Expert**: Break up new vocabulary words into mini-lists and have each student become the "expert" of two or three words. Have students create a card with a definition, illustration, and sentence from the text to share with the class.

▶ **Words Alive:** Have students form groups to come up with actions or poses that illustrate the meaning of each new word on their list after the teacher explains the words' meanings to the group.

▶ **Semantic mapping:** Students write the new word in the center and then around it write a synonym, an antonym, an example, and a non-example of the word. Another take on this is the Frayer Model in which students write the word in the middle of four squares: definition, characteristics, examples, and non-examples.

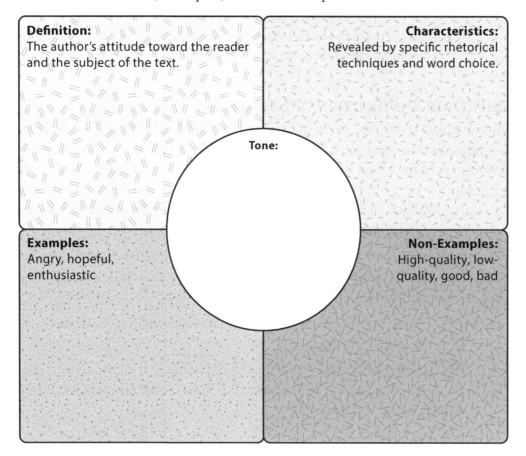

Definition:
The author's attitude toward the reader and the subject of the text.

Characteristics:
Revealed by specific rhetorical techniques and word choice.

Tone:

Examples:
Angry, hopeful, enthusiastic

Non-Examples:
High-quality, low-quality, good, bad

Figure 3.4. Frayer Model

STUDY TIP

When you finish each chapter of this text, write down two or three terms that were new and/or that you believe you will have the most trouble remembering. Use a semantic map or the Frayer Model to help you remember each new term.

Use collaborative learning strategies to tackle challenging nonfiction texts. Students can be divided into pairs for reading activities. They can also be placed in larger groups where each member works on a different part of the text (e.g., one student identifies the main idea of each paragraph, one student identifies the purpose).

Students should be taught and encouraged to use various annotation strategies. They should be encouraged to mark up the text, write in the margins, or use sticky notes. Using **text coding** can help students develop metacognition skills:

▶   ✓=I already know this

▶   X=not what I expected

▶   *=important

▶   ?=question about this

▶   ??=really confused by this

▶   !=surprising

▶   L=learned something new

▶   RR=section needs to be reread

In addition to annotating, students can use systematic **note-taking strategies**:

▶   Have students complete a full or partial outline of the text from a template.

▶   Have students use two-column notes where they put main ideas on one side and important details on the other. This is known as the **split-page method** or the **two-column method**.

▶   Have students use the **Cornell method** of note-taking whereby each page is divided into keywords, notes, and summary.

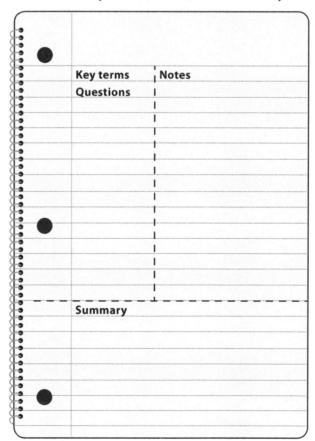

Figure 3.5. Cornell Method for Taking Notes

Finally, give students a toolbox of fix-up strategies for when comprehension breaks down. These might be similar to strategies used for fiction texts. For example:

- Students should know when and how to use the glossary in each textbook.

- Students should have access to a dictionary appropriate for their age and skill level to consult as needed.

- Students should know who to go to and how to ask for assistance when they have exhausted all their independent strategies.

SAMPLE QUESTION

20) A reading specialist is planning a professional development event for first- through fifth-grade teachers focused on strategies to comprehend nonfiction texts. The specialist wants to make sure that there is at least one strategy presented that will be relevant to teachers of the youngest students. Which is the BEST strategy to meet this aim?

   A.   Cornell method

   B.   Words Alive

   C.   two-column method

   D.   text coding

REVIEW

Read the question, and then choose the most correct answer.

1

A reading specialist working with a small group of students asks them to use each of the bold headings in their textbook to generate questions they will answer after reading the chapter. This is a strategy to help students do what?

A.   read with purpose

B.   activate background knowledge

C.   apply fix-up strategies

D.   use context clues

2

Which of the following is the MOST appropriate way for kindergarten students to preview a text?

A.   conducting background research on the setting and author

B.   identifying the protagonist and antagonist

C.   examining the cover and title

D.   underlining possible topic sentences

3

A reading specialist observes middle school students in a social studies class reading a primary and secondary source on the same topic and then comparing the two texts. Which foundational reading skill is the social studies teacher helping students to develop?

A.   activating background knowledge

B.   drawing reasonable conclusions

C.   making connections

D.   annotating the text

4

A teacher asks the reading specialist for advice on taking the class to the library to select texts for sustained silent reading (SSR). What is the BEST advice for the reading specialist to give?

A.   encourage students to find a text at their independent reading level that meets their interests

B.   discourage students from selecting texts about topics they are already familiar with

C.   select texts for students to make they are appropriate

D.   ensure that an Accelerated Reader test exists for each chosen book to monitor comprehension

5

Which of the following is an evaluative question that a student might ask while reading?

A.   How many pet cats did Celeste have?

B.   What might happen to Celeste's cats?

C.   What do I think about Celeste as a person?

D.   How old is Celeste?

6

Which of the following is the MOST appropriate text for independent reading for most fourth-grade students?

A.   a poem at a Lexile level of 1200

B.   a nonfiction text at a Lexile level of 770

C.   a drama at a Lexile level of 1100

D.   a fiction text at a Lexile level of 200

7

Which of the following is a qualitative text measure?

A.   mean sentence length

B.   word count

C.   average word length

D.   knowledge demands

8

A high school teacher teaching a dual-credit US history course to seniors asks the reading specialist for help with the college-level textbook, which is challenging for some students to comprehend. What should the reading specialist recommend?

A.   focusing the class on multimedia texts instead of written information

B.   giving students explicit strategies such as the SQ3R method

C.   reading most of the textbook aloud in class

D.   switching to another textbook for the rest of the year

9

Which of the following reading comprehension strategies could also provide students with opportunities for socio-emotional learning (SEL)?

A.   reciprocal teaching

B.   cloze procedure

C.   list-group-label

D.   embedded phonics

10

Before assigning a historical fiction novel, what should the reading teacher do to give students the necessary background knowledge?

A.   reveal the climax and resolution

B.   provide students with a character trait chart

C.   encourage students to determine the theme

D.   give insights into the setting

Answer Key

Sample Questions

1) A.   Incorrect. Timed reading does not necessarily develop expression.

       B.   Incorrect. Prosody refers to expression, not reading rate.

       C.   Incorrect. Prosody is part of oral reading.

      D.   **Correct.** Having students read from a script would give them practice reading expressively.

2) A.   Incorrect. Reciprocal teaching involves a group working together to comprehend a text. It is not directly related to activation of background knowledge before reading.

       B.   Incorrect. This is a graphic organizer used to help students develop vocabulary skills.

       C.   Incorrect. This is also a vocabulary-building strategy similar to cloze exercises.

      D.   **Correct.** The *K* stands for "What I already know" about the topic. The *W* is "What I want to know," and the *L* is completed after reading to state, "What I learned."

3) A.   Incorrect. Graphophonic cues are aimed at decoding on the word level, not overall comprehension.

      B.   **Correct.** Fix-up strategies are applied when comprehension breaks down.

       C.   Incorrect. Coarticulation of phonemes addresses speaking and oral language, not reading comprehension.

       D.   Incorrect. Using Elkonin boxes would help pre-readers or beginning readers detect phonemes in words. This strategy is not aimed at comprehension.

4) A.   Incorrect. The students seem to be completing assigned reading exercises. Independent reading for pleasure is the issue.

       B.   Incorrect. This additional research would take time and might not generate useful data. Students might have different reasons for not enjoying reading for pleasure that likely cannot all be met by a single program.

      C.   **Correct.** Students who are rewarded might read independently more and then discover they enjoy it.

       D.   Incorrect. Literature on the importance of independent reading might impress upon parents the importance of independent reading, but it would not motivate students. The literature may not even reach all parents or be read by them.

5) A.   Incorrect. All students need oral reading practice.

       B.   Incorrect. Using such low-level texts would not be challenging enough for some students.

C. **Correct.** This activity would allow for differentiation of text complexity.

D. Incorrect. All students need reading instructional time, though it must be differentiated for each student.

6) A. Incorrect. Lexile measures are available in Spanish as well as English and are not applicable only to students whose first language is English.

B. **Correct.** Lexile measures only account for quantitative text features like word length and sentence length. They do not measure content, knowledge demands, and so on.

C. Incorrect. Assigning texts at a high Lexile level would encourage the reading of rigorous texts, as they would have greater quantitative complexity.

D. Incorrect. Lexile measures can be used to measure fiction and nonfiction texts, though typically not poetry and drama.

7) A. Incorrect. Pragmatics are important, but this does not address the situation of multiple skill levels.

B. Incorrect. Analogy-based phonics is helpful for basic decoding but would not be part of the objectives in a sixth-grade general education classroom.

C. Incorrect. Keeping running records would help the teacher monitor oral fluency but would not qualify as independent practice.

D. **Correct.** PALS partner students with a more proficient peer who provides scaffolding to help finish assignments.

8) A. Incorrect. Metacognition refers to the reader's inner thought process while reading.

B. Incorrect. Fix-up strategies use techniques to aid in understanding when comprehension breaks down.

C. **Correct.** Previewing the booklet's title and illustrations and making predictions about the book will help the student determine the genre of the book.

D. Incorrect. The illustrations might provide *some* indication of plot, but they will not allow for "analysis" of it.

9) A. Incorrect. Phonemic awareness is best promoted through texts with rhyme and rhythm.

B. **Correct.** Drama is particularly useful for reader's theater, in which students read parts of a text aloud and develop oral reading skills and prosody.

C. Incorrect. Poetry is more likely than drama to have alliteration.

D. Incorrect. Concepts of print are basic understandings of how print is used to communicate meaning.

10) A. Incorrect. Using an e-reader or digital copy is not directly applicable to the lesson or the students' special needs.

B.   **Correct.** An audio recording would help students challenged by reading written text understand the concepts of rhyme and meter.

C.   Incorrect. Large print would only be appropriate for students with visual impairments.

D.   Incorrect. Poems are not measured for complexity using a Lexile text measure.

11) A.   **Correct.** In this strategy, students listen to a lecture on a topic, read a text, and then discuss similarities or differences in the lecture versus text.

B.   Incorrect. A predict-o-gram involves students predicting how vocabulary will be used in parts of a text and does not apply to having a guest speaker.

C.   Incorrect. Peer tutoring is not the most appropriate activity to use with the lecture. A peer would not be able to assist another student *during* a lecture, as this would disrupt the presentation.

D.   Incorrect. While the novel could be read using reader's theater, this does not incorporate the lecture.

12) A.   Incorrect. Pre-reading strategies might help with overall comprehension and setting a purpose for reading, but they do not directly address the goal of identifying tone.

B.   Incorrect. A list-group-label process is aimed at categorizing words in a list and labeling them as linked to certain ideas. This relates to building vocabulary and specific concepts from the text rather than to identifying tone.

C.   Incorrect. Focusing on morphology and orthography would help students with vocabulary and spelling, not identifying tone.

D.   **Correct.** Identifying specific evocative words will aid students in connecting word choice and tone.

13) A.   Incorrect. A personal narrative is typically written in first person, not second person.

B.   Incorrect. A research report would generally be written in the third person.

C.   **Correct.** Letters are usually written in the second person, so a teacher who wants students to avoid writing in the second person would probably not assign this project.

D.   Incorrect. A compare/contrast essay is typically written in third person.

14) A.   Incorrect. Asking John about his favorite parts of the reading would help him evaluate the text, not identify the main idea.

B.   Incorrect. Having John list all the details would be counter to the goal of identifying the main idea.

C.   Incorrect. Reviewing vocabulary might increase John's understanding but would not directly help him in identifying the main idea.

D.   **Correct.** Asking John what he thought was most important about the text is a simple question that can help him think about the main or central idea.

15)   A.   Incorrect. Students will not necessarily know about conflict just by looking at the cover of the book.

B.   Incorrect. This project is not specifically related to conflict in literature.

C.   Incorrect. Comparing and contrasting daily problems might be an interesting socio-emotional learning activity, but it is not directly related to conflict in literary texts.

D.   **Correct.** Guided storybook reading emphasizing the problem the characters resolve is developmentally appropriate and a good introduction to the idea of conflict in literature.

16)   A.   Incorrect. Determining whether the author's purpose was achieved is another skill tested on these exams, but it does not help confirm answers to questions on *identifying* purpose.

B.   **Correct.** Supporting text evidence is key to confirming answers on such a test and in confirming the author's purpose.

C.   Incorrect. More complex texts, such as those on the ACT and SAT, generally do not state the purpose up front in the introduction.

D.   Incorrect. A call to action is a very good clue to the author's possible purpose in writing and should be considered.

17)   A.   Incorrect. Recorded lectures feature speakers, not authors, so this activity does not meet this objective.

B.   **Correct.** Studying Shakespeare's *Julius Caesar* and comparing it to the relevant information in the history text involves two different texts by two different authors. Students can compare things such as purpose (inform vs. entertain) and why certain points were or were not emphasized.

C.   Incorrect. In this activity, students compare two texts by the same author, so it does not meet the learning objective.

D.   Incorrect. This activity does not feature two different authors.

18)   A.   Incorrect. This question might help students activate background knowledge, but it would not help them determine the main idea.

B.   Incorrect. New facts students learned may or may not be the main idea; they might represent only details or examples.

C.   **Correct.** This question can help students narrow a topic to the main idea.

D.   Incorrect. What students found interesting may or may not be the main idea, though it is a useful strategy for evaluating the text.

19)   **A.**   **Correct.** Graphic text features will help all learners, including English language learners, to understand key concepts visually, even if they lack the vocabulary skills to read the textbook chapter.

B.   Incorrect. Peer tutoring will likely not be helpful, as it is foundational vocabulary that the English language learners may lack.

C.   Incorrect. An audio recording does not directly address comprehension, though it might help students with reading-related learning disabilities.

D.   Incorrect. A lecture might be hard for English language learners to follow.

20) A.   Incorrect. The Cornell method is more appropriate for older students.

B.   Correct. Even first-grade students can "act out" the meaning of new words and would likely find a Words Alive activity engaging.

C.   Incorrect. The two-column method is more appropriate for older students.

D.   Incorrect. Most first-grade students are not reading fluently enough to effectively use text coding.

REVIEW

1) **A.** **Correct.** Having set questions will help students to read with the purpose of answering these questions.

   B.   Incorrect. Questions are more about knowledge that students want to learn, not background knowledge they already have.

   C.   Incorrect. Fix-up strategies are used when comprehension breaks down.

   D.   Incorrect. Making and answering questions out of headings is not using context clues to determine a word's meaning.

2) A.   Incorrect. Conducting research is a previewing method, but it is more appropriate for older students.

   B.   Incorrect. Identifying the protagonist and antagonist would be difficult before reading and is not developmentally appropriate for kindergarten students.

   C. **Correct.** Having kindergarten students examine a text's cover and title is an appropriate previewing technique.

   D.   Incorrect. Topic sentences can usually be identified only after reading the paragraphs. This is not developmentally appropriate for kindergarten students.

3) A.   Incorrect. This activity is not activating background knowledge, as students are not being asked what they already know about the topic or sources.

   B.   Incorrect. Drawing conclusions might be part of students' overall comprehension strategy, but it does not describe this activity.

   C. **Correct.** Students are making text-to-text connections by comparing and contrasting two different texts on the same topic.

   D.   Incorrect. Students are not being asked to highlight, underline, or make notations in the text.

4) **A.** **Correct.** This is good advice for scaffolding students as they self-select texts.

   B.   Incorrect. Some students may have an interest in a certain topic and enjoy reading more about it even if they already are familiar with it.

   C.   Incorrect. This robs students of the opportunity to self-select texts, which is an objective in most states at most grade levels.

   D.   Incorrect. Sustained silent reading is for pleasure; students do not need to be assessed on overall comprehension.

5) A.   Incorrect. This is a literal question.

   B.   Incorrect. This is an inferential question.

   C. **Correct.** Asking this question allows readers to form an opinion about Celeste, which makes it an evaluative question.

   D.   Incorrect. This is also a literal question.

6) A.   Incorrect. Poems are not typically assigned Lexile text measures.

   B.   **Correct.** 770L is an appropriate text measure for a fourth-grade student's level of proficiency.

   C.   Incorrect. Dramas are hard to score with a Lexile measure, and 1100 would be too high for most fourth graders to read independently.

   D.   Incorrect. A level of 200 would probably be too simple for a fourth-grade student.

7) D.   **Correct.** This is the only measure that is qualitative, or based on qualities of the text, versus quantitative. Knowledge demands refers to background information students will need to comprehend a text successfully.

8) A.   Incorrect. In a college-level course, students should be exposed to written information.

   B.   **Correct.** Giving students strategies to help them comprehend a difficult text can be helpful across the content areas.

   C.   Incorrect. There would not be time to read the text aloud in class, and not all students would necessarily comprehend it.

   D.   Incorrect. The textbook likely cannot be changed if it is mandated by the college offering the dual-credit course.

9) A.   **Correct.** In reciprocal teaching, students in a small group are assigned a role and must work together to comprehend a text.

   B.   Incorrect. Cloze procedure is typically an independent exercise.

   C.   Incorrect. List-group-label activities are aimed at vocabulary building.

   D.   Incorrect. Embedded phonics is aimed at decoding on a basic level, not comprehension or SEL.

10) A.   Incorrect. This would spoil the story and might limit student interest.

   B.   Incorrect. A character trait chart is more appropriate for students to fill in while or after reading.

   C.   Incorrect. The theme cannot be identified until the novel is read.

   D.   **Correct.** Students may not be familiar with the historical era in which the novel is set, and having this information about setting can help them better comprehend the novel.

Oral Language and Communication

ORAL LANGUAGE AND READING DEVELOPMENT

Oral (spoken) **language** and the development of reading skills are entwined in children from a young age. Children who understand the role of oral language in communication and how to produce and "consume" oral language will have a head start in learning to read.

Children who have heard or spoken many words will be far more likely to identify words in text. Those who have heard and participated in many conversations will make connections and activate background knowledge as they read. Further, oral language and an understanding of its structures is a seminal component in phonics instruction, which relies on the connection between written language and spoken language.

Storybook reading, which might seem to be aimed solely at creating prereading skills, helps develop oral language skills. As students listen to stories read aloud, they learn vocabulary and syntax they can then use as part of their own expressive language. They also use language to describe what they are hearing and seeing. In this way, most activities aimed at developing overall literacy skills in early childhood will

> **DID YOU KNOW?**
>
> The Record of Oral Language assesses children's oral language skills by having them listen to and repeat a series of increasingly complicated sentences. When children encounter a sentence structure they have not mastered, they will try to repeat the sentence using a structure they are comfortable with.

also help develop oral language skills, and vice versa. However, young children who come from non-print-rich environments and/or who were not read to as very young children may experience delays in both prereading and oral language skills.

Students will have a variety of backgrounds and oral language skills. Assessments such as the **Record of Oral Language (ROL)** can evaluate oral language competency and focus on the development of students' overall language skills.

While students with no or little exposure to many different words do have some disadvantage in learning to read, early intervention to build such vocabulary and basic oral language proficiencies can make a tremendous difference.

For these reasons, oral language development should be nurtured in young children and embedded in all daily interactions in the school setting. The most valuable forms of oral language instruction are practice and modeling. Children learn the components of oral language through observation and experience. Speaking frequently with children and encouraging them to speak with others will help them develop the oral language foundation necessary to be successful with beginning reading instruction.

Nuances related to each student's home language (dialect, register, etc.) should be respected in assessing and building oral language skills in preparation for and in conjunction with reading instruction. While educators might have certain notions of the "right" or "wrong" way to speak, such a distinction does not exist organically. Speech may not be well matched for a particular setting or audience, but it is not "wrong." In assessing and building oral language proficiency in tandem with reading skills, such

DID YOU KNOW?

Pragmatics refers to the way we use oral language (or any form of language) for a practical purpose. Pragmatic use of language is often explicitly taught in early childhood classrooms, where students are reminded to "use their words" to express needs, wants, frustrations, etc.

a distinction should be kept in mind. An overemphasis on speaking English "correctly" without consideration for unique registers and dialects removes language from its pragmatic context and fails to account for the broad diversity within the spectrum of spoken English.

SAMPLE QUESTION

1) A first-grade teacher asks a reading specialist for strategies to build oral language skills in one of her students struggling with class-wide phonics instruction. What is the BEST reason for her to use such a strategy?

A. Better oral language skills will help the student develop relationships with peers.

B. Oral language skills are tied to success in foundational phonics instruction.

C. Oral language skills will help the student better communicate lack of understanding to the teacher.

D. Better oral language skills will make the student feel less self-conscious during oral reading activities.

LANGUAGE ACQUISITION

The developmental sequence of first-language acquisition follows the same pattern in nearly all cases. And while there is variation in the age at which children reach given milestones, each child's acquisition maintains the same gradual pace. Correct usage of the parts of speech emerges slowly, whereas full pattern recognition generally takes place over four stages of first-language acquisition.

In the **pre-speech stage**, infants learn to pay attention to speech, inflection, and rhythm before they begin to speak. In fact, research indicates that they respond to speech more acutely than to other sounds. Brain scans have shown speech to elicit electrical activity in the left side of the brain, where much of the language center is stored in a region called Wernicke's area.

Infants' initial vocalizations may be expressions of discomfort, such as crying or fussing, or the by-product of involuntary actions such as sucking, swallowing, burping, and coughing. However, by two to four months, infants begin vocalizing expressions of comfort, usually in response to pleasurable interactions with a caregiver. These may be grunts or sighs, which later evolve into **cooing** sounds; laughter generally appears at about four months.

The **babbling stage** is unique to the human species. Infants start by controlling the pitch of their vocalizations to create squeals or growls. Next, they change the volume of their sounds to create both quiet and loud sounds. Finally, they learn to produce sounds based on **friction**, such as snorts or "raspberries." Toward the end of this stage, infants learn to create sequences of consonant-vowel sounds that they often repeat in lengthier spans as though they are speaking in sentences.

> **DID YOU KNOW?**
>
> Ninety-five percent of all babbling by babies throughout the world is composed of only twelve consonants: *p, b, t, d, k, g, m, n, s, h, w, j.*

The **one-word stage** is characterized by a child's use of a single word to convey a full meaning. These utterances usually have one of three purposes: to identify an action, to convey an emotion, or to name something.

Often a child's definition of a word is too narrow, called an **underextension**. For example, when a child refers to a stuffed animal as "toy," he or she is underextending the definition of the word *toy*. The opposite holds true as well; children at this stage also frequently **overextend** the definitions of words, as when a child refers to all animals with tails as "doggy."

The **two-word stage** usually occurs around the second year of a child's life. Vocabulary acquisition rates typically begin at one to three

> **DID YOU KNOW?**
>
> Underextensions and overextensions occur with most children and vary from individual to individual. They change frequently over time until the correct definition of the word is learned.

words per week, increasing to as many as ten words per week after about forty words have been learned. Word combinations also begin appearing. Children will form mini sentences with simple semantic relationships. For example, a child might say, "Go bye-bye," as a way of telling someone she is ready to leave.

In the **early multi-word stage**, also known as the **telegraphic stage**, children are mostly understood by their parents and caregivers. They begin using elements of grammar and repeating longer sentences, though they are still unable to create their own. Children at this stage also tend to leave out parts of speech like pronouns, determiners, and modals. But as they mature, children begin to alternate between childlike and adultlike speech, making fewer omissions and using more multi-clause sentences.

By age five, children have reached the **later multi-word stage**. They average four to six words per sentence and can increase their vocabulary by as many as twenty words per day. By age eight, the average child knows approximately 28,300 words.

SAMPLE QUESTION

2) **During which stage of first-language acquisition do children begin using words with intentional meaning?**

   A.   babbling stage
   B.   one-word stage
   C.   two-word stage
   D.   multi-word stage

THE STRUCTURE OF ORAL LANGUAGE

Oral language has three components: phonological, semantic, and syntactic. The structure of oral language is usually entwined with beginning reading instruction.

PHONOLOGICAL COMPONENT

Phonology refers to the system of sounds that make up language. Oral language can be broken down into several parts. The most basic unit of language is the **sound**, or **phoneme**. (Chapter 2 contains a list and detailed description of phonemes.) When any phoneme is spoken aloud, it creates an audible sound known as a **phone**. Phones are further broken down into **allophones**, or specific variants of phonemes. For example, there are several variants of the phoneme /t/. Consider the difference in the way the mouth moves when saying the /t/ sound in *batter*, *bat*, *take*, *water*, and so on. Each pronunciation represents an allophone.

The most common semivowels are:
▶   /w/ when it sounds like /oo/ (*dew*)
▶   /y/ when it sounds like /ee/ (*yesterday*), /e/ (*happy*), or /i/ (*fly*)

There are many ways to categorize phonemes based on how the sound is produced and used within words. All sounds or phonemes can be classified as one of the following:

▶ **vowels**: sounds produced without closing the vocal tract

▶ **diphthongs**: two vowels in the same syllable

▶ **semivowels**: a sound that is voiced similarly to a vowel but acts as a syllable boundary

▶ **consonants**: sounds produced through a partially or completely closed vocal tract

DID YOU KNOW?

The diphthongs are *ai, ay, ee, ea, ie, ei, oo, ou, ow, oe, ue, ey, ay, oy, oi, au, aw.*

Consonants can be further divided based on place of articulation, manner of articulation, and voicing. **Place of articulation** refers to where the sound originates in the mouth and how the parts of the mouth (lips, teeth, alveolar ridge, hard/soft palate, velum, glottis, and uvula) work to make the sound. There are eight places of articulation (shown in Figure 1.1).

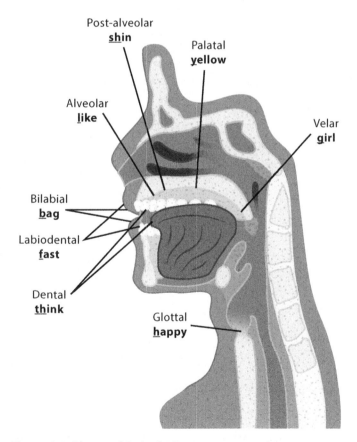

Figure 1.1. Places of Articulation

Manner of articulation refers to airflow and whether it is impeded as the sound is formed. It can be any of the following:

▶ **stop sounds** (or oral occlusive): consonant sounds in which the vocal tract is blocked so that all airflow stops

▶ **fricatives**: consonants produced when the air moving through the mouth creates audible friction

▶ **nasals**: consonants produced when air moves through both the nose and mouth in the production of the sound

▶ **affricatives**: combination between stop sounds and fricatives (e.g., *cherry*)

Voicing refers to how the vocal folds react, whether by vibrating or remaining open. **Voiced sounds** occur when the vocal folds vibrate. **Unvoiced sounds** occur when the vocal cords remain open and do not vibrate.

Alternatively, phonemes can also be placed in two categories based on how the vocal tract configuration changes while the sound is being produced. **Continuant sounds** are spoken through a fixed configuration of the vocal tract. Continuant sounds include vowel sounds, fricatives, and nasals. **Non-continuant sounds** are produced as the vocal tract changes over the pronunciation of the sound. Non-continuant sounds include diphthongs, semivowels, stop sounds, and affricatives.

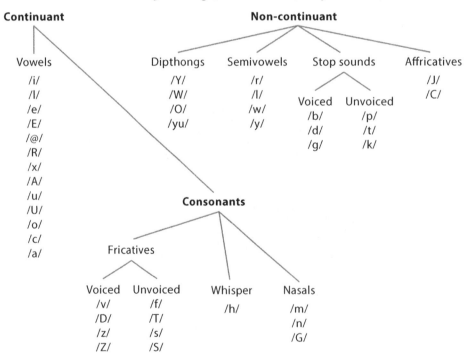

Figure 1.2. Classifying Phonemes

When it comes to reading and oral language instruction, phonemes are categorized with more simplistic terms that describe the way most educators discuss oral phonics instruction:

- **syllables**, or units (typically containing a single vowel sound) within words
- **onsets**, or the beginning consonant sounds of words (_sw_-im)
- **rimes**, or the letters that follow (sw-_im_)

SAMPLE QUESTION

3) A second grader reads the word _book_ as _būk_. This student would MOST likely benefit from instruction in

    A.   syllabication.

    B.   morphology.

    C.   diphthongs.

    D.   pragmatics.

SEMANTIC COMPONENT

The semantic component of oral language refers to the way speakers combine **morphemes**, the smallest units of language that have meaning, to make words. (Chapter 2 contains a detailed discussion of morphemes in reading instruction.) In English, morphemes can be combined in a variety of ways. For example, coffee + maker = coffeemaker, and run + ing = running.

Morphology refers to the forms of words. After very young children experiment with making sounds, they begin to form words. Morphology includes word parts like roots and affixes and various word endings that make a word change in number or part of speech. Those learning English for the first time as children or as second-language learners must learn the construction of words through manipulation of morphemes to create plural construction, adjective or adverb forms, and so on.

Semantics refers to the meaning of words. English dictionaries are the resources containing the semantics of the English language.

SAMPLE QUESTION

4)   Which resource would be MOST helpful to a seventh-grade student building skills in the semantic component of oral language as she reads a text with complex vocabulary?

A.   a chart showing continuant and non-continuant sounds

B.   a chart showing how to form irregular plurals

C.   an age-appropriate dictionary

D.   a chart that shows how to diagram sentences

SYNTACTIC COMPONENT

Syntax refers to the way speakers use morphemes together to make sentences with meaning. The syntactic component of oral language is the last to develop. This development is evident as young children begin by making statements such as "dog go" and then gradually progress to more advanced sentences such as "The dog goes outside."

The syntactic component of oral language governs the way speakers string ideas together. Typically, in English, speakers most often speak in a pattern of subject + verb + object, though there are many variations to this pattern.

SAMPLE QUESTION

5)   A young child says, "Mama go" after being dropped off at school by his mother. What component of oral language is he still mastering?

A.   morphology

B.   syntax

C.   pragmatics

D.   phonology

INSTRUCTIONAL STRATEGIES FOR DEVELOPING ORAL LANGUAGE SKILLS

DEVELOPING LISTENING AND SPEAKING SKILLS

From a young age, children should be encouraged to have conversations with adults and peers as much as possible. Such interactions help children understand the role of oral language in communications. Conversations also show them the best way to use oral language to express needs or preferences, to join a group in play, or to pretend to exist in another world (imaginative play).

Vocabulary development can also be encouraged in young children or English learners through **picture vocabulary cards**, which can then serve as a springboard to incorporate new words into the classroom in both speaking and listening. Listening to and singing songs and rhymes can also aid in both vocabulary development and phonemic awareness. **Guided storybook reading** and whole-group activities that require students to speak and listen, such as **show-and-tell**, also aid in oral language development of young learners.

Figure 1.3. Vocabulary Cards

As students become more proficient with oral language in an organic context, various targeted instructional strategies can aid in development of these skills.

▶   "think-pair-share" activities in which students first think of an idea or opinion about a topic, then pair up with another student or group, and finally share this idea

▶   "ask three then me" activities in which students ask three peers to try to answer a question before asking for the teacher's help

▶   peer tutoring

▶   flexible grouping

▶   collaborative learning

▶   role-play/dramatizations/impromptu dialogues

▶   oral presentations/speeches

▶   debates

▶   discussions

▶   oral reading/recitation

When planning oral language activities, it is helpful to consider the particular skills being targeted. For example, a teacher might want to encourage students to develop prosody as they recite or read a poem or monologue to the class. Another activity might be aimed at having students use oral language in a pragmatic context by first considering audience before planning a speech or oral presentation.

Listening skills can be slower to develop, especially among young children. However, games like Simon Says and others in which students must follow oral directions can be useful and enjoyable. A popular technique with elementary students is **whole body listening**. This strategy gives students explicit instruction in how to listen with their entire body.

- ▶ eyes should be on the speaker
- ▶ ears should be listening
- ▶ mouth should be quiet
- ▶ hands should be in the lap or away from others
- ▶ feet should be still
- ▶ body should be pointed toward the speaker
- ▶ brain should be thinking about what it is hearing
- ▶ heart should be considerate of others

Depending on the student age and context, **active listening** skills can also be taught. Active listening, or reflective listening, describes students' ability to repeat what has been said to check for understanding. Students can use active listening strategies in several ways: asking questions after hearing a speaker or lecture, taking notes that summarize what the speaker has said, and using verbal or nonverbal affirmations of understanding as the person is speaking.

SAMPLE QUESTION

6) A reading and language arts teacher is planning a unit on listening skills for fourth graders. She asks a reading specialist for ideas. Which activity would the reading specialist MOST likely recommend?

    A. having students memorize and recite poetry in front of the teacher for a grade based on inflection and accuracy

    B. having a guest speaker visit the classroom to discuss a topic and answer student questions

    C. having students watch a video and then ask questions about parts they did not understand

    D. having students find a solution to a school-wide problem that affects them all

ORAL LANGUAGE FOR CRITICAL THINKING AND CREATIVE EXPRESSION

Students should also be expected to use oral language to think critically and communicate their thoughts. This process relies on both **receptive oral language**, the ability to understand what is being said, and **expressive oral language**, the ability to use language to communicate ideas appropriately.

Techniques for developing oral language skills for critical thinking and creative expression vary by age level. Strategies for younger students include:

- asking students to describe objects in the room or that they see out the window or outside on a nature walk
- asking students to describe how two objects or pictures are similar or different
- encouraging play with props in the dramatic play center
- encouraging students to pretend to be a character from a story
- asking students to describe another person or themselves aloud

Techniques for developing oral language skills for critical thinking and creative expression for older students include:

- oral discussion or critiques of literature or expository texts
- reciprocal teaching (students become the teachers and guide a small-group reading activity)
- "book club" or book discussion activities in large or small groups
- oral discussions with peers on current events or issues that require critical reflection
- persuasive speeches or presentations
- plays or dramatic performances
- writing and reading a piece of creative writing aloud
- impromptu dialogues or role-plays

SAMPLE QUESTION

7) A ninth-grade English teacher asks a reading specialist how to incorporate oral language for critical thinking into his unit on Shakespeare's *Romeo and Juliet*. Which instructional strategy is the reading specialist MOST likely to recommend?

    A. filling out a graphic organizer before, during, and after reading the play
    B. reading the play aloud with dramatic inflection
    C. holding a class-wide debate on whose fault the tragedy really was
    D. encouraging students to use fix-it-up strategies as they read the tragedy orally

NONVERBAL COMMUNICATION SKILLS

Developing students' nonverbal communication skills is just as important as oral language skills. **Nonverbal communication** refers to any way communication occurs outside of speech. Examples of nonverbal communication are:

- **paralinguistics** (tone, loudness, inflection, pitch)
- facial expression
- gestures
- body language/posture
- proximity
- eye contact

Each of these instructional activities can also focus on nonverbal communication skills as part of overall oral communication. Additionally, activities such as having students play charades or act out a "silent" movie can show them how even nonverbal communication has an impact.

Students can focus on paralinguistics by practicing speaking for an audience and then reviewing an audio or video recording of themselves. They can also analyze audio or video recordings of famous speeches for tone and inflection or other nonverbal communication, such as gestures or eye contact.

Students should receive instruction in formal versus informal speaking and nonverbal communication. In any activity, pragmatics, or the way speech is used to achieve a given purpose, should be emphasized. Again, there is no right or wrong way to speak or communicate nonverbally, only ways that fit or do not fit a given audience or situation.

Educators should not judge culturally nuanced means of nonverbal communication as incorrect or correct but rather should focus on what is most appropriate for a given situation. Students should also be made aware that nonverbal communication varies based on locale, and different cultures have different norms or standards for gestures, eye contact, volume of voice, and so on.

SAMPLE QUESTION

8) A high school teacher asks a reading specialist for feedback on a rubric she has created to assess students on their oral presentations. The rubric includes the following categories:
- unity/adherence to topic
- cohesion and transitions
- well-researched and understood content
- appropriate language use

Which category should the reading specialist suggest the teacher add to the rubric?

A. use of continuant and non-continuant sounds
B. phonological awareness
C. use of transitional expressions
D. nonverbal communication

REVIEW

Read the question, and then choose the most correct answer.

1

A reading specialist notices that a kindergarten student receiving Tier 2 interventions often struggles to pronounce words such as "bread," "hoop," "deal," and "void" in conversation. She should tell the speech language pathologist that the student is struggling with which type of structure?

A.   consonant blends

B.   *r*-controlled vowels

C.   diphthongs

D.   syllabication

2

How is a semivowel distinct from a vowel?

A.   It acts as a syllable boundary.

B.   It is always pronounced as a short vowel.

C.   It contains no phone.

D.   It is always pronounced as a long vowel.

3

Students with hearing impairments are MOST LIKELY to experience difficulties with which of the following components of oral language?

A.   phonological component

B.   semantic component

C.   syntactic component

D.   orthographic component

4

How many morphemes does the word "painted" have?

A.   one

B.   two

C.   three

D.   four

5

Which component of oral language is the last to develop in children?

A.   phonology

B.   semantics

C.   syntax

D.   vocalization

6

Based on changing enrollment and demographic trends, a reading specialist is asked to give a school-wide training on creating learning environments that respect cultural and linguistic diversity but still aim to meet challenging state standards for oral communication. Which of the following strategies should the reading specialist include in the presentation?

A.   strategies to eliminate an accent based on careful and scripted training

B.   strategies to promote code-switching once students enter the school

C.   opportunities to teach strategies for adjusting register based on audience

D.   opportunities to recognize and correct the use of slang and idioms in speech

7

To teach whole-body listening to students, educators should do which of the following?

A.   use incidental learning

B.   give explicit instruction

C.   limit teacher talk

D.   use formal assessments

8

Schools using positive behavior intervention and supports (PBIS) often teach and use active listening because it

A.   can limit misunderstandings.

B.   promotes tolerance for diversity.

C.   is part of the first tier of intervention.

D.   is part of the second tier of intervention.

9

A dramatic play center can promote which of the following?

A.   overall phonics learning

B.   knowledge of orthography

C.   expressive oral language

D.   practice with non-continuant sounds

10

The word "threw" contains

A.   two syllables.

B.   a consonant blend and a semivowel.

C.   a consonant blend and a short vowel.

D.   a consonant blend and a long vowel.

ANSWER KEY

SAMPLE QUESTIONS

1) A. Incorrect. Better oral language skills will help the student develop relationships, but there is no indication that the student needs help with this. The deficiency lies with phonics.

   B. Correct. Phonics connects written language with spoken language, and oral language skills are important for students to get the most out of phonics instruction.

   C. Incorrect. Oral language skills will help the student communicate with the teacher, but she seems aware of the student's lack of understanding. The issue seems to be a skill gap more than an inability to communicate lack of understanding.

   D. Incorrect. The student might still struggle with decoding even with more advanced oral language skills.

2) A. Incorrect. Children are unable to utter complete words during the babbling stage. Instead, they make sounds to express basic emotions.

   B. Correct. Most children first use a single word to express complete ideas.

   C. Incorrect. Children in the two-word stage are able to use more than one word to express their meaning and often modify their intents with descriptors.

   D. Incorrect. Children who have reached this stage are able to express themselves using complete sentences and no longer rely on basic communication to convey meaning.

3) A. Incorrect. *Book* has only one syllable, and the student is correctly pronouncing the word with only one syllable.

   B. Incorrect. Morphology has to do with the form of words, and the student is not reading the word in an incorrect form.

   C. Correct. /oo/ is a diphthong pronounced with a short /ŭ/ sound, not a long /ū/. Instruction in this diphthong would likely be helpful for this student.

   D. Incorrect. It appears that the student is using this word in isolation, not in a pragmatic or real-world context.

4) A. Incorrect. A chart showing continuant and non-continuant sounds applies to the phonological component.

   B. Incorrect. A chart showing irregular plurals does involve the semantic component of language but would not aid the student, as she is reading a text with complex vocabulary. This chart would more directly help the student to write.

   C. Correct. Dictionaries give the definitions of words and could help the student build semantic knowledge as she looks up unfamiliar words.

D.   Incorrect. Diagramming sentences pertains to the syntactic component, not the semantic component.

5)   A.   Incorrect. Morphology refers to the way words are formed. This child is working to form sentences.

     B.   **Correct.** Syntax refers to the way morphemes are combined to make meaning in sentences.

     C.   Incorrect. Pragmatics refers to the way language is used for a particular purpose in a particular situation.

     D.   Incorrect. Phonology refers to the system of sounds that make up language, not the construction of sentences to make meaning.

6)   A.   Incorrect. Recitation promotes speaking skills, not listening skills.

     B.   **Correct.** Questioning a guest speaker would allow students to apply the listening skills they have learned in an authentic context.

     C.   Incorrect. A video activity might help with metacognition and determining what is understood, but this is not *directly* aimed at listening skills, as there may be other reasons students did not understand parts of a video (e.g., lack of background knowledge).

     D.   Incorrect. Collaborative learning does provide a way to practice listening skills, but without explicit instructions to focus on listening, this activity does not directly relate to unit objectives.

7)   A.   Incorrect. Graphic organizers would help students make predictions and consolidate understanding but do not necessarily involve oral language skills.

     B.   Incorrect. Reading the play aloud would perhaps aid in comprehension of the play and help students express themselves creatively, but it does not necessarily encourage critical thinking.

     C.   **Correct.** In a class-wide debate, students have to think about the play critically, form an opinion, and then express that opinion orally.

     D.   Incorrect. This would aid in comprehension but is not a strategy directly related to oral language skills.

8)   A.   Incorrect. Use of continuant and non-continuant sounds would most likely be mastered by high school and is not really a part of assessing a speech or oral presentation.

     B.   Incorrect. Phonological awareness refers to awareness of sounds or phonemes and is not a skill taught in high school.

     C.   Incorrect. Use of transitional expressions could be a subheading of the rubric under "cohesion and transitions," but it is already covered under that section and does not need to be added.

     D.   **Correct.** Nonverbal communication such as eye contact, gestures, posture, and so on should also be assessed as part of a comprehensive assessment of an oral presentation.

REVIEW

1) A.   Incorrect. Only "**br**ead" has a consonant blend.

    B.   Incorrect. None of these words has an *r*-controlled vowel.

    C.   Correct. /ea/, /oo/, and /oi/ are diphthongs, or two vowels in the same syllable.

    D.   Incorrect. Syllabication is not at issue; these are all one-syllable words.

2) **A.   Correct.** Semivowels create a boundary at the end of a syllable.

    B.   Incorrect. Semivowels have a unique pronunciation and are not strictly short or long.

    C.   Incorrect. A phone is a spoken sound, so semivowels are phones.

    D.   Incorrect. Semivowels are not categorized as long or short vowel sounds.

3) **A.   Correct.** The phonological component of oral language refers to the way sounds make language.

    B.   Incorrect. The semantic component is related to the meaning and forms of words.

    C.   Incorrect. The syntactic component is related to stringing words into sentences.

    D.   Incorrect. Hearing impairments are not necessarily related to difficulties in spelling.

4) **B.   Correct.** Paint + ed is two morphemes. Morphemes are the smallest units of meaning in words. Endings that indicate tense or singularity or plurality are considered morphemes.

5) A.   Incorrect. Phonology, the concept that oral language uses sounds to convey meaning, is one of the first components to develop.

    B.   Incorrect. Semantics, the meaning of words, develops early in many children, although children may underextend or overextend word meanings.

    C.   Correct. Syntax, successfully stringing words into sentences, is the last part of oral language to develop. Young children may say things like "Dog go!" to mean "The dog goes."

    D.   Incorrect. Even infants begin to vocalize or make sounds. This skill tends to develop early.

6) A.   Incorrect. Eliminating an accent is not respectful of cultural and linguistic diversity. Many students may have accents that do not impede overall communication.

    B.   Incorrect. Students should not be asked to code-switch upon entering the school. In social situations with friends at school, certain dialects and registers are appropriate.

C.   **Correct.** Students should understand that oral communication in different dialects and registers is not right or wrong, good or bad. Students should adjust their communication style based on audience and situation.

D.   Incorrect. Slang and idioms in speech are not bad or wrong. They might be appropriate or inappropriate for a given audience or situation.

7)   A.   Incorrect. Whole-body listening must first be taught explicitly, not incidentally.

B.   **Correct.** Teachers should introduce the components of whole-body listening through explicit and direct instruction.

C.   Incorrect. Teachers will likely need to talk and model to help students understand each part of whole-body listening.

D.   Incorrect. Some parts of whole-body listening may be hard to fully observe and assess through formal assessment measures.

8)   A.   **Correct.** Active listening allows the listener to confirm understanding of what the speaker has said, which can limit misunderstandings.

B.   Incorrect. Tolerance for diversity is important in any school, but active listening is not targeted at this.

C.   Incorrect. Active listening is simply a part of everyday communications, not an intervention strategy.

D.   Incorrect. Active listening is part of appropriate behaviors that, when demonstrated, would eliminate the need for interventions.

9)   A.   Incorrect. Dramatic play centers can promote socio-emotional learning and cognitive and language development but not necessarily phonics learning.

B.   Incorrect. Dramatic play centers are not targeted at spelling instruction.

C.   **Correct.** At dramatic play centers, students can practice expressing themselves through oral language.

D.   Incorrect. Non-continuant sounds such as diphthongs and stop sounds are important to practice speaking, but dramatic play centers don't target this.

10)   A.   Incorrect. "Threw" has only one syllable.

B.   **Correct.** /thr/ is a consonant blend, and /w/ acts as a semivowel.

C.   Incorrect. The /ew/ is not a short vowel sound.

D.   Incorrect. The /ew/ sound is not a long /e/ sound.

Writing Skills and Processes

From a very young age, children understand that written language is a way to communicate. As they develop reading and writing skills, children learn that writing is a means to both express and receive information. When they produce writing, they are giving a reading experience to others. When they consume writing, they are engaged in their own reading experience. Both reading and writing help students develop pre-reading skills like letter-sound correspondence and phonemic awareness. For example, a student who titles a drawing "M" to denote it as an image of their mother understands that the symbol "M" stands for the sound /m/ and is part of communicating the meaning of "mother."

As students grow and develop more advanced literacy skills, writing-related activities like spelling practice can increase reading comprehension. Students who are exposed to high-frequency words in spelling or writing practice activities will strengthen their knowledge of these words. Since word identification skills are strongly linked to reading fluency, writing activities should be integrated with reading instruction and activities as much as possible.

Some theorists believe reading and writing are so interconnected that one cannot occur without the other. Even when students lack the motor skills to write themselves, many educators believe that writing can and should still be a meaningful part of literacy instruction.

One strategy that illustrates this belief is the **Language Experience Approach (LEA)**. In this approach, learners and teacher first have a shared experience. They might, for example, visit the school garden as a class. Teachers or students then document the shared experience, usually with photographs. Students refer to the photographs when writing about the experience. With scaffolding from the teacher as necessary, students create a text about the shared experience. They then read the story aloud (with scaffolding as needed), noting any needed revisions. The final story is read aloud again, often accompanied by teacher-directed comprehension questions.

LEA helps students connect writing and reading because they are involved in both the creation of written language to communicate an experience and the reading of the written language used to communicate what happened.

SAMPLE QUESTION

1) **Preschool children should be encouraged to experiment with letters and text to label pictures they draw because this**
    A.   strengthens receptive vocabulary.
    B.   develops gross motor skills.
    C.   contributes to an understanding of text as meaning.
    D.   encourages the transition from artistic to written expression.

DEVELOPMENTAL STAGES OF WRITING

A child's journey to writing happens in phases and is influenced by encouragement from parents, teachers, and caretakers. **Writing development** involves three areas:

1. conceptual knowledge (understanding the purpose of writing)
2. procedural knowledge (understanding how to form letters and words)
3. generative knowledge (using words to communicate a meaning)

Even children as young as two begin to draw pictures they use to communicate ideas. These images are their first written representations. This drawing develops into **scribbling**, which looks like letters. Wavy scribbling or mock handwriting may appear as children are exposed to print-rich home environments and classrooms. This is followed by forms that look like individual letters and then forms with actual letters that resemble individual words strung together.

In the **transitional writing stage**, children begin writing letters separated by spaces, although real words are generally not yet being formed. Even in the transitional writing stage, however, many children successfully copy letters and words from environmental sources. Writing a child's name or the name of a common classroom object on a card for a child to copy can encourage transitional writing. Be mindful, however, that writing is still emergent, and children may invert letters or fail to accurately copy letters.

Table 4.1. Stages of Emergent Writing

Stage	Example
Drawing	

Stage	Example
Scribbling	
Wavy scribbles	
Letter-like forms	
Letter strings	
Transitional writing	
Invented and phonetic spelling	My NAM IS HANA
Word and phrase writing	DOG / PIG
Conventional spelling and sentences	HANNAh

As children learn sounds, they begin a phase of **invented spelling**. They start communicating words and ideas more clearly, though many words may have only a beginning and ending sound. This stage is a natural part of the process of emergent writing. Children should be allowed to express ideas and practice writing without an overemphasis on spelling errors. Explicit spelling instruction will generally begin in the early elementary grades. Students will have plenty of time and practice to master these skills when they are developmentally ready.

As children gain more knowledge of sounds and words, they will begin writing whole words, first with single letter-sound constructions like "dog," "hat," and "fun." This progresses to the correct spelling of more words and eventually to stringing together words to make phrases and short sentences.

It is important to see writing as a process and recognize that it can be affected by many factors. For example, students with conditions that impact fine motor skills functioning or young children with developmental delays in associated domains may have difficulty learning to write fluently. Expectations should be tailored to the individual student. Teachers should encourage and praise effort rather than result as young people are developing these skills.

Table 4.2. Developmental Stages of Writing

Stage	Age	Students in this stage...
Preconventional	3 – 5	▶ are aware that print conveys meaning, but they rely on pictures to communicate visually. ▶ include recognizable shapes and letters on drawings. ▶ can describe the significance of the objects in their drawings.
Emerging	4 – 6	▶ use pictures when drawing but may also label objects. ▶ can match some letters to sounds. ▶ copy print they see in their environment.
Developing	5 – 7	▶ write sentences and no longer rely mainly on pictures. ▶ attempt to use punctuation and capitalization. ▶ spell words based on sound.
Beginning	6 – 8	▶ write several related sentences on a topic. ▶ use word spacing, punctuation, and capitalization correctly. ▶ create writing that others can read.
Expanding	7 – 9	▶ organize sentences logically and use more complex sentence structures. ▶ spell high-frequency words correctly. ▶ respond to guidance and criticism from others.

Stage	Age	Students in this stage...
Bridging	8 – 10	▶ write about a particular topic with a clear beginning, middle, and end. ▶ begin to use paragraphs. ▶ consult outside resources (e.g., dictionaries).
Fluent	9 – 11	▶ write both fiction and nonfiction with guidance. ▶ experiment with sentence length and complexity. ▶ edit for punctuation, spelling, and grammar.

SAMPLE QUESTION

2) **During free-choice center time, a kindergarten teacher notices that one of her students has gone to the writing center, taken a piece of lined paper, and written several misspelled phrases. What should the teacher do?**

   A.   explain the correct spelling of each word

   B.   praise the student for the attempt and choosing to practice writing

   C.   provide hand-over-hand guidance for the student to erase and rewrite the words

   D.   target the student for more explicit spelling instruction

PRINCIPLES OF EFFECTIVE WRITING

As students become more proficient writers, revising and examining their own writing and that of others, they should be mindful of what makes written communication effective. Successful writing has a central **focus**, or main idea (often referred to as a **central idea** in state and national standards). Brainstorming and other pre-writing activities can help students maintain focus as they plan a piece. While students will mainly be exposed to professional writing that has already been edited, having them identify the author's focus across a broad range of texts will increase reading and writing capability.

Additionally, students should identify how the author uses details, examples, and other elements as part of overall concept development. They should be critical of how authors support their arguments and determine whether the evidence is sufficient. Students can then use these skills to critically reflect on their own writing and decide whether they have adequately proven a point.

DID YOU KNOW?

Effective writing skills are a key component of success in higher education. Students who must take remedial or developmental college courses in writing and/or math (estimated at 40 – 60 percent) are less likely to complete their degree program on time or at all.

A knowledge of basic text **organization** will also help students become critical readers and effective writers. While there are many ways to organize and structure text, most effective writing has an **introduction**, several supporting details organized in a logical sequence, and a **conclusion** that wraps up the focus of the piece. It is helpful to have students practice labeling these parts in various texts. But even very young children can understand the idea of text organization by being shown the beginning, middle, and end of a story. As students edit and revise their work, they should organize their ideas so that the reader can follow the information in a logical pattern.

Each piece of writing also has a unique **style**, or approach. Style can describe the author's choice of words. Style also includes sentence and paragraph structure. Both word choice and structure can make a piece **formal**, **informal**, or somewhere in between. Additionally, all texts have a **tone** or attitude the author takes toward the subject or audience. A writer's tone might be hopeful, sarcastic, pessimistic, and so on.

One part of selecting a style and tone is the intended purpose and audience. Students should pay attention to the reader of their piece. A formal style is appropriate for writing a letter to the principal asking for a longer recess. A note to a friend would probably be written in an informal style. When reading any text, students should consider why an author chose a particular style convention or tone: Did the writer intend to argue a point to a hostile audience? Inform a group of students about the difference between income and expenses? Was the style formal or informal?

Mechanics are the structural elements of writing and include punctuation, capitalization, spelling, grammar, and general conventions of usage. Like most procedural knowledge of writing, this proficiency may vary among students and grade levels. A kindergarten class, for example, may be focused on a unit about capitalizing the letter *I*, whereas a second-grade class may be working on forming the past tense of verbs.

Teachers should not presume knowledge of Standard English conventions among students whose first language is not English. Correct use of prepositions, irregular verbs, and pronouns may be particularly challenging for these students until they get more experience with common usage patterns. Teachers should always aim for growth, not perfection, when helping students develop skills in editing their writing for errors in mechanics. These skills continue to build throughout a student's schooling.

SAMPLE QUESTION

3)   A reading specialist is helping a ninth-grade English teacher develop a rubric that she will use to score student writing. Which of the following categories would appear on the rubric under the heading of "mechanics"?

A.   word choice

B.   style

C.   punctuation

D.   tone

THE RECURSIVE WRITING PROCESS

Students should understand that writing is a process and that even professional writers put their work through several phases before releasing the finished product. A **recursive writing process** means that writers may return to a previously completed part of the process. Also known as the **authoring cycle**, this process includes several phases in which ideas are transformed into written form to effectively communicate meaning:

1. Plan   **4.** Edit

2. Draft   **5.** Publish

3. Revise

The first step in planning is to **brainstorm** ideas, which can take many forms. Teachers might have the class generate ideas for topics and write them on the board or screen. Students can then create their own **webs** or **outlines** to organize their ideas.

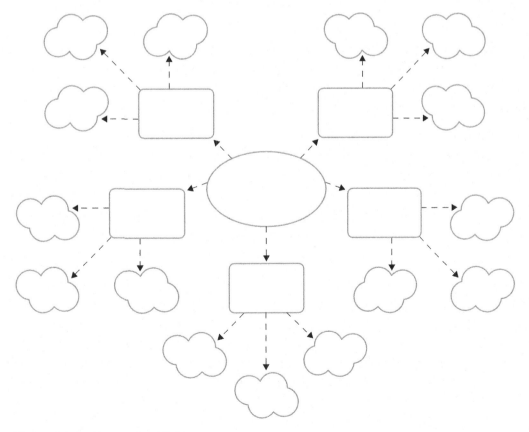

Figure 4.1. Brainstorming Web

This initial planning can help students organize their overall point and supporting details. These activities can be based on a book they have read, their opinion of the work (e.g., "I liked the book," "I did not like the book," "My favorite/least favorite part was...") and reasons for their opinion. Students might also write a simple expository piece introducing a topic and then using supporting details to inform the reader. Brainstorming activities can also help students organize the events they want to describe when writing narratives.

After brainstorming, students **draft** their piece and connect their ideas with an introductory statement, support, and concluding section. With scaffolding, students then go through a **revision** process where they address weaknesses in the writing. For example, they may need to add more supporting details or connecting words ("because," "also," "then") to improve clarity. They can then **edit** for capitalization, end marks, and spelling.

Teachers can help students in the revision process by giving them a simple checklist to help ensure they have met certain criteria. One such checklist is the **COPS mnemonic**, which stands for Capitalization, Organization, Punctuation, and Spelling.

Teachers can also use peer and teacher feedback as part of the revision process. Receiving feedback helps students understand that the main purpose of writing is to communicate ideas, so having other readers offer their perceptions and suggestions is an important part of revision.

Students should **publish** their work after the final copy is created, particularly if the writing project was significant in scope. Having students read their work aloud is one simple and immediate way to publish a piece (as well as a way to link reading and writing), as is posting it on a classroom or school bulletin board. Teachers may have students organize and bind their work into a simple book with string or brads or collect student work into a class-wide literary sampler.

If a teacher uses student portfolios in the classroom, students can prepare their pieces for inclusion in a digital or physical folder. This may involve transcribing the piece digitally, adding illustrations, or matting it on construction paper. Teachers should also emphasize that sharing the work with others is an important part of publishing. This is a great way to build a home–school connection while encouraging students to share their work with parents. Teachers should also show student work samples or portfolios at parent conferences to further build the home–school connection.

4)   A high school English teacher sponsors a creative writing club that meets weekly after school. He asks the reading specialist for advice on a high-impact way to publish student work and share it with the school community. What should the specialist suggest?

   A.   invite administrators to attend one of the club meetings and listen to students read their work

   B.   encourage students to read their pieces at home to their family members

   C.   plan a digital or print literary journal that can be shared across the school

   D.   teach students to use publishing and graphic design software to format their pieces

INSTRUCTIONAL STRATEGIES FOR DEVELOPING WRITING SKILLS

Teachers and reading specialists can use many strategies and activities to help students develop strong writing skills throughout the writing process.

PLANNING

1.   **Data dump** is an informal prewriting method whereby students write down a topic and then any words that immediately come to mind. For example, a student might write "environmentalism" and then list terms like "climate change, pollution, endangered animals, etc." After a data dump, students select only the words that most closely pertain to their chosen topic.

2.   In **guided pre-writing**, the class or group of students come up with ideas and/or a writing structure. The teacher helps by visually projecting ideas or writing them on a board. Mapping, outlining, webbing, and listing are common strategies for guided pre-writing.

3.   **RAFT** is a pre-writing method that encourages students to consider their purpose, audience, and organization pattern. Students think about the following questions:

   ▷   **Role** of writer: what perspective will you as the writer take?

   ▷   **Audience**: who will read the piece?

   ▷   **Format**: how will you communicate your message (e.g., story, essay, drama)?

   ▷   **Topic**: what will you write about?

4. **Media or tech-enabled planning** involves students watching a video, looking at images, or searching for ideas online. This can be a useful strategy for students who are stuck or who do not have an opinion on an issue or a clear topic to write about.

DRAFTING

1. **Framed paragraphs** are a scaffolding technique to help students write paragraphs. Framed paragraphs are fill-in-the-blank templates that students use to write their own paragraphs. For example, an "empty" frame for a persuasive paragraph might be something like:
    I think that _____. The first reason I think this is because _____. The second reason I think this is because _____.
    Lastly, I believe that _____. For these reasons _____ should _____.

2. **Paragraph or essay hamburgers** encourage students to plan a paragraph or essay with the topic sentence or introduction as the top "bun" and the concluding sentence or concluding paragraph as the bottom "bun." The supporting details or body paragraph are the middle parts of the "hamburger."

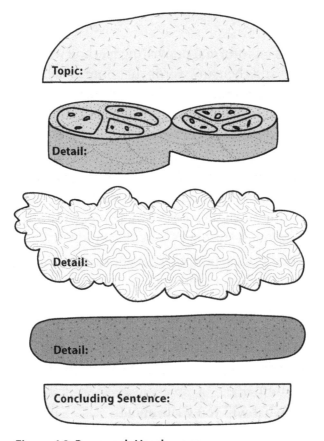

Figure 4.2. Paragraph Hamburger

3. **Shared or interactive writing** is a process whereby writers are scaffolded by "experts," usually teachers. In shared writing, the teacher scribes for the students, who must give explicit direction in what to write. This can be an effective method for students who have difficulty with the physical task of writing. In interactive writing, students compose the written piece, but the teacher serves as the subject matter expert who facilitates the process.

In both methods, the teacher helps scaffold learning as needed. This might involve asking leading questions ("What should happen after _____?"), providing ideas for transitions or breaks ("Let's start our next sentence with 'Additionally,'"), or even providing more explicit instruction to reinforce concepts ("Now, we need to add supporting details. What supporting details can we add?"). Shared or interactive writing helps students see and participate in an effective model for writing, which can give them confidence and strategies to use in independent writing assignments.

REVISION AND EDITING

1. **Modeling or think-alouds** can be used with a sample piece. This can be teacher- or student-authored (with student permission and name removed as requested) but should involve whole-class input. The piece can be projected on a screen and edited through a "track changes" feature in a word-processing program or even copied onto a transparency and written on. This process is helpful, as it allows students to participate in and experience the revision and editing process. Teachers can encourage input from the class and model strategies to revise writing, such as reading aloud, identifying and refining thesis and topic sentences, and so on.

2. **Conferencing or peer review** can also be used after first modeling the process and providing guidelines to students. Research proves that the most successful writing conferences are structured and occur when students have a clear idea of what type of feedback they should provide and how to give feedback in a constructive way.

3. **Self-assessment** should also be taught as part of the revision process. Students can be given a checklist or rubric from which to assess their own drafts and make necessary revisions.

SAMPLE QUESTION

5) A third-grade teacher wants to encourage students to organize their thoughts into a coherent paragraph. Which of the following instructional strategies BEST meets this goal?

    A. data dump

    B. self-assessment

    C. hamburger method

    D. COPS mnemonic

Spelling, Usage, and Mechanics

Spelling Instruction

The mechanics of writing will generally involve explicit **spelling** instruction, which will likely be part of a program's curriculum. It is important to view spelling as part of a developmental continuum and not overemphasize correct spelling too early when preschool students are still forming mock letters or letter strings. However, a standard **continuum of spelling** can be referenced to tailor spelling instruction appropriate to grade level while always keeping in mind the differing developmental levels within the classroom.

Table 4.3. Continuum of Spelling	
By the end of first grade, most students should be able to correctly spell short words with . . .	short vowel sounds with a consonant-verb-consonant (cat, dog, pin) pattern [CVC]
	vowel-consonant pattern (up, egg) [VC]
	simple consonant-vowel pattern (go, no) [CV]
	consonant blends and digraphs in simple and high-frequency words (chat, that) [CCVC]
By the end of second grade, most students should be spelling words with . . .	final consonant blends (rant, fast, bend, link) [CVCC]
	regular long vowel patterns (ride, tube) [CVC]
	double consonant endings (lick, fuss)
	more complex long vowel patterns (suit, fail)
	r-controlled vowels (near, bear, hair, are)
By the end of third grade, most students should be able to spell words with . . .	diphthongs (coil, soon, enjoy, wow)
	soft g's and c's (dice, hedge)
	short vowel patterns (head, sought)
	silent consonants (tomb, known, gnaw, wrote)
	advanced digraphs and blends (phase, character, whose)
	contractions
	soft g's and c's (dice, hedge)
	short vowel patterns (head, sought)
	silent consonants (tomb, known, gnaw, wrote)
	advanced digraphs and blends (phase, character, whose)
	contractions
	two-syllable words
	compound words
	words with suffixes that show number or degree (fastest, foxes)
By the end of fourth grade, most students should be able to spell words with . . .	special spelling rules such as doubling the final letter on CVC words when adding certain suffixes (napping, saddest)

Spelling instruction should be explicit and systematic, focusing on **orthographic knowledge**, or an understanding of the system by which spoken language is communicated in writing. To develop orthographic knowledge, students must have certain foundational skills based on an understanding of the three layers of linguistic information:

▶ alphabetic: recognition of letter-sound correspondence and sounding out from left to right

▶ pattern: understanding more complex patterns that might not be simple left to right, such as long vowel digraphs or open and closed syllables

▶ meaning: understanding meaning in word parts that do not change with pronunciation, such as "sign" and "signature"

To spell, students need skills in visualization and auditory sequencing. **Visualization** is the ability to recall the spelling of a word and write it based on a stored mental image. **Auditory sequencing** is the ability to identify a word's sounds in the proper order. These skills are linked to both reading and spelling proficiency and are important foundations.

There are three primary approaches to spelling instruction.

1. The **basal approach** is rooted in the notion of **orthographic patterns** or spelling generalizations such as consonant doubling, adding prefixes and suffixes, dropping the silent *e* when adding a suffix, and so on. This approach involves a set curriculum with spelling lists that gradually increase in difficulty. Research suggests that these lists are most effective when grouped by orthographic pattern and when they contain high-frequency words that students can decode when reading.

2. The **developmental approach** involves individualizing spelling instruction based on the developmental level and needs of individual students. This approach uses the research-backed strategies of the basal approach but does not rely on a single spelling list or spelling continuum or curriculum for all students. The developmental approach is gaining in popularity and is characterized by practices like focusing on words that are within a student's instructional level, defined by a list of words that students can spell with 40 – 90 percent accuracy.

3. The **incidental approach**, sometimes called the student-oriented or student-centered approach, teaches spelling in an authentic context. Instead of using a published curriculum, it relies on words students encounter in reading across the content areas. This method is less effective than the other two approaches, but it is still used in some programs that employ a whole-language literacy approach.

Spelling instruction should focus on instruction and assessment. Examples of research-backed spelling instructional activities include:

▶ Word sorts: students sort words based on orthographic features. For example, students might sort words with long and short vowel sounds or words that end in –*ch*.

▶ Phonogram study: students practice reading and writing words that contain certain sounds, like /ou/, or word endings, like –*ink*.

▶ Writing sorts: students divide spelling words into columns based on similar orthographic patterns.

▶ Spelling notebooks: students learn a spelling rule (or exception to it) and then list words that demonstrate it.

▶ Cover-copy-compare: students study word spellings, cover them up, and then spell them independently, checking afterward for accuracy.

It is important to provide opportunities for students to apply spelling skills in writing. Students can write a paragraph or essay using words from a spelling list or words with a certain orthographic pattern. Students must be explicitly taught that the purpose of studying spelling is to become a competent writer, not a perfect speller. Students must receive many opportunities to *apply* spelling skills as part of the drafting and revision process.

Regardless of specific activities and approaches, educators should assess spelling proficiency in multiple contexts. This means that assessment of student progress should not rely solely on traditional spelling tests. It should include authentic assessments, both formal and informal, as educators monitor students' overall writing development.

SAMPLE QUESTION

6)   A fourth grader writes the following sentence: *I should have called him, but he wuld not have been home.*

What type of spelling instruction should his teacher use to help him revise this sentence?

A.   draw his attention to the correctly spelled phonogram in the sentence

B.   point out the incorrectly spelled word and have him write the word spelled correctly five times

C.   have him read aloud the sentence he has written to identify and correct his spelling error

D.   use an incidental approach and try to develop opportunities for him to see the word spelled correctly in another text

MECHANICS INSTRUCTION

Mechanics instruction used to focus on drills, and many students did not understand the connection between explicit study of grammatical conventions and their own writing. In recent years, however, most classrooms use a more integrated or holistic approach where mechanics and writing are taught together.

Many teachers and contemporary educational publishers focus on how a certain grammatical convention conveys a message in a particular way, instead of focusing on structure of language in isolation, which is not as helpful and may hinder oral and written language development. For example, capitalization and punctuation may not be necessary or appropriate when texting. However, in a formal expository essay for an academic audience, attention to these details is essential.

Further, correct punctuation such as commas and semicolons helps readers follow a writer's message and clearly see the relationship between ideas. For instance, short, choppy sentences structured in a nearly identical way may not appeal to or interest certain audiences.

Some best practices and instructional techniques for teaching mechanics in context are discussed below.

1. **Writing workshop** is an organizational framework for teaching the writing process that includes a mini-lesson, work time, and share time. The mini-lesson can provide mechanics instruction for students to incorporate into their writing.

2. **Targeted mechanics instruction** can be used with an individual student or at the class level. For example, after grading a student-authored short story, a teacher may need to provide explicit instruction in apostrophe use as a targeted lesson to the entire class. Or perhaps a teacher notices that only one or two students are struggling with correct use of apostrophes. The teacher could then provide individualized instruction, perhaps through published exercises in a text or on a digital platform.

3. Teachers can use **mentor texts** to teach grammar. Mentor texts describe high-quality writing (often published) that students can emulate in their own writing. These types of texts can be used to teach punctuation, capitalization, dialogue, sentence structure, style, format, and appropriateness to audience.

4. Teachers can give students **writing assignments** to practice and demonstrate understanding of key components of mechanics. For example, students can write a paragraph with two compound sentences and two complex sentences or an essay in which they identify and circle all the object or subject pronouns they used.

5. Teachers can encourage reading and **analysis** of structure. After reading texts, students can consider how the texts use conventions to create meaning and engage the reader. Possible questions for analysis include:

    ▷   How are pronouns used to create perspective?

    ▷   How is sentence structure used to create tone and mood?

    ▷   How are sentences and dialogue punctuated? How does this help the reader?

    ▷   How might the meaning of the text have shifted if different choices in mechanics had been used?

6. Teachers can encourage varied **writing exercises** for different purposes and encourage writing every day. Not all writing exercises have to be formal or instructional. Educators should allow time for freewriting as well as for writing that will be graded in part based on use of mechanics appropriate to the audience and situation.

7. Teachers should be mindful and respectful of dialects and registers. **Dialect** is an overall characteristic of a group of speakers. For example, certain English speakers are said to speak in a dialect based on geographic location (e.g., a Southern drawl or a Boston accent). A **register** is a variation in language based on audience or situation. Students may slip into various dialects and even registers as they write. Educators should not be critical of such variations. Rather, they should encourage students to think about a given audience when they write and how they can most clearly communicate their message with that audience in mind.

SAMPLE QUESTION

7) **A reading specialist is providing a list of mentor texts to help the sixth-grade English teaching team provide instruction on punctuation of dialogue. Which type of texts will the list MOST LIKELY include?**

    A.   autobiographies about well-known people

    B.   persuasive essays with expert quotations

    C.   long narrative poems with multiple speakers

    D.   short stories with multiple characters

INQUIRY AND RESEARCH

THE RESEARCH PROCESS

Research and library skills are an important part of developing overall student literacy. There are seven steps in the research process:

1. **Identifying and focusing on the topic**. This might be as simple as having students pick a topic they want to learn more about or develop a research question they wish to answer—before searching online.

2. **Finding background information and conducting a preliminary search**. This involves getting a general overview of a topic and possible subtopics. During this stage students may Google a topic or read the Wikipedia page about a particular topic.

3. **Locating materials**. This could involve work at the library and online. Teachers should encourage students to explore a wide variety of possible resources. Depending on the research topic, students should seek out **primary sources**, or firsthand accounts. Primary sources may be speeches or diaries, surveys or census data, photographs of an event,

and several other media that give eyewitness accounts of an event. Many primary sources are available online, and many sites organize these sources into an accessible format for students. Many materials that students find will also be **secondary sources**, or non-firsthand accounts. These include the majority of books, articles, and web pages devoted to a topic.

> **DID YOU KNOW?**
>
> Some state standards require students to know the differences between primary and secondary accounts, so this type of analysis should be part of the research process.

4. **Evaluating sources**. Students should determine if certain sources are useful and accessible to them. For example, a library database may generate results for articles in publications the library does not have. Some resources may be overly technical or written for an older audience. Students should also make sure they have **credible sources** written by experts. This stage in the research process might be a good point to introduce the different types of information available on the internet and the elements that make a source more reliable (listed author, .edu or .org domain, publication date, and so on).

5. **Note-taking**. Note-taking may involve the use of formal note cards or simply jotting down main ideas. As developmentally appropriate per student age, teachers should ensure students understand the idea of paraphrasing, or changing the author's words into their own, as they take notes. Paraphrasing can help students prevent **plagiarizing**, or presenting someone else's words as their own work.

6. **Writing**. This includes organizing all the notes into sentences and paragraphs. Students should be aware of the overall organization of their work as they introduce a focused topic, provide support, and write a conclusion. Depending on the age group teachers work with, they may have students make a poster to present their research instead of writing a formal paper.

7. **Citing sources**. This may include in-text **citations** and preparing a **bibliography**. To simplify these elements for young students, teachers might have them simply list titles of books and authors. Students in the upper elementary grades can create more sophisticated bibliographies in MLA style. MLA is generally regarded as the simplest citation style and the one students are first introduced to.

These steps can be simplified for very young students and depending on the scope of the research project. However, even kindergartners can gather information from sources to answer a simple research question, and first-grade students can contribute to a class-wide research project with teacher support. The key is introducing students to the various parts of the research process while providing scaffolding as needed to support them as they explore new outlets for their developing literacy.

SAMPLE QUESTION

8) **Which of the following is a primary source appropriate for a third-grade class to use as part of a research project?**

    A.   an article in a history journal written by a noted scholar of WWII at a 770 Lexile level

    B.   photographs of soldiers taken during WWII available online

    C.   a documentary video about American pilots in WWII made by public television

    D.   transcripts of an interview with a WWII pilot at a 1400 Lexile level

DIGITAL TOOLS

Increasingly, schools are using digital learning tools in their curricula. Many schools have one or more subscriptions to various educational technology platforms that may enhance student learning and digital literacy, which is defined as the ability to find, use, and create digital information. **Media literacy**, a key part of digital literacy, is students' ability to access, analyze, evaluate, and communicate information in both digital and physical form.

Some students may be experienced with accessing digital information at home on computers, tablets, or phones. However, not all students will have the same level of **digital literacy**. Teachers should explicitly direct students in strategies for finding and assessing the usefulness of digital information. The internet has created an unlimited platform for disseminating information. Students must be taught early not to trust all sources equally and how to determine the validity and usefulness of a given source.

Digital tools also enable students to differentiate literacy instruction through adaptive software programs that target practice for individual skill level. Technological tools can also aid students with special needs or limited English proficiency through their daily activities in the classroom. Devices and applications that allow nonverbal children to communicate and those that help English language learners quickly translate new words may become indispensable learning aids.

Teachers should also incorporate digital tools into the writing process as appropriate. This may include the use of word processing or presentation software to help with student drafting and revising and even the use of digital storytelling sites, which help students create and publish visual stories. The classroom or school may have a website or social media page for publishing stu-

DID YOU KNOW?

There are many intentionally fake sites on the internet designed to help students practice determining whether online information is legitimate. One example is found at https://zapatopi.net/treeoctopus, where students can learn about the Pacific Northwest Tree Octopus.

dent-created content. Before publishing any student work online, however, always check with administration and get parental consent.

SAMPLE QUESTION

9) A reading specialist is trying to convince one of the school's fourth-grade teachers to incorporate more technology into his lessons to meet new district standards. The teacher did not grow up with technology and does not think his students need it. What is one argument in favor of technology the reading specialist might make to help the teacher see its value?

    A. Students play video and computer games at home, so they should use technology at school too.

    B. Technology may help the teacher differentiate instruction for struggling readers.

    C. The district standards are always based on what is best for students, so he should heed them.

    D. Technology is not bad as long as it is strictly controlled by the teacher.

REVIEW

Read the question, and then choose the most correct answer.

1

A second-grade teacher wants to build student writing skills as well help them develop basic skills in summarization. Which of the following activities BEST meets her goals?

A.   written retellings

B.   neurological impress

C.   shared writing

D.   word experts

2

A teacher hangs a poster in the classroom that says, "I before E except after C or when sounded like ay as in neighbor and weigh." This poster gives an example of

A.   a continuum of spelling.

B.   a graphophonic cue.

C.   a phonogram.

D.   an orthographic pattern.

3

Auditory sequencing describes the process of

A.   forming oral language in the proper sequence.

B.   focusing on the main idea of spoken language.

C.   identifying sounds in the proper order in a word.

D.   differentiating between long and short vowel sounds.

4

Which of the following is characteristic of the writing workshop organizational framework?

A.   share time

B.   reading mentor texts

C.   embedded phonics

D.   semantic feature analysis

5

Writing instruction in preschool usually focuses on which of the following?

A.   semantics and morphology

B.   spelling remediation

C.   the alphabetic principle

D.   syntax and mechanics

6

A sixth-grade student receiving literacy interventions writes the following introductory paragraph for his autobiographical essay:

My name is Joel my friends sometimes call me Joe. I have lived in Boston all my life I enjoy baseball fishing and marshal arts. After school. I live in a large house my two brothers live there to.

Which type of targeted mechanics instruction should the interventionist plan?

A.   basic orthography

B.   sentence structure

C.   basic capitalization

D.   preposition use

7

Which of the following describes the BEST way for a kindergarten teacher to integrate technology into the writing process?

A.   teaching students to use the spell- and grammar-check feature in word-processing software

B.   structuring research assignments that require students to search online databases

C.   using software that allows students to drag and drop pictures to create a story

D.   allowing time each day for students to complete online punctuation drills

8

In which type of writing would students be MOST LIKELY to use a dialect or register and still communicate a message effectively?

A.   an expository essay

B.   a free-verse poem

C.   a research paper

D.   a biographical essay

9

Which of the following assessment methods would be MOST effective to gauge student writing progress over time?

A.   norm-referenced assessment

B.   criterion-referenced assessment

C.   dynamic assessment

D.   portfolio assessment

10

Purposeful instruction in the mechanics of writing should focus on which of the following relationships?

A. mechanics and communication

B. semantics and pragmatics

C. inductive and deductive reasoning

D. mechanics and vocabulary

ANSWER KEY

SAMPLE QUESTIONS

1) A.   Incorrect. Receptive vocabulary is an understanding of words that are heard or read. It is not related to labeling pictures.

B.   Incorrect. Gross motor skills involve the development of large muscle groups, not the small muscles developed through writing.

C.   Correct. This activity helps young children understand that written language is used to communicate meaning.

D.   Incorrect. It is not developmentally appropriate to expect preschoolers to transition from artistic to written expression. Preschoolers should be encouraged to use both forms of expression together.

2) A.   Incorrect. The student will likely not retain this information. The writing center is for practice, and the student is in the invented spelling stage.

B.   Correct. Practice is essential to developing writing and spelling skills, so praise is appropriate because the student chose this activity. Further, the student is likely in the normal and necessary invented spelling stage.

C.   Incorrect. While hand-over-hand guidance may be appropriate in cases where motor skills are still developing or students are reluctant to write, this student has already written the words. Erasing and rewriting the invented spelling is unnecessary and may be discouraging.

D.   Incorrect. This invented spelling is a normal stage, as students develop more accurate spelling skills through practice.

3) A.   Incorrect. Word choice would probably fall under the heading of "style."

B.   Incorrect. Mechanics refers to the basic structural elements of language; style refers to tone, word choice, and other factors.

C.   Correct. Punctuation is a major part of the mechanics of writing.

D.   Incorrect. Tone is not a part of the mechanics of writing. Tone refers to the writer's attitude toward the topic or audience.

4) A.   Incorrect. Having only administrators attend the club meetings is not the most high-impact way to publish student work.

B.   Incorrect. This only shares the work with the student's family, not the school community.

C.   Correct. A school-wide literary journal is an effective way to publish and distribute creative writing in a high school.

D.   Incorrect. Learning to use the software might be helpful, but it does not ensure that the work is shared with the school community.

5) A.   Incorrect. A data dump would only help students generate ideas, not organize them coherently.

B.   Incorrect. Self-assessment is an important part of the revision process, but it is not targeted at paragraph cohesion.

C.   Correct. The hamburger method helps students understand what sentences go where in a paragraph and how they can structure a paragraph to communicate a point.

D.   Incorrect. The COPS mnemonic is helpful for revising and editing but is not directly related to organizing ideas into a coherent paragraph.

6)   **A.   Correct.** This is an evidence-based spelling strategy. The student can be prompted to recognize that "should" and "would" have similar orthographic patterns and should be spelled similarly.

B.   Incorrect. Rewriting incorrectly spelled words correctly multiple times has not been proven to yield results. This might also be discouraging to the student.

C.   Incorrect. Reading the sentence aloud is unlikely to help the student recognize a spelling error, since he has spelled the word phonetically.

D.   Incorrect. The incidental approach is not effective in this context. The student will likely not make the connection to his own writing.

7)   A.   Incorrect. Autobiographies are not likely to have a lot of dialogue.

B.   Incorrect. This text would show how to punctuate quotations but not necessarily dialogue or speech between characters.

C.   Incorrect. Poems, even those with multiple speakers, are usually not punctuated with quotation marks.

D.   Correct. Students can see a model of dialogue punctuated correctly and then structure their own work in a similar way.

8)   A.   Incorrect. While this is a reasonable Lexile level for a third-grade student, it is not a primary source.

B.   Correct. This is a primary source that is easily accessible to third-grade students.

C.   Incorrect. This is a good resource, but it is not a primary source.

D.   Incorrect. This is a primary source, but the Lexile level is too high for third-grade students.

9)   A.   Incorrect. This reasoning will probably not be convincing.

B.   Correct. This is one benefit that may help his students and that he might have a hard time arguing against.

C.   Incorrect. He likely already disagrees with these standards since he does not want to implement them.

D.   Incorrect. This is a general statement and does not directly reference how technology might help his students.

REVIEW

1) **A.**   **Correct.** With written retellings, students retell a story they have read in a shorter form in their own words.

   B.   Incorrect. Neurological impress helps build automatic and sight word recognition.

   C.   Incorrect. Shared writing does not necessarily meet the goal of summarization, as it usually does not involve first reading a text.

   D.   Incorrect. Word experts helps build vocabulary skills.

2) A.   Incorrect. The continuum of spelling is the process by which words of increasing degree of difficulty are introduced.

   B.   Incorrect. Graphophonic cue is another word for decoding: when a student reads a word based on its component letters and sounds.

   C.   Incorrect. A phonogram is a single sound unit, such as /a/ or /sh/.

   D.   **Correct.** This is a common spelling convention, or orthographic pattern, present in English.

3) A.   Incorrect. Auditory sequencing is foundational knowledge needed for spelling, not for oral language.

   B.   Incorrect. Any spoken language exercise is part of listening comprehension.

   C.   **Correct.** Auditory sequencing involves identifying sounds in order within a word.

   D.   Incorrect. Distinguishing between long and short vowel sounds is part of phonemic awareness or overall phonics knowledge.

4) **A.**   **Correct.** The writing workshop approach involves a mini-lesson targeted to a particular facet of writing, work time in which students draft, and then share time in which they share their writing for feedback.

   B.   Incorrect. Mentor texts are helpful, but they are not only a characteristic of a writing workshop approach.

   C.   Incorrect. Embedded phonics refers to teaching phonics in the context of authentic reading. It is not related to writing workshop.

   D.   Incorrect. Semantic feature analysis is a vocabulary acquisition strategy.

5) A.   Incorrect. Semantics and morphology are not developmentally appropriate for a preschool student.

   B.   Incorrect. Preschool students are still using invented spelling, which is developmentally appropriate.

   C.   **Correct.** By using the alphabetic principle, students begin to understand that written language is part of a "code" in which letters stand for certain sounds that create meaning.

   D.   Incorrect. Syntax and mechanics are too advanced for a preschool student.

6) A.   Incorrect. There are only two incorrectly spelled words, and both are homonyms. The student seems relatively proficient in basic orthography.

    B.   Correct. The student's writing is mostly run-on sentences and fragments, indicating that he needs explicit instruction in sentence structure.

    C.   Incorrect. There is not a significant number of capitalization errors.

    D.   Incorrect. Prepositions are not used incorrectly.

7) A.   Incorrect. Spell- and grammar-check features are not developmentally appropriate for kindergarten students.

    B.   Incorrect. Kindergarten students would have trouble completing this activity, as their ability to read online information is still limited.

    C.   Correct. This is a developmentally appropriate way to integrate technology into the writing process. Even before students are able to write in the most traditional sense, they can experience the writing process by selecting images to insert into the story.

    D.   Incorrect. Punctuation drills in isolation are ineffective and not developmentally appropriate for kindergarten students.

8) A.   Incorrect. Expository writing usually requires a formal, academic style.

    B.   Correct. Informal language could communicate a message just as effectively in a poem written without a set structure.

    C.   Incorrect. A research paper typically requires formal, academic language.

    D.   Incorrect. A biographical essay also typically requires more formal language.

9) A.   Incorrect. A norm-referenced assessment would only compare a student's writing scores with those of other students.

    B.   Incorrect. A criterion-referenced assessment is more of a snapshot in time than an ongoing record of progress.

    C.   Incorrect. A dynamic assessment integrates teaching or demonstration into the assessment. It does not track progress over time.

    D.   Correct. A portfolio shows student progress over a span of time. Writing samples will hopefully show growth and increased proficiency and complexity.

10) **A.   Correct.** Successful mechanics instruction encourages students to see that mechanics help communicate meaning to the reader.

    B.   Incorrect. Mechanics isn't really about semantics or the meaning of words.

    C.   Incorrect. Inductive and deductive reasoning are not directly related to mechanics.

    D.   Incorrect. Mechanics and vocabulary/word choice are two distinct things.

Assessment and Diagnostic Teaching

MEASUREMENT CONCEPTS

Assessment is the process of gathering information from multiple sources to understand what students know. It also measures how they are progressing and if any problems have arisen in their development. Assessment of student learning and progress in reading is ongoing and should occur every school day.

Assessments are conducted in many areas of development, including cognitive, socio-emotional, and physical. Assessments can be used for a variety of purposes:

▶ identifying developmental delays

▶ evaluating student mastery of learning objectives

▶ designing appropriate interventions

▶ gauging efficacy of program delivery

▶ determining placement of students within programs

Data from assessments can then be used to make decisions. These decisions might be related to an individual student, a classroom, or even an entire school or district. Much educational research relies on assessment to yield data that can be applied broadly in other educational situations. One role of the reading specialist is to conduct such assessments and use the results to improve reading performance among individual students, within classrooms, and on a school-wide level.

Assessments are ranked based on two factors: reliability and validity. **Reliability** is the rate at which the assessment produces the same outcome every time. One way to think about reliability is in terms of consistency across many different test takers and testing scenarios. A test has low reliability if it does not produce accurate results each time it is given.

Ideally, each assessment would give the same results even when administered multiple times to the same student under the same conditions. Unfortunately, this is not the case. Even assessments that are thought to be reliable have measurement error. **Measurement error** refers to all the variations that impact an examinee's performance. Some variations are testing conditions (e.g., quietness of the room, behavior of the test administrator) or the emotional state of the test taker. Assessments of very young children often have significant measurement error compared to those of older children.

Additionally, many reading assessments conducted in English may contain errors or be ineffective when used with students with limited English proficiency. Particular attention should be paid to matching the assessment to the student needs and intended purpose.

Validity is quite different from reliability. It refers to whether the findings the assessment instrument seeks to measure are accurate and backed by research and evidence. If the assessment does not measure what it is supposed to measure (achievement, personality, intelligence, or something else), then it lacks validity even if it is reliable and produces consistent results each time.

> **STUDY TIP**
>
> Think of the concept of test reliability as you would a person who is reliable. A *reliable* person behaves as expected every time. A *reliable* assessment instrument does too.

Assessment data is generally quantitative, or numerical, and qualitative, or nonnumerical. **Quantitative** data is gleaned from standardized assessments such as a numerical IQ or performance in the fifteenth percentile. **Qualitative** data is usually obtained through interviews with parents and teachers and observational records. Both types of data should be considered in initial evaluation for reading interventions or special education services and in ongoing assessment of student learning.

> **STUDY TIP**
>
> Use the roots of the words to remember quantitative and qualitative data. Quantitative data is a quantity. Qualitative data is the quality of something.

SAMPLE QUESTION

1) A reading specialist gives a published, criterion-referenced reading assessment instrument to a third-grade student on two different occasions within a week. The student scores much higher on the first assessment. This assessment has measurement error as well as

   A. reliability issues.

   B. validity issues.

   C. a biased norming group.

   D. a small norming group.

STANDARDIZED ASSESSMENTS

There are numerous **standardized** published assessment instruments. These instruments have standardized questions or criteria and are administered in a consistent manner. Most professionals agree that standardized assessments reveal only one part of any student's learning situation and level of mastery of individual objectives. Standardized assessments provide one way to gather data to help with individualized planning and instruction.

NORM-REFERENCED ASSESSMENTS

Standardized assessments fall into two categories: norm-referenced and criterion-referenced. Norm-referenced assessments measure an individual student against a group of other test takers, typically those of the same age or grade level. Results are reported in a percentile ranking.

Norm-referenced tests are most often used to measure achievement, intelligence, aptitude, and personality. Achievement tests measure what skills a student has mastered. These often fall under categories like reading and mathematics.

Achievement tests are generally multiple choice and require test takers to answer a standardized set of questions. Popular achievement tests include:

- Iowa Test of Basic Skills (ITBS)
- Peabody Individual Achievement Test
- Wechsler Individual Achievement Test (WIAT-III)
- Stanford Achievement Test

Another type of norm-referenced assessment is the aptitude test. Like achievement tests, **aptitude tests** measure learned abilities such as mathematics and verbal reasoning. They also help predict the course of future learning. The SAT and ACT are two very common aptitude tests used to predict the probability of a student's success in a college environment.

> **DID YOU KNOW?**
>
> The first exams offered by the College Board (which now produces the SAT) were administered in 1901. The sections were English, French, German, Latin, Greek, history, mathematics, chemistry, and physics. Instead of the multiple-choice format of most of today's standardized tests, questions were in essay format. Student responses were graded as very poor, poor, doubtful, good, and excellent.

Intelligence tests are another norm-referenced assessment. They are used to measure overall intellectual functioning, problem-solving skills, and aptitude for learning. The most commonly used intelligence tests are:

- Stanford-Binet Intelligence Scales (SB5)
- Wechsler Intelligence Scale for Children (WISC-V)

▶ Woodcock-Johnson III Tests of Cognitive Abilities

▶ Differential Ability Scales (DAS-II)

▶ Universal Nonverbal Intelligence Test (for students with certain communication disorders)

Intelligence tests can help determine giftedness in children and the presence of an intellectual disability. Intelligence tests are also used in tandem with achievement tests to note patterns or discrepancies in IQ and academic achievement. These discrepancies may be the result of a specific learning disability or another condition that might require special services.

Personality tests are also norm-referenced tests. They measure a student's tendency to behave in a certain way. Often these tests are administered to parents and children together.

Because norm-referenced tests compare students to one another, the results must be given in a format that makes possible such a comparison. The most common way to do this is the **percentile**. A percentile is a score that shows where a student ranks in comparison to ninety-nine other students. For example, a percentile of 81 would mean that the student in question has performed equal to or outperformed eighty-one out of the other ninety-nine students who took the same test. A percentile of 14 means that the student only performed equal to or outperformed fourteen of the other ninety-nine test takers.

These percentiles are usually determined early in the development of a standardized norm-referenced assessment using an early group of test takers known as a **norming group**. Depending on the assessment instrument, these norming groups may be students in a particular school (school average norms) or district (a local norm group). They may also be students with a particular diagnosed exceptionality or special learning situation (special norm group). More often, they are national norm groups. These groups are carefully selected to be representative of the nation as a whole. One criticism of norm-referenced tests is that national norm groups are not always current and truly representative. Students might be taking a test that has not been recalibrated with a new norming group in some time.

Norm-referenced tests base their percentiles on the bell-shaped curve, also called the normal curve or the normal distribution. Often tests are modified so the results will generate a bell-shaped curve. This distribution of scores has three primary characteristics:

▶ It is symmetrical from left to right.

▶ The mean, median, and mode are the same score and are at the center of the symmetrical distribution.

▶ The percentage within each standard deviation is known.

Not all standardized assessment instruments use percentile. There are also **grade-equivalent scores**, which provide a result in a grade level. This means that the student's performance is equal to the median performance corresponding to other students of a certain grade level. For example, if a student scores at a tenth-grade reading level, that would mean their score was the same as the median for all tenth graders who took the test. Some assessment instruments also use an age-equivalent score, which simply compares a student's results to the median score of other students of a certain age.

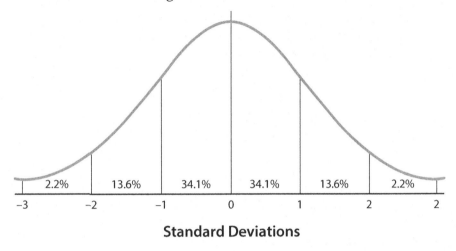

Figure 5.1. Bell-Shaped Curve (normal distribution)

SAMPLE QUESTION

2) **Harvey scores in the 89th percentile on the Stanford Achievement Test, an annual norm-referenced test. What do these results mean?**

    A. He got 89 percent of the questions correct.

    B. Eighty-nine percent of students did the same as or better than Harvey did.

    C. Harvey did the same as or better than 89 percent of students.

    D. Harvey did well enough to be part of the norming group.

CRITERION–REFERENCED TESTS

Criterion-referenced tests measure an individual's performance as it relates to a predetermined benchmark or criteria. These tests are generally used to measure a student's progress toward meeting certain objectives. They do not compare test takers to one another but rather compare student knowledge against the set criteria. Criterion-referenced tests include everything from annual state tests to those created by teachers or educational publishers to assess mastery of learning objectives.

One new incarnation of the criterion-referenced test used by many states is **standards-referenced testing** or **standards-based assessment**. These tests measure a student's performance against certain content standards as defined by each grade level and subject. They are typically scored in categories such as basic, proficient, and advanced; or unsatisfactory, satisfactory, and advanced. Most annual state accountability tests such as STAAR, PARCC, and many others are standards-based, criterion-referenced tests.

SAMPLE QUESTION

3) A reading interventionist wants to use the class-wide results of a criterion-referenced test as a starting point to meet with a fourth-grade teacher about improving vocabulary knowledge among students. Which assessment results should she reference?

   A. Iowa Test of Basic Skills

   B. annual state accountability test

   C. results from a phonics screener

   D. results from running records

TYPES OF ASSESSMENTS

FORMAL AND INFORMAL ASSESSMENTS

Most programs try to maintain a balance between formal and informal assessment measures. **Formal assessments** refer to test results that are reported in either a percentile or percentage format. Standardized tests, chapter or unit tests, and end-of-course exams are all examples of formal assessments.

Informal assessments evaluate students outside the traditional written test format. These assessments help give a more complete picture of ongoing progress. At times, particularly when students experience stress in high-stakes testing scenarios, informal assessments might provide more accurate results.

Informal assessments include observation, portfolios, projects, presentations, and oral checks, among others. Informal assessment should be ongoing and should guide instruction alongside formal assessment. Informal assessments popular in terms of student literacy development include:

- ▶ oral reading checks
- ▶ oral comprehension checks
- ▶ running records
- ▶ phonics screeners
- ▶ exit tickets
- ▶ informal writing assignments/journaling

Another popular informal reading assessment is the **Informal Reading Inventory (IRI)**. This assessment includes a word list to determine which level of the assessment should be given. It also features an oral reading and silent reading portion. The assessment pinpoints the independent, instructional, and frustrational reading level for each student. The results can then be used to differentiate instruction and choose appropriate reading material for the reading level of each student.

Both formal and informal assessments can be used to gather information and guide instruction. Some students, however, simply do not perform well on formal assessments or may have test anxiety. In these instances, informal assessments are often a better measure of student knowledge.

SAMPLE QUESTION

4) A reading specialist wants to assess student retainment of skills at the end of a small-group intervention aimed at vocabulary acquisition. Which method of assessment should the specialist use?

   A.   administer a norm-referenced assessment

   B.   ask students to write down three new words they learned

   C.   ask students to write three words with long vowel sounds

   D.   administer a standardized achievement test

FORMATIVE AND SUMMATIVE ASSESSMENTS

Assessments—whether formal, informal, authentic, or more traditional—can also be either formative or summative. **Formative assessment** refers to the ongoing monitoring of student progress toward learning objectives. Formative assessments are often informal assessments whereby teachers seek more information to streamline instruction. For example, a kindergarten teacher may give frequent formative assessments by asking each student to read words from a sight word list or consonant blend chart. This will help the teacher determine each student's progress in learning to read. It will also provide appropriate and targeted instruction in areas where there is most need.

Formative assessments can also be more formal. Examples include a short quiz over the day's material or a concept map or outline that students submit for grading. However, formative assessment tends to be low-stakes assessment: assessment that does not carry a high point value. Formative assessment does not significantly impact a student's course grade or chances of promotion to the next grade.

STUDY TIP

Formative assessments are used while students are *forming* their knowledge. Summative assessments are used to add up all of student learning into one lump *sum*.

Summative assessment is designed to evaluate student learning after the end of a defined unit of study. It compares student knowledge to the initial learning objectives that were addressed throughout the unit of study. It, too, may be formal or informal but may often take the form of a unit test, midterm or final exam, or a final paper or project. Summative assessments are generally high-stakes assessments because they carry high point values. They are often critical to a student's overall grade, their ability to pass a course, or promotion to the next grade.

A middle ground between a formative assessment and a summative assessment is the **benchmark assessment**. This type of assessment is more formal than a formative assessment but is not a high-stakes standardized summative assessment.

Benchmark assessments are sometimes called interim assessments or predictive assessments. They track student progress and determine the degree to which students are on track to perform well on future summative assessments.

Many states use benchmark assessments before the annual standards-based assessment to determine which students need interventions to help prepare for the high-stakes test. They can also be used to evaluate overall school or district goals and whether the school or district is on track to achieve those goals.

In some cases, benchmark assessments are less formal. For example, a first-grade teacher using a leveled-reader program may employ a benchmark assessment to determine when her students are ready to move to the program's next level. Similarly, a kindergarten teacher whose goal is to have his students know all the Dolch Sight Words might give them benchmark assessments over smaller sections of the list.

SAMPLE QUESTION

5) A sixth-grade reading teacher gives a daily warm-up quiz with a low point value that covers some of the material discussed the day before. What type of assessment is he giving?

A. a benchmark assessment

B. a low-stakes formative assessment

C. a norm-referenced assessment

D. a high-stakes summative assessment

AUTHENTIC ASSESSMENTS

One important trend in student assessment is authentic assessment. **Authentic assessment** measures the student's ability to use knowledge in a direct, relevant, often real-world way.

In an authentic literacy assessment, students apply reading and writing skills in a pragmatic or practical way. For example, high school students might work on writing a resume or a profile on a professional networking platform. These are both examples of an authentic assessment of skills in writing for a formal audience. Or, a fifth-grade teacher might give students brochures for places to explore on a field trip and ask them to read and summarize the high points of each brochure. These are authentic literacy assessments since they measure literacy skills in a pragmatic context.

Authentic assessments offer opportunities to go much deeper than a traditional written test. There are numerous examples, many of them cross-curricular, that can be used to assess reading and writing skills in an authentic context. Teachers across multiple disciplines can collaborate to design projects that assess multiple skills. For example, a science teacher and an English teacher might work together to have students research and summarize a scientific article to earn a grade for English and then design an experiment based on the article for a grade in science.

SAMPLE QUESTION

6) A tenth-grade English teacher wants to create an authentic assessment to evaluate students' skills with writing in coherent paragraphs. Which assignment would be best?

    A. directing students to give a presentation to the class on something they know how to do well

    B. asking students to analyze the way paragraphs are used in a newspaper article on a topic of their choice

    C. assigning students to write the draft of an email they will eventually send to someone

    D. having students use a graphic organizer to organize their thoughts into paragraphs before writing an essay about an assigned topic

DIAGNOSTIC ASSESSMENTS

Diagnostic assessments are used to determine what students already know. Many teachers give diagnostic assessments at the beginning of the school year or before each unit of study. This helps calibrate the level of instruction and can help track progress over time when diagnostic assessments are compared with summative assessments.

Diagnostic assessments are particularly important when teachers are implementing pyramid planning as part of the Universal Design for Learning. For example, a teacher discovers through a diagnostic assessment that most of her first-grade students do not know all the letter sounds. It would be unreasonable to expect all her students to be reading sentences by the end of the first unit of study.

Diagnostic assessments can uncover learning gaps that teachers will need to address. For example, a second-grade teacher discovers that many of his students lack knowledge of long vowel sounds. This teacher will need to give explicit instruction in that topic before presenting a unit on spelling that requires students to drop the *e* and add a suffix.

Diagnostic assessments can also be used at the beginning of the year to identify students at risk of not meeting reading learning objectives and to differentiate instruction and plan interventions for these students. Meeting each student at their current learning situation is important in setting goals and targeting instruction.

7)   **Mrs. El-Badawi is a kindergarten teacher who wants to find out her students' level of phonemic awareness at the beginning of the school year so she can target her instruction. Which is the BEST type of assessment?**

   A.   formative assessment

   B.   diagnostic assessment

   C.   summative assessment

   D.   play-based assessment

DYNAMIC ASSESSMENTS

Dynamic assessment has become quite popular, particularly in the field of speech-language pathology. It is based on Lev Vygotsky's theory of the zone of proximal development. Vygotsky posited that what a learner can do alone is negligible when compared to what they can do with the aid of a more skilled peer or adult. In a dynamic assessment, some instruction is embedded into the assessment.

While there are many ways to conduct a dynamic assessment, it typically involves a pretest, some type of intervention, and then a posttest. This process is called **test-teach-retest**. In this way, a child's initial skills can be compared to the skills he or she displays after receiving instruction for improvement. This type of assessment can be very helpful in measuring a student's ability to learn new skills.

Proponents of dynamic assessment say that it can help uncover learning potential and that it is more modifiable and responsive to the individual student. Critics point to its heavy reliance on the skill and even personality of the assessor. Assessors who make a student uncomfortable, for example, may not produce reliable or valid results.

8)   **Dr. Kim has Anna place number tiles on a board in a certain pattern. He then shows Anna how to place the tiles correctly on the board. Then he asks Anna to try placing the tiles again. What type of assessment is Dr. Kim administering to Anna?**

   A.   dynamic assessment

   B.   benchmark assessment

   C.   criterion-referenced assessment

   D.   multi-perspective assessment

PEER, SELF-, AND MULTI-PERSPECTIVE ASSESSMENTS

Teachers and parents are not the only ones who can participate in student assessment. Peers can also be very helpful in providing feedback on student learning. **Peer assessment** is the assessment of student work by peers.

Peer assessment is widely used in higher education, particularly in large online classes in which instructors are unable to give feedback on each student's work. If students receive appropriate guidance and practice, peer assessment can be used effectively in many secondary and even some elementary classrooms. While most peer assessment will not result in a formal grade, it can be invaluable to help students revise their work before submitting it for grading.

In a peer assessment, students are given a rubric or list of criteria and asked to assess another student's work based on this rubric or set of criteria. They are also asked to offer specific feedback for improvement. This process can help students who are unsure of how to revise or edit their work, as they are given clear and actionable suggestions.

Peer assessment can also be used during collaborative learning. In this model, the teacher asks for feedback from the group about the level of each member's participation. This can be particularly helpful if much of a group project happened outside of school. This way, the teacher can get some idea of each group member's contributions. This type of assessment is usually more effective when clear criteria for evaluation are set. The teacher might, for example, ask group members to fill out a chart showing which parts of the project each member completed individually and which parts were completed together.

Multi-perspective assessments are also used during cooperative learning activities. In this type of assessment, peers, the individual student, and teachers all collaborate to assess learning outcomes. This can be helpful when parts of a group project occur both in and out of the classroom. In this type of assessment, the teacher may weigh input from different assessors differently when computing the total overall grade. For example, the teacher evaluation of the finished project may count for 75 percent of the grade, the peer assessment of group members for another 10 percent, and the student's self-assessment for the remaining 15 percent.

> **DID YOU KNOW?**
>
> Any comprehensive evaluation for special education services will be multi-perspective since a multidisciplinary team, alongside a child's parents, will be participating in the process.

Peer assessment and multi-perspective assessment can be used in conjunction with **self-assessment**. This is a student's evaluation of their individual progress toward learning goals. Self-assessment is a critical part of any child's overall education. It helps students become self-directed learners who devise and meet learning goals with little help from others. Self-assessment should be a large part of formative assessment. Students who are self-assessing can actively seek out the resources they need to meet learning objectives without waiting for teachers to realize they need them.

Usually, self-assessment must be explicitly taught. There are many strategies for this. Often, students are given an example of work that meets certain criteria and then asked to compare their work to this example. In other cases, students are asked to simply assess their degree of understanding of a concept. This could be anything from having students respond in journals or interactive notebooks to prompts such as "Today I learned..." or "I am still unsure about..." Students might use simple symbols like a checkmark or a happy/sad face to indicate their degree of mastery of a given concept.

SAMPLE QUESTION

9) After a group project–based learning assignment, a high school reading specialist asks each group member to fill out an evaluation of their team members. What method of assessment is this?

    A.   peer assessment

    B.   multi-perspective assessment

    C.   self-assessment

    D.   formative assessment

ASSESSING EMERGING READERS

Students who are not yet fluent readers will need specific assessment techniques to ensure they are mastering foundational skills that form the building blocks of later reading instruction. Since concepts of print are the first stage of reading development, these skills must be mastered thoroughly. Most of the time, these assessments are informal and might include any of the following:

▶ asking students to point to the parts of a book (e.g., title, front cover, back)

▶ presenting students with a book and observing as they interact with it

▶ asking students to point to a word, sentence, or picture

As students progress to developing phonetic awareness or overall phonemic awareness, assessment is also conducted in a highly interactive manner. Students might be asked to clap out sounds or words, think of rhyming words, repeat words or sounds, and so on.

Once students begin to work on letter recognition and sound-symbol knowledge, a letter chart or letter-sound chart can be used as assessment tools. Students can cross off each letter or letter sound once it is mastered. The same assessment method with a chart or list can be used for sight words (often with a Dolch Word List), consonant blends, digraphs, diphthongs, and other challenging sounds.

There is an important distinction between children's ability to sing the alphabet song or point to and say letters or sounds in order (which many master quite early) and the different (though related) skill of letter and letter-sound recognition in isolation. For this reason, it is a good idea to always assess phonics skills in different contexts. For example, students can be asked to point to certain letters or sounds (/b/, /ch/, /i/) in a book or story. This type of **embedded phonics** assessment ensures that students can transfer knowledge and apply it in connected texts.

In addition to more structured assessment methods like charts and lists, phonics skills can be assessed through any number of hands-on activities. Students can play with letter/sound cards or magnets and form or dissect words. Students can match up cards with different rimes and onsets or different target consonant or vowel sounds.

In assessing decoding, or the ability to sound out a word and glean meaning, an oral assessment approach continues to be the gold standard. There are many assessment tools designed specifically to aid in assessing such skills, including the popular **Quick Phonics Screener**, which assesses a student's ability to read a variety of sounds and words.

When assessing decoding skills, it is important to note student strengths and weaknesses. But teachers must also develop a general idea of the student's overall approach and "word-attack skills," or methods of decoding unfamiliar words. Attention to how students approach any oral reading task can provide significant information on strategies they are already using, as well as those they do not use but might find beneficial. Though the age of the student certainly comes into play, sometimes older students still mastering decoding might be able to verbalize the way they approach such challenging words. Questions posed to the student about strategy or method can also yield valuable information.

In addition to these methods, there are also several published assessment instruments for pre-readers and emerging readers.

- ▶ Letter knowledge and phonemic awareness can be assessed using the **Dynamic Indicators of Basic Early Literacy Skills (DIBELS)** and the **Early Reading Diagnostic Assessment (ERDA)**.

- ▶ The **Comprehensive Test of Phonological Processing (CTOPP)** and **Phonological Awareness Test (PAT)** can also be used as instruments to assess phonemic awareness.

- ▶ Other instruments that assess early reading skills include the **Texas Primary Reading Inventory (TPRI)**, **Test of Word Reading Efficiency (TOWRE)**, and even the kindergarten version of the **Iowa Test of Basic Skills (ITSB)**.

Regardless of the assessment instruments used, assessing emerging readers can be challenging since young children often find assessment scenarios intimidating. Any single assessment is only as useful as it provides part of the full picture. The fullest picture of a student's pre-reading development can best be gleaned through observation and input from both parents and teachers. Portfolios, observational records, checklists, and other informal assessment methods can provide much insight into the development of emergent readers.

10) **A kindergarten teacher who wants to assess student mastery of phoneme blending would MOST likely**

   A.   ask students to add affixes to various root words.

   B.   have students match up cards with onsets and rimes and say each word.

   C.   ask students to remove a letter from a word, add a new one, and read the new word.

   D.   have students point to items in the classroom that begin with a certain letter sound.

ASSESSING READING SKILLS AND STRATEGIES

Assessing each student in an individual oral context is not always possible. This can make assessing reading skills and metacognitive reading strategies a challenge. Further, it is often hard to fully assess any one student's individual thought process. With these caveats, assessing reading skills and strategies with an eye for gaps that might be addressed through intervention is an important task of the reading specialist.

Word-attack skills can be assessed through observation and oral reading. Teachers should take note of what happens when students encounter words they do not know. Do they immediately ask for help? Skip over the word? Reread the word? Slow down? Speed up? Assessing word-attack skills relies on observation of students as they read aloud but also on the assessment of underlying skills that lead to a strong word-attack tool kit. Do students make use of all text features and graphic elements? Do they sound out the word or make inferences based on roots and affixes? Do they use context clues?

> **HELPFUL HINT**
>
> Asking comprehension questions after listening to students read is a simple, effective way to monitor oral comprehension.

Assessment of vocabulary typically happens in the context of breadth (the number of words one knows) or depth (the ability to use the vocabulary in varied and nuanced ways). It also happens in the context of an isolated assessment (a vocabulary test) or as an embedded assessment as an adjunct to another assessment, such as one of reading comprehension or oral fluency.

Such assessments can also be context-independent: "What does *contortion* mean?" or context-dependent: "What does the word *contort* mean in the following sentence?" Educators should consider what "bank" they will draw vocabulary from in order to assess students. Typically, teachers assess vocabulary students will need to comprehend the language of classroom instruction, the textbook, and any literature the class will read. Reference materials such as the *EDL Core Vocabularies* define "target" words per grade level. Published standardized vocabulary instruments such as the classic **Peabody Picture Vocabulary Test (PPT)**, which requires no reading or writing, can also be used to assess individual students.

Assessing oral fluency is generally done by assessing reading accuracy, prosody, and automaticity. This can be tracked in numerous ways. Teachers may keep **running records** that track accuracy, self-correction, and use of fix-up strategies and word attack skills. Running records use forms so teachers can mark errors, self-corrections, and how students use cues to make meaning of texts. These forms are filled out as the student reads the same text the teacher has.

Figure 5.2. Running Record

Students can also be measured for oral reading skills using various fluency norms charts that indicate average words read correctly per minute per grade. While several standard measures exist, one of the most researched is the **Hasbrouck-Tindal oral reading fluency chart**. This chart measures progress over the course of the school year and from grade to grade. It compares students in percentiles with their peers on a scale of words read correctly per minute.

Table 5.1. Hasbrouck–Tindal Oral Reading Fluency Chart

	Words Correct Per Minute (50th percentile)		
Grade	**Fall**	**Winter**	**Spring**
1	---	29	60
2	50	84	100
3	83	97	112
4	94	120	133
5	121	133	146
6	132	145	146

Comprehension while reading silently can be assessed through cloze exercises. In these exercises, words are removed from the text and students must fill them in. There are other written exercises aimed at determining level of comprehension. Some students might struggle to answer written questions. Therefore, a full assessment of silent reading comprehension should include an oral component as well.

As previously mentioned, one of the most common assessments is the Informal Reading Inventory (IRI). There are multiple versions created by various entities. One of the more popular versions is **Pearson's Qualitative Reading Inventory (QRI)**. These assessments include oral reading of word lists that assess accuracy of word identification. The QRI also contains passages and questions that assess both oral and silent reading comprehension. Standardized norm-referenced test batteries such as the Iowa Test of Basic Skills and Stanford Achievement Test, as well as several criterion-referenced tests such as the Partnership for Assessment of Readiness for College and Careers (PARCC), also test reading comprehension.

As in all types of reading assessment, comprehension assessment does not require a lengthy formal written test. Simply asking students to recount or retell a story they have read or to recall the most important or interesting parts of a text can provide valuable data. Further, self-assessment should be ongoing and explicitly taught to all readers to monitor comprehension. As students self-assess, they can apply fix-up or fix-it-up strategies as needed when comprehension breaks down.

SAMPLE QUESTION

11) **A reading teacher asks her sixth-grade students to skim the text and turn the bold paragraph headings into questions. After the students have read the text silently, the teacher asks them to write answers to each of the questions. What skill is the teacher assessing?**

A.   identifying tone

B.   recalling main ideas

C.   activating background knowledge

D.   making inferences

USING ASSESSMENT DATA

Data from reading assessments can be used in many ways. In schools using a **Response to Intervention (RTI)** framework, all students should be screened for reading proficiency early and often. Ongoing assessment (progress monitoring) should be implemented as reading interventions occur.

In an RTI framework, a reading specialist may conduct universal screenings with any number of assessment tools and then determine which students would benefit from interventions. The reading specialist will then use this data to determine goals for students identified as "at risk" of not meeting reading objectives. These students will receive early intervening services (Tier 2 intervention) through many possible avenues, though small-group reading instruction is the most common.

As these Tier 2 interventions occur, the reading specialist/interventionist will continue to monitor progress and use assessment data to determine if the student is responding or needs more intensive intervention (Tier 3). This type of intervention is usually in a smaller group and of a greater frequency and longer duration.

When reading specialists are working as co-teachers or as direct providers of intervention services, they will also use assessment data to:

- ▶ differentiate instruction for all students (Tier 1 interventions) including but not limited to:
  - ▷ assessing the independent, instructional, and frustrational reading levels for each student and selecting appropriate texts
  - ▷ providing scaffolds and supports for individual students per the principles of the Universal Design for Learning
  - ▷ using data for flexible grouping strategies that group students by skill level for optimal instruction but constantly reassess and adapt based on student progress
- ▶ plan and conduct small-group interventions (Tier 2 or Tier 3) by:
  - ▷ assessing skill gaps where students need additional instruction or practice
  - ▷ grouping students for interventions based on similar instructional goals/learning needs (keeping in mind principles of flexible grouping)

Assessment data can and should also be used on a macro level to make improvements to instruction and support teachers across the content areas. A reading specialist might use reading assessment data in a variety of contexts, such as:

- determining individual classrooms/grade levels that might need additional support
- determining grade-level or school-wide curricular needs
- determining efficacy of classroom/grade-level or school-wide curricular or intervention approaches
- designing intervention approaches or teacher support systems on a school-wide level
- recognizing trends across grade levels (e.g., students are not adequately prepared for instruction on spelling words with *r*-controlled vowels at the beginning of second grade)
- providing planning or instructional recommendations to teachers
- identifying teachers or classrooms to serve as mentors
- planning topics for professional development events

The way assessment data is used on a school-wide level will vary based on the duties and roles of the reading specialist at any particular school, but these are some of the most common uses of such information.

SAMPLE QUESTION

12) **After reviewing the data from annual standards-based assessments, a reading specialist sees that results show most third- and fourth-grade students are struggling with the meaning of homographs. Which area of instruction would the reading specialist MOST likely recommend to the third- and fourth-grade reading teachers to aid students in determining the meaning of homographs?**

   A.   roots and affixes

   B.   graphophonic cues

   C.   context clues

   D.   analogy-based phonics

REVIEW

Read the question, and then choose the most correct answer.

1

Which of the following is a characteristic of a bell-shaped curve?

A.   The mean, median, and mode are all different scores.

B.   The mean, median, and mode are all exactly 70 percent.

C.   It is symmetrical from left to right.

D.   It is larger on the right than the left.

2

After her sixth-grade son takes a norm-referenced test, a parent receives a score report saying that his reading performance is at a ninth-grade level. How should the parent interpret these results?

A.   Her son should skip a grade in order to find material challenging enough for his abilities.

B.   Her son took a test containing reading material that was well above grade level.

C.   Her son scored the same as the median score of tenth graders who took the same test.

D.   Her son's score on the test was three times better than his sixth-grade peers.

3

How do criterion-referenced tests differ from norm-referenced tests?

A.   They are standardized assessment instruments.

B.   They measure performance against a benchmark.

C.   They are usually multiple-choice assessments.

D.   They are both scored electronically.

4

Which type of diagnostic assessment would give a first-grade reading teacher the most information on students' knowledge of consonant blends?

A.   a group activity in which students take turns placing letter tiles in boxes for each phoneme

B.   a whole-class choral reading activity in which students read a paragraph with multiple consonant blends

C.   an individual assessment with a phonics screener or similar targeted list of words and sounds

D.   an activity in which students write down the sounds they hear while words are read aloud

5

A preschool teacher wants to assess the level of her students' print awareness during the first week of school. Which of the following supplies does he need?

A.   a phonics screener

B.   an Informal Reading Inventory (IRI)

C.   the Iowa Test of Basic Skills

D.   a book with print and pictures

6

A reading specialist wants to provide strategies for elementary school reading teachers to use to assess oral fluency growth over time. Which of the following strategies should the specialist recommend?

A.   running records

B.   digital portfolios

C.   time sampling

D.   observational records

7

A reading specialist wants to get qualitative data on the efficacy of the school's current reading intervention program. Which method should the specialist use?

A.   aggregate results from criterion-referenced tests

B.   aggregate results from norm-referenced tests

C.   results of interviews with teachers

D.   results of oral reading inventories

8

A reading specialist is attending a transition planning meeting for an eleventh-grade student with a specific learning disability (SLD) related to reading. Which of the following assessment instruments would MOST LIKELY help the student determine transition goals?

A.   an intelligence test

B.   a standards-based assessment

C.   an achievement test

D.   an aptitude test

9

Which of the following statements is the BEST reason for educators to avoid relying on standardized assessment instruments as the sole criteria for determining a reading-related learning disability?

A.   All assessment instruments lack reliability and validity.

B.   All assessment instruments have some measurement error.

C.   All assessment instruments overidentify students for specific learning disabilities.

D.   All assessment instruments are norm-referenced and require careful interpretation.

10

A reading specialist is mentoring a first-year fifth-grade teacher on using assessment data effectively. After checking the results of a summative assessment on Greek and Latin roots, the specialist notes that fewer than 50 percent of students achieved mastery. What is the BEST action for the reading specialist to recommend to the teacher?

A.   reconfigure ability-based reading groups based on assessment results

B.   plan for reteaching and reinforcement of unit objectives

C.   refer low-performing students for more intensive interventions

D.   attend a professional development event on reaching reluctant learners

ANSWER KEY

SAMPLE QUESTIONS

1) **A.** **Correct.** Reliability refers to how often the test gives the same result. This test clearly has some issues with reliability, as the student should score with similar results on multiple assessments in a short time frame.

    B. Incorrect. Validity refers to whether the assessment actually gives data on the skills it seeks to measure. This is not necessarily the same as producing the same result each time.

    C. Incorrect. Norming groups are only used for norm-referenced tests, not criterion-referenced tests. Further, this would not necessarily impact the results in two subsequent testing scenarios with the same student.

    D. Incorrect. Again, norming groups are used for norm-referenced tests, not criterion-referenced tests. Further, the size of the norming group would not be directly related to the lack of test reliability. This is more related to interpreting scores/performance.

2) A. Incorrect. Percentile refers to how well one student performed in relation to others.

    B. Incorrect. The reverse is true.

    C. **Correct.** Harvey's score was equal to or better than 89 percent of students to whom he is being compared.

    D. Incorrect. The norming group is the initial group of test takers used to formulate the percentile.

3) A. Incorrect. The Iowa Test of Basic Skills is a norm-referenced assessment.

    B. **Correct.** Most annual state accountability tests are standards-based assessments that are criterion-referenced based on state standards. This would help the reading interventionist phrase the needs in a concrete and standards-aligned way.

    C. Incorrect. A phonics screener is not the most appropriate assessment to discuss vocabulary knowledge.

    D. Incorrect. Running records can provide data on oral reading progress but not necessarily vocabulary knowledge.

4) A. Incorrect. A norm-referenced assessment would be too broad in scope and time consuming. It would not give the specialist the needed data about this small session.

    B. **Correct.** This is a short, informal assessment that gives the specialist the needed data about what has been retained from the session.

    C. Incorrect. This would assess phonics skills, not vocabulary acquisition.

D.   Incorrect. A standardized achievement test would be too broad and time consuming. It would not yield data about knowledge retention from this session.

5)   A.   Incorrect. A benchmark assessment is generally the middle ground between a formative assessment and a summative assessment. On the other hand, a daily warm-up quiz is a low-stakes formative assessment.

   B.   Correct. A daily warm-up quiz is a low-stakes formative assessment. It is designed to be an ongoing monitoring of student learning and has a low point value.

   C.   Incorrect. Norm-referenced assessments compare results to other students and are generally made by large publishers, not by teachers.

   D.   Incorrect. A daily warm-up quiz has low point value and assesses ongoing learning, so it is a low-stakes formative assessment.

6)   A.   Incorrect. A class presentation is authentic assessment, but it does not address the teacher's intended point of evaluation because the students do not write paragraphs.

   B.   Incorrect. This assignment is also authentic assessment, but it does not address students actually writing in paragraphs.

   C.   Correct. This assignment is authentic assessment because students will actually send the email to someone, so the assessment has a real-world application. It also allows the teacher to assess the students' use of paragraphs.

   D.   Incorrect. Using a graphic organizer would help students organize their writing, but it is more of an organizational strategy than an assessment.

7)   A.   Incorrect. Mrs. El-Badawi is not trying to monitor her students' ongoing learning but rather to assess what they already know.

   B.   Correct. A diagnostic assessment will help Mrs. El-Badawi determine her students' existing knowledge of phonemic awareness.

   C.   Incorrect. Summative assessments occur at the end of study. Mrs. El-Badawi wants to offer an assessment at the beginning of the school year, not the end.

   D.   Incorrect. While a play-based assessment might be useful for this age group, it will not give information on phonemic awareness.

8)   **A.   Correct.** A dynamic assessment uses a test-teach-retest format.

   B.   Incorrect. Benchmark assessments track student progress toward objectives.

   C.   Incorrect. A criterion-referenced assessment involves students meeting a particular objective criterion. It is not clear that this is a criterion-referenced test.

   D.   Incorrect. There appears to be only one assessor.

9) **A.**   **Correct.** Students assessing other students is peer assessment.

   B.   Incorrect. Multi-perspective assessment involves self-assessment and teacher assessment in addition to peer assessment.

   C.   Incorrect. Students are assessing each other, not themselves.

   D.   Incorrect. The assessment is made at the end of a long project (per the definition of project-based learning), so it is a summative assessment, not a formative assessment.

10) A.   Incorrect. Manipulating roots and affixes can help students decode challenging words and master new vocabulary, but it will not assess mastery of phoneme blending.

   B.   **Correct.** When students say the onset and rime together, they are blending both phonemes together.

   C.   Incorrect. This helps students manipulate sounds and analyze the structure of words, but it does not assess phoneme blending.

   D.   Incorrect. This activity assesses knowledge of letter sounds, not the ability to blend sounds together.

11) A.   Incorrect. The tone of the text is generally not revealed by paragraph headings.

   B.   **Correct.** The paragraph headings and the questions generated from them are clues to the main idea of each paragraph. Asking students to answer the questions requires them to recall main ideas from the text.

   C.   Incorrect. There is no reference to students connecting their background knowledge with the text. They are simply using the text features.

   D.   Incorrect. In this practice, students should be turning the paragraph headings into literal questions, not necessarily inference questions.

12) A.   Incorrect. Instruction in roots and affixes can help students determine the meaning of many words but most likely not homographs, which are words that are spelled the same but have different meanings.

   B.   Incorrect. Graphophonic cues help students decode unfamiliar words. They will not aid in determining the meaning of a homograph in context.

   C.   **Correct.** The context of the sentence in which the homograph is written will clue its meaning. Instruction in looking for context clues will aid students in determining the meaning of these types of multiple-meaning words.

   D.   Incorrect. Analogy-based phonics would help students use word parts they already know to decode new words. This does not apply directly to determining the meaning of homographs and is more about decoding unfamiliar words.

REVIEW

1) A.   Incorrect. In a bell-shaped curve, the mean, median, and mode are all the same score.

B.   Incorrect. The mean, median, and mode are all the same score but not necessarily 70 percent.

C.   Correct. A bell-shaped curve is perfectly symmetrical with the mean, median, and mode score at the center.

D.   Incorrect. The curve is perfectly symmetrical.

2) A.   Incorrect. There are other ways for this student to find more challenging material. Further, this is only reading performance, not all academic performance.

B.   Incorrect. The grade level results compare performance among different groups of students; they are not a direct representation of material on the test.

C.   Correct. The grade-equivalent score means that he scored the same as the median score of tenth graders who took the same test.

D.   Incorrect. His score was likely better than many of his peers but not necessarily three times better.

3) A.   Incorrect. Both types of tests are standardized assessment instruments.

B.   Correct. Criterion-referenced tests measure student performance against a predetermined benchmark or criteria. Norm-referenced tests compare student performance against other students.

C.   Incorrect. Both types of assessments are usually multiple-choice.

D.   Incorrect. Both types of assessments are usually scored electronically.

4) A.   Incorrect. A group activity might assess phonemic awareness if the teacher were paying close attention to each student. However, this is impractical and would be hard to administer, especially focusing only on phonemes that are consonant blends.

B.   Incorrect. It would be virtually impossible to hear individual students as they read in unison.

C.   Correct. An individual assessment is the best way to determine individual student knowledge.

D.   Incorrect. This would not necessarily assess blends because two letters are making a single sound.

5) A.   Incorrect. A phonics screener assesses phonics skills.

B.   Incorrect. An IRI is for students who are already reading.

C.   Incorrect. The Iowa Test of Basic Skills assesses early reading skills, not print awareness.

D.   **Correct.** The teacher could ask students to point to the title, front, back, a word, or a letter.

6) A.   **Correct.** Running records is an effective way to assess oral fluency over time.

B.   Incorrect. Oral fluency cannot easily be assessed through a digital portfolio.

C.   Incorrect. Time sampling is used to record frequency of behavior.

D.   Incorrect. Observational records would not give a good indication of oral reading fluency development over time.

7) A.   Incorrect. Results from criterion-referenced tests would yield quantitative data, not qualitative data.

B.   Incorrect. Results from norm-referenced tests would also yield only quantitative data.

C.   **Correct.** Interviews would allow teachers to share their thoughts about the current program and would provide qualitative data.

D.   Incorrect. Results of oral reading inventories would also provide quantitative data.

8) A.   Incorrect. Intelligence tests determine eligibility for special education services.

B.   Incorrect. Standards-based assessments measure the degree to which students have mastered certain standards or objectives.

C.   Incorrect. Achievement tests measure academic performance.

D.   **Correct.** An aptitude test like the ASVAB would help the student to determine future plans.

9) A.   Incorrect. This is not true of all assessment instruments; many have good reliability and validity.

B.   **Correct.** All assessment instruments will have some measurement error based on testing conditions and the test taker's emotional state.

C.   Incorrect. Some assessment instruments are highly sensitive, but this cannot be said about all assessment instruments.

D.   Incorrect. Not all assessment instruments are norm-referenced. Some are criterion-referenced.

10) A.   Incorrect. Since half of students did not master the objectives, reteaching is necessary. The issue does not appear to be a matter of grouping.

B.   **Correct.** Since so many students did not meet learning objectives, reteaching and reinforcement are needed.

C.   Incorrect. Half of the class receiving interventions may not be practical. It is better to reteach this unit since so many students did not master objectives.

D.   Incorrect. There is no indication that students were reluctant to learn the material. All that is known is that half of students did not master objectives.

Meeting the Needs of Individual Students

English Language Learners

Second-Language Acquisition

Researchers agree that **second-language acquisition** occurs, much like first-language acquisition, through a series of stages. Learners must pass through each of the five stages on their way to proficiency, though the time spent in each stage varies from person to person.

The first stage—**preproduction**—is also known as the **silent period**. Though these learners may have upward of 500 words in their receptive vocabulary, they refrain from speaking. However, they will listen and may copy words down. They can respond to visual cues such as pictures and gestures, and they will communicate their comprehension.

Sometimes students will repeat what they hear in a process called parroting. This can help them build their receptive vocabulary, but it should not be mistaken for producing language.

In the **early production** stage, learners achieve a 1,000-word receptive and active vocabulary. They can now produce single-word and two- to three-word phrases and can respond to questions and statements as such. Many learners in this stage enjoy musical games or word plays that help them memorize language chunks (groups of related words and phrases) they can use later.

English language learners have a vocabulary of about 3,000 words by the time they reach the **speech emergence stage** of second-language acquisition. They are able to chunk simple words and phrases into sentences that may or may not be grammatically correct. They respond to models of proper usage better than they do to explicit correction.

At this stage, learners are more likely to have conversations with native English speakers, as they are gaining confidence in their language skills. These students can understand simple readings when reinforced by graphics or pictures and can complete some content work with support.

By the **intermediate fluency stage**, English language learners have a vocabulary of about 6,000 words. They can speak in more complex sentences and catch and correct many of their errors. They are also willing to ask questions to clarify what they do not understand. Learners at this stage may communicate fairly well, but they have large gaps in their vocabulary and in their grammatical and syntactical understanding of the language. They are often comfortable with group conversations as long as any difficult academic vocabulary is limited.

Second-language learners reach **advanced fluency** when they have achieved cognitive language proficiency in their learned language. They demonstrate near-native ability and use complex, multi-phrase and multi-clause sentences to convey their ideas. Though learners at this stage still have accents and sometimes use idiomatic expressions incorrectly, they are essentially fluent.

As language learners progress through levels of study, they usually develop an interlanguage to aid them in their progression. **Interlanguage** is the learner's current understanding of the language they are learning. It is a rule-based system that develops over time. It tends to blend aspects of the learner's first language with those of the second.

Interlanguage is often characterized by the learner's tendency to overgeneralize speaking and writing rules in the new language. For example, when students learn that most English verbs in the past tense end in –ed, they might apply this rule to all verbs. The learner then creates an interlanguage rule by continuing to conjugate irregular verbs incorrectly. Over time, these rules are adjusted and readjusted according to feedback, and the interlanguage evolves as the learner moves toward proficiency.

When language learners stop progressing and the development of their interlanguage stops, their understanding can become fossilized. **Fossilization** is the point in second-language acquisition when a learner's growth freezes, and further linguistic development becomes highly unlikely.

SAMPLE QUESTION

1) Lucia enjoys listening to songs in English. She memorizes the choruses and sings them to herself. She notes words she does not recognize and integrates phrases from the songs into her everyday language practice. When asked about the songs, Lucia responds in single words and short

phrases but struggles to compose complete sentences. What stage of second-language acquisition might Lucia be in?

A.   preproduction

B.   early production

C.   speech emergence

D.   intermediate fluency

FIRST–LANGUAGE INFLUENCE ON SECOND LANGUAGE

Students' native languages will always impact their learning of English. The influences will occur in all parts of language learning, from grammatical understanding to vocabulary acquisition to syntactical awareness. They are bound to transfer their understanding of their first language to their studies of English to make sense of what they are learning.

Transfer occurs when a student applies knowledge of a first language to another. Transfer can be both positive and negative. **Positive transfer** occurs when students find similarities between their native language and English and use those similarities to help them learn.

For example, a Spanish-speaking student may recognize the English verb "to comprehend" because it looks like the Spanish verb *comprender* ("to understand"). Visually similar words like these are **cognates**. Words that look similar but are different in meaning are **false cognates**. The Spanish verb *comprar*, for example, means "to buy," not "to compare." Students who are learning a new language should understand that both cognates and false cognates exist.

> **DID YOU KNOW?**
>
> Students' ability to recognize cognates and use them as a tool for understanding a second language is called **cognate awareness**.

Negative transfer, also called interference, occurs when students incorrectly apply rules from their native language to their learning of English. For example, a Spanish-speaking student may place an adjective after a noun ("the house red") because of the noun-adjective structure in Spanish. However, in English the adjective comes before the noun ("the red house").

Code-switching is also frequent among language learners. Students mix words from their first language in with the language they are learning. This happens when they have forgotten a term or do not know how to express themselves in the second language. For example, a Spanish-speaking student who is looking for the bathroom and cannot recall a vocabulary word might ask, "Where is the *baño*?" This type of linguistic back-and-forth is very common with bilingual and multilingual individuals.

Finally, students' **accents** will impact their learning and pronunciation of English. Often speakers will substitute the sounds of their first language for ones they think are the same in English. For example, some Spanish speakers may pronounce the /v/ sound like the English *b*.

Additionally, stresses and intonations of words can be carried from first languages. Both of these speech patterns can change the meanings of English words (for example, the meanings of the words "read" and "read"), leading to an unclear message.

SAMPLE QUESTION

2) Jamie has just moved from Mexico to Texas, where his mother enrolled him in an ESOL class. A few weeks in, Jamie is still reluctant to speak because he mixes in words from his first language with the English he is learning. Which linguistic behavior is Jamie demonstrating?

   A.   code-switching

   B.   cognate awareness

   C.   difficulty with accent

   D.   language interference

ASSESSMENT OF ENGLISH LANGUAGE LEARNERS (ELLS)

Because English language learners need differentiated instruction, they should be identified as soon as possible. Title III of Part A of ESSA requires states to hold English language learners to the same rigorous standards as all students. These students must receive high-quality, early targeted interventions to increase English proficiency and stay on track to meet grade-level objectives.

The first and most common step in identifying English Language learners (ELLs) is the **home language survey**. Many states and districts mandate that parents complete this upon student enrollment. This survey is short (fewer than ten questions) and available in multiple languages. An example survey is shown in Figure 6.1.

The home language survey is not the end of the process. Some parents might fear that their child will be placed in "lower-level" classes, so they may say that English is spoken in the home when it is not. In other cases, students who speak a language other than English at home may be fluent in both languages and require no language learning supports at school. However, in many states and districts, all students who use a language other than English at home must receive further assessment to determine the need for English language learning services. Some commercially available assessment instruments include:

1.   Bilingual Syntax Measure (BSM) of listening and speaking

2.   IDEA Proficiency Test (IPT)

3.   Language Assessment System (LAS Links)

4.   WIDA-ACCESS Placement Test

5.   Woodcock-Muñoz Language Survey–Revised (WMLS–R)

6.   Student Oral Language Observation Matrix (SOLOM) (particularly useful if the second language is not Spanish)

Student Name: _____ Grade: _____ Date: _____	
Parent/Guardian Name: _____ Parent/Guardian Signature: _____	
Right to Translation and Interpretation Services	1. In what language(s) would your family prefer to communicate with the school? _____ _____ _____
Eligibility for Language Development Support	2. What language did your child learn first? _____ 3. What language does your child use the most at home? _____ 4. What is the primary language used in the home, regardless of the language spoken by your child? _____ 5. Has your child received English language development support in a previous school? Yes_____ No_____ Don't Know_____
Prior Education	6. In what country was your child born? _____ 7. Has your child ever received formal education outside of the United States? (Kindergarten – 12th grade) Yes_____ No_____ If yes: Number of months: _____ Language of instruction: _____ 8. When did your child first attend a school in the United States? (Kindergarten – 12th grade) _____ Month Day Year

Figure 6.1. Home Language Survey

Some states also use scores below a certain threshold on standardized achievement tests as possible indications of limited English proficiency, particularly for older students (grade 2 and above).

State requirements for qualifications to administer ELL assessments vary. In some locations, ESOL or bilingual education teachers might give such assessments. In others, reading specialists are responsible, particularly if they are proficient in the student's first language.

Reading specialists work closely with teachers and administrators specially trained in second language acquisition to make sure the assessment process is thorough and expedient.

If a reading specialist conducting an assessment determines that the student needs to be tested for English proficiency, they should consult with the appropriate specialist to ensure the student is assessed by the most qualified individual.

The assessment is typically followed by an interview with the student's parents or guardians, with an interpreter as needed. This step is crucial, as it can give relevant background on the student's prior educational experiences and other factors that might not be apparent through the home language survey and the assessment.

In some states, particularly those with many English language learners, a **Language Proficiency Assessment Committee** (LPAC) may be formed. An LPAC is composed of relevant educators and administrators. This committee recommends placement of ELLs into certain courses and creates a plan for their success. (These committees are similar to an IEP but focus on language-learning goals.) Depending on the school's student population and resources, reading specialists may participate on such committees. However, they must be aware of student plans and monitor their implementation as part of students' overall literacy development.

Reading specialists must consider all aspects of a student's learning situation. Formal assessment measures like standardized tests and other high-stakes assessments may not fully reflect an ELL's abilities. Educators should use frequent, ongoing informal assessment measures to help confirm any placement decisions made through standardized assessments.

Students who require special education services or reading intervention services are in another category. Many schools and districts use a multidisciplinary approach to identify students for special services. This approach requires input from special education teachers, ESOL teachers, reading specialists, school psychologists, and others.

Students who are misplaced (e.g., a student is thought to have a second language acquisition issue when they actually have a learning disability) will not receive appropriate services and programming.

Further, it is not unusual that a student might need English language learning support *and* qualify for special education services. ESOL teachers may initiate referrals for special education services as appropriate. A student might need evaluation by multiple professionals before the best services to meet individual needs are found.

SAMPLE QUESTION

3)   **Which is the MOST appropriate question to ask parents or guardians during an interview as part of a comprehensive assessment of English language learning?**

A.   "Do you value education in your home?"

B.   "Has your child attended school before?"

C.   "Why did you come to the United States?"

D.   "Why do you believe learning English is important?"

INSTRUCTION OF ENGLISH LANGUAGE LEARNERS

Like all learners, ELLs need developmentally appropriate systematic instruction to build content knowledge and English proficiency. While students are working to master content-specific standards, they will also be working to master **English Language Proficiency (ELP) standards**. Such standards may be created by the state or by the WIDA Consortium (a group of state and government agencies that uses a shared set of ELPs). These standards aim to help students develop language proficiencies related to language arts, mathematics, science, social studies, and the social and instructional language of the school environment.

> **DID YOU KNOW?**
>
> Some schools use bilingual education to transition to solely English instruction. Other schools use full English immersion with ESOL services, through co-teaching, pull-out services, or sheltered or specialized classes

Within a broader framework of overarching ELPs, educators should create language objectives for ELLs that correspond with each lesson's focus. In schools with a large population of English language learners, some classes may be "sheltered." These classes focus on the content area and English language learning, with an emphasis on developing language objectives in conjunction with content area proficiency.

However, if ELL students are taught in the general education setting, content area teachers will need to embed English learning objectives in their lessons. They will also need to modify lessons and assessments to meet the needs of all learners. This might include strategies such as:

▶   using picture dictionaries or electronic translators

▶   eliminating portions of assignments or assessments students may not have background knowledge of

▶   using peer tutors or collaborative learning strategies that build on each student's strengths

▶   using multimedia or visual elements to aid in understanding

▶   pre-teaching core vocabulary or vocabulary scaffolding such as digital texts with click-through definitions

▶   limiting teacher talk and, when used, avoiding colloquialisms and speaking slowly

▶   verifying that instructions are understood before students begin a task

▶   providing both a print and oral version of instructions

- ▶ using manipulatives or authentic learning situations whenever possible
- ▶ providing copies of lecture notes or allowing audio recording

When conducting assessments with English language learners, some common strategies include:

- ▶ giving students a word bank or other explicit prompting
- ▶ allowing a test to be read aloud or to be completed orally in its entirety
- ▶ giving written assessments with simplified language
- ▶ administering assessments in smaller portions
- ▶ allowing students to use a dictionary or translating device on tests and/ or allowing for extra time or unlimited time
- ▶ not penalizing for spelling or grammar errors (as appropriate)
- ▶ using informal assessment measures such as observational records or oral assessments whenever possible

Reading and English/language arts teachers are in a slightly different position from content area teachers. They must teach basic literacy skills along with the foundations of English as a language students might not be familiar with. Their focus will be on best practices in reading instruction with an emphasis on the needs of English language learners.

Phonemic Awareness: English phonemes are distinct and should be taught explicitly, particularly for sounds that do not exist in the student's native language. However, sounds that are present in the native language and are already known can be transferred rapidly. In this case, instruction in phonemes should focus on those that differ from the student's first language.

Systematic Phonics Instruction: As with all learners, systematic phonics instruction is effective with students whose first language is not English. Decoding through phonics is a two-step process: Teachers must give ELLs the tools to sound out words. But these students must also be able to make meaning of the words based on their oral language vocabulary, which should be developed in tandem.

In addition, automatic word recognition (sight reading) can be very helpful for ELLs. It can speed up reading rate and sometimes prevent difficulties encountered when words deviate from standard phonetic structures.

Fluency: Reading fluency follows oral language fluency. However, ELLs may have trouble with strategies like reading aloud in front of others. They may lack confidence and focus on mistakes instead of growth over time. Oral reading practice with English language learners should be carefully orchestrated, making use of a trusted peer whenever possible.

Vocabulary: Vocabulary instruction for ELLs will vary considerably from their native-speaking classmates. ELLs will need instruction in idioms and basic "connector words" like "because," "and," and so on. They will also need explicit and direct instruction in the vocabulary of the classroom. This includes words frequently used in giving instructions, words associated with subject area, high-frequency words used in speech and texts, and all vocabulary necessary to understand a text. Whenever possible, vocabulary should be taught explicitly and backed up with images or objects.

Comprehension: Comprehension must be carefully scaffolded in a variety of ways. Teachers should provide as much background knowledge as possible to students unfamiliar with aspects of American culture. ELLs, like developing readers, are better able to comprehend text with low complexity. Such texts should be used to build comprehension skills. Graphic organizers, visual aids, and films or multimedia elements to promote comprehension may also be helpful.

Cultural Sensitivity: Awareness of cultural differences is important for all students. It is especially relevant for English language learners, who may be unfamiliar with elements of American culture that many people take for granted. Assumptions about religious beliefs, dietary preferences, clothing choices, family structures, and so on should be avoided. Teachers should select a variety of texts and curricular resources to promote an understanding of diverse cultural perspectives. While many publishers now promote multicultural awareness, teachers should consider curricular resources that include diverse authorial voices.

SAMPLE QUESTION

4) A reading specialist is helping a high school teacher make her unit on *Romeo and Juliet* more accessible to English language learners. Which is the BEST suggestion for the reading specialist to make?

   A. provide an alternate dramatic text on a different topic for ELL students to read

   B. encourage ELL students to use context clues as they read the play to identify new vocabulary

   C. pre-teach important roots and affixes to ELL students to aid in their decoding of new words in the play

   D. give ELL students a list of words used frequently in the play with their definitions

STUDENTS WITH READING DIFFICULTIES AND DISABILITIES

LEGAL ISSUES RELATED TO READING DISABILITIES

Today's special education landscape has been shaped by federal legislation over the last fifty years. Before federal legislation mandating school access, many individuals with disabilities were institutionalized rather than given opportunities for education. In institutions, systemic neglect and abuse was common. In the 1960s, alongside other civil rights movements, the disability rights movement raised public awareness of the treatment of individuals with disabilities. The federal government responded with legislation supporting educational opportunities for people with disabilities.

In 1965, Congress enacted the **Elementary and Secondary Education Act (ESEA)**, which seeks to improve student academic achievement through supplementary educational services as well as increased educational research and training. It also provides financial assistance to schools servicing a high percentage of students from low-income families (Title 1 funding). ESEA was the first legislation to provide states with direct financial assistance to support the education of students with disabilities.

> **DID YOU KNOW?**
>
> In 1970, only one in five children with disabilities attended US schools. In fact, many states at that time had laws excluding students with certain disabilities from school.

A major civil rights victory for individuals with disabilities came with the **Rehabilitation Act of 1973**, which ensures all students with disabilities a right to public education. **Section 504** of the Rehabilitation Act prohibits programs that receive federal financial assistance from discriminating on the basis of disability. As federally funded institutions, public schools are required to ensure that students with disabilities receive a comparable education to those without disabilities. If a student with a disability does not qualify for services under IDEA, they may still receive support through a 504 plan. Under Section 504, students with disabilities may receive related services, accommodations, and modifications to ensure equal access to education.

The most comprehensive civil rights legislation for individuals with disabilities to date is the 1990 **Americans with Disabilities Act (ADA)**. The ADA prohibits discrimination on the basis of disability in the workplace and in all public places (e.g., restaurants, parks, schools, businesses). The passage of the ADA has led to increased community access, accessibility of public transportation, and more equal employment opportunities for individuals with disabilities. As a comprehensive civil rights law, the ADA provides another layer of legal protection for the right of students with disabilities to have equal access to public education.

The first legislation targeting educational rights was the 1975 **Education for All Handicapped Children Act** (EHA, also referred to as **P.L. 94-142**). This act expands educational rights for students with disabilities. The legislation ensures that students with disabilities can access any accommodations, modifications, related services, and specially designed instruction needed to make adequate educational progress in a public school setting.

Congress reauthorized EHA as the **Individuals with Disabilities Education Act (IDEA)** in 1990 and again with amendments in 1997 and 2004. Part B of IDEA provides for services for students between the ages of three and twenty-one, while Part C provides for early intervention services for students from birth to three years old.

Since its original authorization, IDEA has operated under six foundational principles:

- ▶ **Free Appropriate Public Education (FAPE)**: FAPE maintains that students with disabilities have a right to an education at no additional cost to parents. (Parents of students with disabilities are still responsible for school fees that apply to all students.) The education is required to meet the student's unique educational needs in a public school setting.

- ▶ **Appropriate and nondiscriminatory evaluation**: Evaluations must be completed by a team of trained professionals (e.g., teachers, school psychologists) and should include information from parents. Evaluations should address all areas of concern, and materials must be sound and nondiscriminatory. Evaluations must be conducted in a timely manner, and reevaluations must occur a minimum of every three years.

- ▶ **Individualized Education Program (IEP)**: An IEP is a legal document developed by the IEP team (parents, general educators, special educators, administrators, related service providers) that reports present levels of performance, annual goals and objectives, accommodations, modifications, related services, and specially designed instruction to help students make adequate educational progress.

Table 6.1 IEP versus Section 504 Plan

	IEP	Section 504 Plan
Law	Individuals with Disabilities Education Act (IDEA)	Section 504 of the Rehabilitation Act of 1973
Department	Department of Education	Office of Civil Rights
Eligibility	a disability as defined in IDEA that impacts educational performance	a disability that impacts a major life function
Included	specialized education services, accommodations, modifications, related services	accommodations, modifications, related services
Age	0 to 21 years	no age limits
Location	schools through grade 12	school through grade 12, college, work

- ▶ **Least Restrictive Environment (LRE)**: Students with disabilities must be provided supports with nondisabled peers to the maximum extent appropriate for them to make educational progress. This includes access to the general curriculum, which ensures that students with disabilities have access to the same curriculum as their nondisabled peers. LRE emphasizes placement in the general education classroom with supplemental aides and services as much as possible.

▶ **Parent (and student) participation**: Parents must have a shared role in all special education decisions, including IEP reviews, evaluation, and placement decisions.

▶ **Procedural safeguards**: Parents must receive written notice of procedural safeguards, parent and student rights, meetings, and all educational decisions. Parents have access to all student educational records. Parents may take due process measures in the event of a disagreement between the parent and a school district.

The most recent authorization of IDEA is the **2004 Individuals with Disabilities Education Improvement Act**. IDEA 2004 expands procedures for identifying students with learning disabilities to include identification through response to intervention. IDEA 2004 also includes several changes to align with the 2001 **No Child Left Behind (NCLB)** legislation. The main purpose of NCLB is to improve the academic performance of all students through increased accountability for results, emphasizing research-based instruction, and ensuring such instruction is delivered by highly qualified teachers (HQT).

In 2015, Congress passed the **Every Student Succeeds Act (ESSA)** to replace NCLB, effective starting the 2017 – 2018 school year. ESSA rolls back many of the federal education requirements, giving power back to the states. Under ESSA, states are required to create accountability plans, track state-set accountability goals, and incorporate accountability systems (e.g., state assessments, English language proficiency, postsecondary readiness, and school safety). ESSA removes the federal HQT requirement of NCLB. However, each state must set expectations for ensuring HQTs are providing instruction. Moreover, ESSA maintains the state assessment requirements of NCLB and Title I funding for schools.

SAMPLE QUESTION

5) **Which of the following would NOT be a service provided to a student under a 504 plan?**

A.   occupational therapy

B.   testing accommodations

C.   extra transition time between classes

D.   specially designed instruction

CHARACTERISTICS OF READING DIFFICULTIES AND DISABILITIES

Students progress toward full literacy at different rates. Those who do not meet or are at risk of not meeting grade-level expectations have reading difficulties, which are different from reading disabilities. Students with **reading difficulties** are falling behind grade-level expectations in reading but do not qualify for special education services under the category of specific learning disability (SLD). **Reading disabilities** are formally diagnosed learning disabilities. These students will typically qualify for special education services and are served through an IEP.

Students who qualify for special education services under another category (such as intellectual disability, speech and language impairment or developmental disability) may have other disabilities that cause reading difficulties. Their IEP may list reading-related modifications and accommodations even though they have not been diagnosed with an SLD.

Reading difficulties fall into three categories:

1. **Specific word-reading difficulties (SWD)** describe students who have trouble reading or decoding individual words. They may also have below-average fluency and comprehension levels because they struggle to decode on the word level. When presented with texts they are able to decode, however, these students may have strong reading comprehension skills.

2. **Specific reading comprehension difficulties (SRCD)** are experienced by students who can decode on a basic level but lack the vocabulary knowledge or inferencing skills necessary to comprehend texts fully.

3. **Mixed reading difficulties (MRD)** describe students who have deficits in both decoding and comprehension.

Reading disabilities fall into three categories:

1. **Phonological deficits** occur when students struggle with word recognition due to weak phonological processing. These students face a range of challenges, including trouble with letter-sound correspondence, sounding out words, and spelling. Seventy to 80 percent of students with a reading-related learning disability have phonological deficits. These deficits are usually described by the term **dyslexia**, sometimes called **language-based learning disability (LBLD)**.

2. **Processing speed/orthographic processing deficits** occur when students do not read quickly or accurately. Orthographic coding differs from phonological coding in that it does not rely solely on letter-sound correspondence and knowledge but rather on memory (of letters, groups of letters, or entire words) to decode. This type of deficit is typically milder than a phonological deficit and may be co-occurring or distinct from a phonological deficit. There is some debate as to whether this type of deficit is a subtype of dyslexia or a distinct disability.

3. **Specific comprehension deficits** describe issues with vocabulary, language learning, and abstract reasoning. Comprehension deficits might co-occur with phonological or processing deficits as well as with other conditions, particularly

DID YOU KNOW?

Dyslexia is a very common SLD thought to affect at least 15 percent of the global population.

Autism Spectrum Disorder (ASD). This type of deficit is also referred to as **hyperlexia** because word recognition skills are average or even advanced.

6)   **Specific comprehension deficits often co-occur in students diagnosed with**

  A.   dyspraxia.

  B.   dysgraphia.

  C.   Autism Spectrum Disorder (ASD).

  D.   Emotional Disturbance (EBD).

ASSESSING READING DIFFICULTIES AND DISABILITIES

Universal screening is an assessment process for possible reading difficulties. It usually takes place three times per year. Schools use different assessment measures for screening, but the most common are:

▶   **Curriculum-Based Measurement (CBM)** is an informal assessment in which a student reads aloud a passage from the core reading curriculum. The student reads for about one to five minutes, while the teacher records the number of words read correctly. This value of number of words correct is compared to the target for the month and year based on predefined standards related to grade and age.

▶   Published measurements include the **Dynamic Indicators of Basic Early Literacy Skills (DIBELS), Woodcock Reading Mastery Test–Revised (WJ–R), and Texas Primary Reading Inventory (TPRI).** These are more formal assessments that generate more detailed reports than a simple CBM.

Whatever assessment instruments are used to screen for reading difficulties, they should meet the following criteria:

▶   sensitivity: degree to which an instrument detects at-risk students

▶   specificity: degree to which the instrument avoids false positives

▶   practicality: brevity and simplicity of the assessment

▶   consequential validity: refrains from inequity in identification and is shown to lead to effective intervention

Different states, districts, and schools may establish different criteria for labeling students as at-risk for reading difficulties. Some use a threshold measure, for example: "students who score lower than X or who read fewer than X words correct per minute." Others use norm-references such as national or state averages. Still others develop their own criterion and may label performance as satisfactory/unsatisfactory or high-risk/low-risk.

Students identified as at-risk during universal screening should be provided support using the response to intervention (RTI) framework. The student may be referred for evaluation of eligibility for special education services at any point during this process based on school district policy and the student's situation. These services may enable some students to receive more targeted or appropriate interventions than with existing Tier 2 and Tier 3 intervention frameworks.

DID YOU KNOW?

Because of the desire to identify all students who might benefit from interventions for reading difficulties or disabilities, some educational researchers believe the rate of "false positive" identification to be as high as 50 percent.

If students are referred for evaluation for special education services, various instruments can be used to determine the presence of reading-related disabilities (including but not limited to dyslexia). These test for skills in phonological awareness; decoding; fluency and comprehension; and rapid naming, a skill linked to reading fluency. Some of these assessment measurements are:

▶ Comprehensive Test of Phonological Processing (CTOPP-2)

▶ Phonological Awareness Test (PAT-2: NU)

▶ Test of Word Reading Efficiency (TOWRE-2)

▶ Gray Oral Reading Test (GORT-5)

▶ Rapid Automatized Naming Test (RAN/RAS)

▶ relevant subtests of the Woodcock–Johnson III (WJIII) or the Wechsler Individual Achievement Test (WIAT-III)

RTI and referral for special education services are not mutually exclusive. Tier 2 and 3 reading interventions are used for students with reading difficulties whether or not they qualify for special education services. Targeted reading interventions are not meant as a replacement for special education services.

The model for RTI and/or special education interventions differs among schools. Some schools use a sheltered reading intervention class period for all identified students. The class is made up of students with specific learning disabilities, students with other disabilities that impact reading performance, and students who have reading difficulties but do not qualify for special education.

In another school model, students who qualify for special education services might receive services from special education teachers, while students with reading difficulties receive services from reading interventionists.

Not all schools and districts use an RTI framework. In some settings, students may participate in less formal types of interventions such as voluntary before- or after-school tutoring, summer school, or summer reading programs.

In any model, reading specialists and interventionists should use **progress monitoring** to determine the efficacy of interventions. Curriculum-based measurements are the most popular method of progress monitoring. There are many print and digital tools to organize and analyze this information. Additionally, several publishers and education technology companies provide digital platforms for ongoing progress monitoring, usually with a per-student, subscription-based fee.

Analyzing data collected through progress monitoring is a core part of a reading specialist's duties, particularly if they are leading a team of interventionists or working in a dual role as an interventionist. Based on this data, the educator must determine the best plan of action for each student. This might include collaboration with other professionals such as special educators, ESOL teachers, school psychologists, educational diagnosticians, and so on. Educational specialists may have different focuses, but they all share the same goal: student progress in reading.

SAMPLE QUESTION

7)   **Asking first-grade students to write the letters of the alphabet as a screening measure for reading difficulties is ineffective because it**

   A.   lacks practicality.

   B.   relies too heavily on background knowledge.

   C.   lacks sensitivity.

   D.   relies too heavily on quantitative data.

INSTRUCTING STUDENTS WITH READING DIFFICULTIES AND DISABILITIES

Students with reading difficulties and disabilities that impact reading performance need explicit, systematic, direct instruction. This model of instruction and practice should be reinforced across settings. For example, students still mastering letter-sound correspondence can practice with charts or flashcards at home.

Additionally, instruction must be based on each student's needs as revealed through assessment and data collection. Instruction not targeted in this way may be ineffective and/or may only increase student frustration.

Instructional strategies and intervention techniques for students with reading difficulties and disabilities are generally provided either to increase word identification or decoding on the word level or to increase overall comprehension. Specific strategies and interventions are discussed below.

Scaffolding refers to the supports used by teachers or sometimes peers during classroom activities. Scaffolds should be built into all lessons per the Universal Design for Learning (UDL), which states that all students should be able to learn from the same curriculum.

Shaping refers to providing incremental reinforcers and is also helpful in instructing students with reading difficulties and disabilities. As students progress, for example, by memorizing more grade-level high-frequency words, they should receive frequent, positive feedback from educators. This feedback is important for students who struggle with reading, as they may not receive consistent positive reinforcers (e.g., high grades, praise from peers) that other students who excel academically typically receive.

Students with reading difficulties on the word level benefit most from phonics instruction, particularly phoneme blending, phoneme segmentation, and phoneme deletion or substitution practice activities. Synthetic (e.g., Elkonin boxes) or analogy-based phonics approaches (e.g., sorting words into categories based on similarities in structures) are popular instructional methodologies for these students.

Intensive, scripted synthetic phonics programs such as Direct Instruction programs (published under names like *Reading Mastery, Corrective Reading, Horizons,* and *Funnix*) are also empirically based and generally effective. However, there is some controversy surrounding them, as they use principles of behavioral analysis such as stimulus-response-feedback as the primary means of instruction.

Students with reading difficulties on the comprehension level benefit most from instruction and interventions that help them develop metacognition to self-assess understanding and apply strategies to integrate information and synthesize it with existing knowledge. Such strategies include semantic mapping or other visual organizers; reciprocal teaching (see chapter 3); and the **PQ4R method**, an extension of the SQ3R method (see chapter 3). In the PQ4R method, students preview the reading material, generate questions, and read to answer the questions. After that, they reflect on what they have read, recite or retell from memory what they have read, and then review the material for any missed information.

In addition to the instructional strategies above, students with disabilities that impact reading, like dyslexia, can benefit from certain accommodations. **Accommodations** are changes to materials or instructional methodologies that allow all students to learn the same material as their peers.

- ▶ Materials Accommodations
    - ▷ underlining or highlighting the key words in directions
    - ▷ chunking assignments or presenting them in smaller increments
    - ▷ using a glossary or list of key vocabulary terms
    - ▷ using chapter-by-chapter, page-by-page, or even paragraph-by-paragraph reading guides
    - ▷ using assistive technology
        - ▷ audio recordings or books on tape
        - ▷ e-readers or tablets
        - ▷ text-to-speech software
- ▶ Instructional Accommodations
    - ▷ clarifying directions through oral repetition and providing a written version
    - ▷ implementing daily routines to clarify expectations
    - ▷ providing visual aids whenever possible
    - ▷ encouraging the use of mnemonic devices

> ▷   providing students a hard copy of notes
> ▷   implementing frequent review and reinforcement activities at the end of each lesson
> ▷   reviewing previously learned concepts at the beginning of a new lesson
> ▷   creating opportunities for additional or extended practice
> ▷   using peer learning strategies

At times, students with reading disabilities will also need modifications to what they are expected to learn. **Modifications** will usually be listed on the student's IEP and may include a reduced number of questions or items on assessments, different grading criteria, and so on. Reading specialists may collaborate with special education teachers to develop and monitor accommodations and modifications for students with learning disabilities that impact reading performance.

SAMPLE QUESTION

8)   A reading specialist is mentoring a new tenth-grade English teacher. One of her students with dyslexia is very frustrated and feeling overwhelmed by the assigned novel the class is reading. What should the reading specialist recommend?

A.   have the student read the CliffsNotes version of the novel instead of the novel

B.   encourage the student to read at least fifty to one hundred pages each day

C.   give the student an audio recording of the book to aid in comprehension

D.   read the entire novel aloud in class, asking a different student to read orally each day

HIGH–ACHIEVING STUDENTS

Reading specialists frequently offer strategies for students with reading difficulties, but there are also students who need greater challenges. As part of the **Universal Design for Learning (UDL)**, all classrooms should use an approach that meets the needs of all learners and allows all students to access the same curriculum. Teachers can meet the needs of high-achieving students with a pyramid approach to plan lessons.

HELPFUL HINT

Not all states mandate specific services for gifted and talented education. What are your state's requirements for gifted education?

Another widely used model for advanced learners is **Renzulli's Triad Enrichment Model**. This model encourages three types of learning experiences:

1.   exploratory opportunities

2.   learning experiences in which thinking processes are developed

3.   investigative activities

In this model, students typically have some sort of authentic experience with a topic. For example, they might take a field trip to visit a working farm. Then they are instructed on how to research and prepare a multimedia presentation on agriculture in the local community. This empowers them to investigate agriculture in the community and prepare a multimedia presentation.

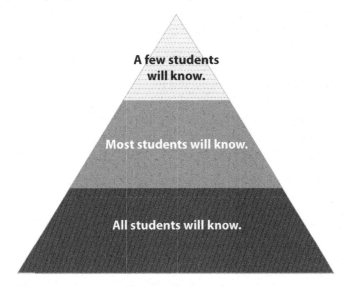

A few students will know.

Most students will know.

All students will know.

Figure 6.2. Universal Design for Learning

The following are ways to encourage a love of reading and a deeper exploration of texts by advanced readers in the classroom:

▶   Encourage choice of texts. Some students may be ready for more complex texts that are above the Lexile measure for their grade level. These students may find books or passages at grade level boring or redundant. Allowing advanced readers to choose their own materials can encourage them to explore topics of interest and increase engagement. Of course, educators should consider students' reading capabilities and socio-emotional development. Some more complex texts contain mature themes or subject matter that might not be appropriate for younger readers.

▶   Allow for appropriate pacing. Some students may benefit from **acceleration**, or moving through the curriculum at a faster rate than peers. **Curriculum compacting** allows students who have already mastered parts of the curriculum to skip those areas and move on to new material.

▶   Extend learning through independent projects, project-based learning, or other methods that encourage critical thinking and deeper comprehension of texts.

Independent learning is an appropriate enrichment activity for advanced readers, but it does not replace explicit instruction, which high-achieving students also benefit from. Advanced learners should not be given "busy work" or simply be given the entire class period for independent reading.

Reading specialists should work with teachers to devise enrichment activities that extend *purposeful* learning to enhance and extend the core curriculum. Such activities allow for student choice and exploration of individual interests. For example, in a class reading the novel *Across Five Aprils*, an advanced learner might extend purposeful learning by preparing a presentation on the Civil War and presenting it to the class as part of the introduction of the novel. This keeps the student engaged in class-wide activities and benefits all learners in the classroom.

SAMPLE QUESTION

9) An assignment in which students select a novel and then create a PowerPoint presentation summarizing its plot is appropriate for an advanced reader because it

   A. allows for student choice.

   B. includes elements of technology.

   C. makes use of curriculum compacting.

   D. promotes homogenous grouping.

REVIEW

Read the question, and then choose the most correct answer.

1

How is bilingual education distinct from English as a second language instruction?

A.   Bilingual education does not focus on developing English language skills.

B.   Bilingual education is conducted in English, the students' native language, and an additional language.

C.   ESL instruction is full English immersion, while bilingual education is not.

D.   ESL instruction occurs outside of the school day, while bilingual education occurs inside the school day.

2

After extensive observations and progress monitoring, a special education teacher, reading specialist, and ESL coordinator decide to move a student from a self-contained special education classroom to a self-contained ESL classroom. What action must they take before making the change?

A.   create a 504 Plan for the student

B.   create an IEP for the student

C.   get input from the principal

D.   get input from the parents

3

Under IDEA, a student with a disability may be placed in a self-contained special education classroom if

A.   he or she is determined to have an emotional/behavioral disturbance (EBD).

B.   it is determined to be the least restrictive environment (LRE).

C.   the school has available slots in such a classroom.

D.   the general education teachers feel uncomfortable meeting the student's needs.

4

Why has universal screening for reading difficulties become standard practice for most elementary schools?

A.   It allows for a more systematic process of selection of a reading curriculum.

B.   It provides further data to support the efficacy of phonics instruction.

C.   It can identify at-risk students for prompt early intervention.

D.   It allows paraprofessionals to take a more active role in reading assessment.

5

Which of the following statements is always true of response to intervention (RTI) frameworks?

A.   They are needed in all individual education programs (IEPs).

B.   They require an extended school day for participants.

C.   They use progress monitoring to determine effectiveness.

D.   They do not include students eligible for special education services.

6

Which of the following is the MOST appropriate accommodation for a student diagnosed with dyslexia?

A.   fewer questions on a written test

B.   an audio recording of a book

C.   a picture board for oral communication

D.   a rubric for grading writing that does not take off points for spelling errors

7

"Hyperlexia" is a term that describes students with reading deficits in which of the following areas?

A.   phonology

B.   processing speed

C.   orthographic patterning

D.   specific comprehension

8

A reading specialist is working with a group of students with specific word-reading difficulties (SWD). Which type of instructional intervention is MOST useful for these students?

A.   a focus on vocabulary knowledge and inferencing skills

B.   practice with synthesis and summarization

C.   explicit, systematic phonics instruction

D.   instruction aimed at increasing reading rate and prosody

9

A reading specialist conducting a curriculum-based measurement (CBM) determines that a third-grade student is reading at a rate of 150 words correct per minute. What next step should the specialist take?

A.   refer the student for evaluation for special education eligibility

B.   recommend possible enrichment opportunities to the student's teacher

C.   place the student in a cohort for Tier 2 interventions aimed at developing fluency

D.   place the student in a cohort for Tier 3 interventions aimed at developing fluency

10

Students who do not make progress during reading-focused interventions as part of an RTI framework are

A.   referred for evaluation for special education services after the parents give their consent.

B.   referred to a language proficiency assessment committee for further evaluation after the parents give their consent.

C.   placed into a self-contained special education classroom for the next semester.

D.   placed into a grade below the one they are currently in.

ANSWER KEY

SAMPLE QUESTIONS

1) A.   Incorrect. Lucia is using language chunking to retain phrases and groups of words more successfully. Language chunking does not occur in preproduction.

    B.   Correct. Lucia is using language chunking and song lyrics to build vocabulary. These are features of early production.

    C.   Incorrect. Lucia has not yet reached speech emergence, since she cannot create multi-word responses to questions and statements.

    D.   Incorrect. Lucia's inability to speak in complete sentences indicates that she has not yet reached intermediate fluency.

2) **A.   Correct.** In code-switching, students mix in words from their first language when they speak their second language.

    B.   Incorrect. Students who recognize similarities between words in first and second languages are demonstrating cognate awareness.

    C.   Incorrect. Students who struggle with accents are usually mixing sounds or tones from their first language with their second language.

    D.   Incorrect. Students who confuse the structure of first and second languages are said to be experiencing interference.

3) A.   Incorrect. Parents might find this question offensive and think the interviewer believes that non–English speakers do not value education.

    B.   Correct. This is a crucial piece of information since ELLs may have experienced disruptions or delays in schooling due to their journey to the United States.

    C.   Incorrect. This personal information is not the interviewer's concern in determining educational planning.

    D.   Incorrect. This question will not lead to information about the student's background and academic history.

4) A.   Incorrect. Using a different text deviates from grade-level standards and does not provide access to the curriculum for all learners.

    B.   Incorrect. Context clues may not help ELL students determine the meaning of new vocabulary, especially in a play with archaic language.

    C.   Incorrect. Roots and affixes might help ELL students decode some vocabulary, but words in a Shakespearean play are quite complex and will need to be explicitly defined.

    D.   Correct. Common Shakespearean words like "thine," "thou," and so on may be new to ELLs. They should be concretely defined before the students read the play.

5)   A.   Incorrect. Related services may be provided through a 504 plan.

       B.   Incorrect. Accommodations may be provided through a 504 plan.

       C.   Incorrect. Transition time may be provided through a 504 plan.

       D.   **Correct.** Specially designed instruction is provided as part of an IEP but not under a 504 plan.

6)   A.   Incorrect. Dyspraxia affects coordination and motor skills development.

       B.   Incorrect. Dysgraphia affects handwriting.

       C.   **Correct.** Specific comprehension deficits commonly co-occur in students with ASD.

       D.   Incorrect. There is no direct link between specific comprehension deficits and EBD, nor are they commonly co-occurring.

7)   A.   Incorrect. This is a short and simple assessment measure, so it does not lack practicality.

       B.   Incorrect. Knowledge of the letters should be mastered by first grade and is not background knowledge.

       C.   **Correct.** This assessment measure would not identify students at risk for reading difficulties; it is not sensitive enough. Many students can write the letters but might not, for example, know the sound each letter corresponds with.

       D.   Incorrect. Some useful screening assessments do rely heavily on quantitative data (e.g., how many vowel sounds or consonant blends are known or unknown).

8)   A.   Incorrect. Assigning an abridged version of the book does not give the student the same access to the curriculum.

       B.   Incorrect. A long daily reading assignment will likely make the student feel more overwhelmed.

       C.   **Correct.** Access to an audio recording of the book will help the student feel less overwhelmed and also scaffold comprehension, as the focus is on listening skills versus reading skills.

       D.   Incorrect. Reading the novel aloud in class would take up too much class time.

9)   **A.**   **Correct.** Research indicates that student choice of reading material is a particularly effective strategy for advanced readers.

       B.   Incorrect. Technology should be integrated into learning experiences for all students, not just advanced readers.

       C.   Incorrect. Curriculum compacting allows students to skip certain parts of the curriculum they have already mastered.

       D.   Incorrect. Homogenous grouping is beneficial to all students in many cases, but it does not apply to this scenario, as the project seems an independent rather than collaborative one.

Review

1) A.   Incorrect. Both methods focus on developing English language skills.

   B.   Incorrect. This would be trilingual education! Bilingual education is part in English and part in the native language of students.

   C.   Correct. ESL instruction is conducted in English, with appropriate scaffolds to aid in understanding.

   D.   Incorrect. Both types of programs typically occur within the school day, though there are more ESL classes for adults in the evening than bilingual programs for adults.

2) A.   Incorrect. A 504 Plan is not required for a change in placement.

   B.   Incorrect. An IEP should already have been done if the student is receiving special education services.

   C.   Incorrect. Input from the principal may be helpful, but it is not required.

   D.   Correct. This is a requirement under IDEA. Parents must have input in placement decisions.

3) A.   Incorrect. Students with EBDs are usually placed in a self-contained classroom only if it is determined to be the least restrictive.

   B.   Correct. While the goal is for all students to learn in the general education classroom, this environment might not allow for maximum educational progress. In this case, a self-contained classroom might be determined to be the LRE.

   C.   Incorrect. Available classroom space is not a valid reason for such a placement.

   D.   Incorrect. If the LRE is the general education classroom, the general education teachers must implement the IEP and meet the needs of all students.

4) A.   Incorrect. Universal screening is not related to curriculum selection.

   B.   Incorrect. Universal screening identifies students at risk of not meeting reading goals.

   C.   Correct. Universal screening, or screening of all students, allows for early and prompt interventions for students who might have reading difficulties.

   D.   Incorrect. These screening measures are usually conducted by teachers, not paraprofessionals.

5) A.   Incorrect. Some students with IEPs may participate in an RTI, but these are two separate frameworks.

   B.   Incorrect. Some interventions occur during the school day.

C.   **Correct.** A key component of RTI is progress monitoring. This is the only way to determine if more intensive interventions are needed or if existing interventions should be continued.

D.   Incorrect. Interventions may include students eligible for special education services.

6) A.   Incorrect. Changing the number of questions is a modification, not an accommodation.

B.   **Correct.** A picture board allows the student the same access to the curriculum and does not change the core content.

C.   Incorrect. Dyslexia is primarily a reading-related disability. Most students with dyslexia can communicate orally.

D.   Incorrect. Changing the grading criteria is a modification, not an accommodation.

7) A.   Incorrect. Phonological deficits are most closely associated with dyslexia or a language-based learning disability (LBLD).

B.   Incorrect. Processing-speed deficits are often part of dyslexia.

C.   Incorrect. Orthographic patterns are letter patterns, which would point to issues related more to dyslexia than hyperlexia.

D.   **Correct.** Hyperlexia, or specific comprehension deficits, describes issues with vocabulary, language learning, and abstract reading. Individuals with these deficits, however, have average or advanced word recognition skills.

8) A.   Incorrect. Focusing on vocabulary and inferencing is more appropriate for students who have specific reading comprehension difficulties (SRCD).

B.   Incorrect. Synthesis and summarization are more helpful for students with SRCD.

C.   **Correct.** Word-reading difficulties are best addressed with phonics since these students are struggling to decode on the word level.

D.   Incorrect. Prosody is not targeted instruction since these students need to practice on improving decoding.

9) A.   Incorrect. There is no indication that the student has a disability or needs special education services.

B.   **Correct.** This student is likely quite advanced and may benefit from enrichment opportunities.

C.   Incorrect. This student seems to be excelling without reading interventions.

D.   Incorrect. This student does not seem to need intensive fluency interventions.

10) A.   **Correct.** Part of the goal of RTI is to determine the need for special education services and provide referrals as necessary.

B.   Incorrect. This group would likely have met already to determine a student's need for language learning support. This referral would not be made after RTI.

C.   Incorrect. A student cannot be placed in a self-contained special education classroom without first qualifying for special education services.

D.   Incorrect. This might be appropriate if a student's birth date, age, or past schooling is in question, but moving a student to the grade below the current grade is not a common practice.

Leadership and Professional Skills

THE LEADERSHIP ROLE OF THE READING SPECIALIST

THE ROLE OF THE READING SPECIALIST

Because literacy skills are the foundation of all academic success, more districts and schools are recruiting reading specialists to serve on teams in various roles.

Until recently, the role of the reading specialist was to work directly with students, usually by providing pull-out remediation services. Today, reading specialists have taken on a broader role. While reading specialists might still conduct response to intervention (RTI) services at the Tier 2, 3, or even Tier 4 levels, the scope of their work goes beyond this.

> **DID YOU KNOW?**
>
> Reading specialists go by different titles depending on the school or district. Some titles are literacy specialists, literacy coaches, reading coaches, reading interventionists, and instructional specialists.

Reading specialists work to improve reading outcomes in a school community. The model of reading intervention at most schools has changed from a *remediation* model to a *prevention* model. Along with other school personnel, reading specialists can help reduce the number of students requiring special education services through early intervention and high-quality universal instruction. They can also reduce the number of students requiring Tier 2 and 3 interventions.

The reading specialist generally covers four areas:

1. **Assessment**. Reading specialists conduct and analyze assessments on a student, classroom, grade, or school-wide level. They might design and facilitate universal screening measures as part of an RTI framework, interpret results of school-wide reading standards-based assessments, and help teachers create rubrics or other assessment frameworks to monitor student progress.

2. **Instruction**. Reading specialists support classroom teachers in reading instruction in many ways. They devise and facilitate plans for differentiated instruction, model instructional techniques, or observe teachers and students to make curricular and instructional recommendations.

    In some settings, reading specialists work as co-teachers in classrooms, providing targeted instruction or interventions. In others, they see students in a reading resource room for pull-out services. In still others, Tier 2 and 3 intervention services might be provided by paraprofessionals or a contracted third-party intervention provider. In such cases, the reading specialist on staff might plan and oversee such efforts.

3. **Serving as a school-wide resource**. Regardless of the setting, a reading specialist must serve as a resource to all in the school community—general education teachers, special education teachers, paraprofessionals, and administrators—for evidence-based reading instructional practices. Reading specialists might consult with educators on planned targeted intervention strategies, differentiated instruction as part of Tier 1 interventions, or methods for embedded literacy across the content areas.

4. **Collaboration with stakeholders**. Educators in a reading specialist role might spearhead literacy initiatives at the school. They communicate with parents and the community about new initiatives and standards-based accountability. They also encourage home-school connections related to promoting reading development. Finally, they conduct frequent and ongoing progress communications with parents in an RTI framework.

SAMPLE QUESTION

1) A reading specialist observing a second-grade classroom notices that during the fast-paced lesson, most students are not participating and seem to find the material too challenging. The teacher is well ahead of the district-mandated scope and sequence, but benchmark assessments show that many of the students are not on target to meet end-of-year objectives. What is the BEST action for the reading specialist to take?

    A. conduct a class-wide assessment of oral reading fluency and share the results with the teacher

    B. plan a meeting with the teacher to work on pacing of instruction to meet the needs of all students

    C. identify the students with the greatest reading needs and refer them for special education services

    D. encourage the teacher to stop all whole-class instruction and focus on working with students one-on-one

DEVELOPING READING PROGRAMS

An effective reading program is important, but it requires high-quality teaching. Developing reading programs also means supporting the teachers who will be using them.

A reading specialist will first conduct a **needs-assessment** to determine an action plan. The reading specialist will meet with the district or school literacy team to discuss possible improvements and district or school goals. After this, data is collected and analyzed. Some types of data include:

▶ standardized test results (e.g., comparing annual state tests and trends from year to year)

▶ teacher interviews or questionnaires (Are teachers satisfied with the current literacy support? The current curriculum resources? What other support or resources would they like to have?)

▶ student/parent surveys (e.g., Ask students and parents if current supplemental services are helpful, how they feel about their progress and the level of school/home communication regarding reading progress.)

▶ classroom observations (What type of differentiated instruction is used? How effective is it? Is the curriculum being used effectively? Are supplemental tools or resources needed?)

▶ resource evaluations (Do students have access to technology? library time? paraprofessionals for small-group instruction?)

After analyzing the data, reading specialists consider school needs and capacity to implement changes or programs. While most public schools will likely be using an RTI framework to screen for and provide early intervention services, that framework may not be effective. Reading specialists should consider the following questions as they assess current processes:

▶ Are many students missing core instructional time to receive pull-out services?

▶ Is high-quality evidence-based instruction and differentiated reading instruction happening in every classroom?

▶ Are pull-out or push-in intervention services aligned with specific objectives?

▶ Is ongoing progress monitoring taking place?

▶ Are there adequate resources for core and supplemental reading instruction? Should another program be purchased?

▶ Is there congruency/consistency of literacy instruction and interventions across classrooms?

▶ Is literacy being promoted on a school-wide level? Are parents active partners in the reading development of their children?

Budget, school/district policies, and specific needs will guide next steps. Large-scale changes to a reading program or curriculum may take time to implement. Proposals must be prepared and considered by district decision-makers. However, a needs-assessment should be conducted as soon as possible to facilitate a plan for implementation.

Reading specialists might have several roles in setting up a reading program, depending on the school or setting. However, they will generally be improving or maintaining literacy levels on a school-wide basis. They might supervise a group of reading paraprofessionals or interventionists, mentor teachers, provide push-in or pull-out intervention services, conduct assessments, and provide professional development activities for school staff.

SAMPLE QUESTION

2) Designing an intervention program that takes place outside of core instructional time is ineffective because students

    A.   might miss opportunities to receive more individualized attention.

    B.   are frequently misidentified as needing such services when they are just unmotivated.

    C.   can miss out on instruction in the main classroom.

    D.   tend to be less focused than when receiving such interventions after school.

PROMOTING STAFF DEVELOPMENT

One of the reading specialist's most important responsibilities is providing instructional support to classroom teachers. They should help teachers provide the highest-quality literacy instruction to all students. This work involves five components:

1. **Explaining instructional theory.** Reading specialists should work with school staff to help them understand research-based best practices. For example, a reading specialist working with a first-grade teacher should not just say, "Read more connected texts." Instead, the reading specialist should explain that using connected texts to reinforce and practice phonics skills in context is an effective part of systematic phonics instruction. The reading specialist should answer teacher questions enthusiastically and provide resources (e.g., position statements, case studies, and journal articles) to help teachers understand and implement high-quality instruction.

2. **Modeling or Demonstration.** Reading specialists should be master reading teachers themselves. They should model or demonstrate new techniques or practices in classrooms to help teachers and paraprofessionals see high-quality instruction in action.

3. **Observation.** Reading specialists should observe ongoing reading instruction as much as possible. This allows them to share successful

techniques used in one classroom with other teachers. It also helps them observe teacher progress toward particular goals with a class or group of students.

4. **Feedback/Reflection**. In some settings, reading specialists will help provide constructive and actionable feedback to teachers. They may also act as instructional or literacy coaches. They should practice humility and patience, modeling their own processes as reflective practitioners.

5. **Supporting collaboration**. One of a reading specialist's most crucial roles is getting everyone "on the same page"—devoted to improving reading and literacy instruction across the school. When a teacher works alone and does not share best practices, only that teacher's students benefit. Reading specialists who observe classrooms frequently can help the administration pair newer teachers with mentor teachers for effective reading instruction.

Reading specialists advise teachers on reading instruction in a collegial way. They should neither judge nor evaluate a teacher's job performance. That is the responsibility of the principal or administrator who conducts formal classroom evaluations. Some teachers might be unenthusiastic about a reading specialist observing their classrooms or working with them to improve instruction. The school leadership or the principal should clarify the reading specialist's role and make sure the school is united in its efforts to improve instruction and student performance.

SAMPLE QUESTION

3) **A sixth-grade teacher asks the reading specialist for feedback on a research project she is planning. Each student will choose a young-adult author to research online at home. They will then bring in printouts of two or three online articles for a note-taking activity the following day. What is the BEST suggestion the reading specialist can make?**

   A. assign the students an author instead of allowing them to choose, since they might choose an uninteresting text

   B. have students print out and take notes on the articles for homework so they can practice working independently

   C. discourage students from using online sources for research because most are biased and outdated

   D. allow students to find and print out the articles at school, since not all students have a computer or printer at home

PROFESSIONAL DEVELOPMENT

As the resident reading expert, the reading specialist should be engaged in ongoing **professional development**. This includes attending conferences, reading articles, conducting action research, and so forth.

Reading specialists should be highly involved with the professional development activities of the school. They might plan or oversee literacy-related professional development activities and events. Because of this, reading specialists must be proficient in working with adult learners, as these learners provide such opportunities for a school's instructional staff. Research indicates that effective professional development for educators:

▶ is perceived as pertinent/relevant to each teacher's classroom

▶ uses authentic experiences and active learning

▶ is collaborative and allows for multiple perspectives

▶ provides modeling of best practices

▶ uses ongoing coaching

▶ includes feedback and reflection

▶ allows for adequate time for new skills to be put into practice

Teachers are more likely to support professional development activities and opportunities when they are embedded into existing activities and contexts. These might include departmental meetings, in-service events, professional learning communities (PLCs), and study groups. Such activities are more effective than those layered on top of a teacher's already full schedule.

When reading specialists support the "real-life" implementation of new initiatives or instructional strategies in the classroom and are willing to provide hands-on assistance, teachers are more likely to use new methods effectively.

Reading specialists should base professional development decisions on school need as revealed by data analysis. For example, a reading specialist might note that fourth- and fifth-grade students have deficits in using roots and affixes as clues to meanings of unfamiliar words based on results from state assessments. They might then hold a professional development event focusing on roots and affixes for fourth- and fifth-grade teachers. To prepare for the event, the reading specialist should identify evidence-based strategies and theories to present. After the event, the reading specialist can follow up with teachers to help them implement new techniques and strategies.

Outside of more traditional or formal professional development presentations led by reading specialists, these professionals might engage in any or all of the following to provide professional development:

▶ modeling a strategy or technique in the classroom

▶ co-planning a lesson

▶ co-teaching a lesson

▶ observing implementation of a strategy or technique and providing feedback

▶ forming or leading a professional learning community (PLC)

▶ videotaping instruction and then analyzing the tape with the teacher

▶ helping teachers plan or prepare for conferences or parent education events

SAMPLE QUESTION

4) **The principal has asked the reading specialist to plan and conduct a two-hour professional development event focused on "strategies for sight word acquisition." A veteran first-grade teacher has already successfully implemented several instructional strategies for this topic. How can the reading specialist BEST draw on this knowledge after the formal PD event?**

A. ask the teacher to create a slide presentation to share with other teachers

B. encourage the teacher to develop a written evaluation to monitor teacher understanding of sight words

C. work with the principal to help other teachers observe the successful first-grade sight word lessons in action

D. enlist the teacher to review and provide feedback on the lesson plans of all teachers for a six-week period following the event

DEVELOPING THE READING CURRICULUM

Different schools and districts might have different approaches to reading instruction. However, most research agrees that effective curricula are:

▶ systematic (clear, logical order of instruction)

▶ explicit (direct and unambiguous)

Additionally, most elementary settings and some secondary settings need several types of curricula to address the needs of all students.

A **core reading program (CRP)**, also known as a basal reading program, helps students learn to read through five core areas (phonemic awareness, phonics, fluency, vocabulary, and comprehension). This program is designed for the regular classroom and includes scaffolds or means of differentiation for all learners. A CRP provides student materials (e.g., textbooks, workbooks, readers, software, assessments) and teacher materials (e.g., teacher's editions, teacher's guides, lesson plans, scope, and sequence).

The "completeness" of any program may vary, but many CRPs are sold as comprehensive packages. Any core reading program must be aligned to the standards of the state, district, or school. A CRP is often decided upon on a district level because of the need for consistency or standardization across grade levels, typically at least K – 3 or even K – 6.

A **supplemental curriculum** is used when the core program does not provide enough practice in certain skills to meet the needs of all students in a school or classroom. It may be a stand-alone phonics, spelling, or vocabulary curriculum. Such a curriculum is an adjunct to an existing successful CRP. For example, a school's core reading program might be producing great results in terms of phonics, fluency, and comprehension, but it does not give students enough exposure to advanced vocabulary. The school might then augment this CRP with a supplemental vocabulary program.

Supplemental curricula are usually designed for the general classroom for all students and for Tier 1 interventions that occur as differentiated instruction in the context of the daily classroom activities. Other types of curricula may be used in an RTI framework for students needing more intensive interventions (Tier 2 and 3).

A **specific intervention program** provides supplemental instruction on one or more key areas of reading development to a small number of students. These target certain core areas. For example, McGraw Hill's *Corrective Reading* is an intervention curriculum aimed at using direct instruction to address phonics and comprehension deficits. Such programs include placement or diagnostic tests to start students at the appropriate point in the curriculum. They also include a recommended scope and sequence to help students fill in skill gaps as quickly as possible.

A **comprehensive intervention program** provides remediation or intervention in all five areas of reading. These programs are often used with students who need an additional class period of reading instruction or more intensive interventions than those provided within the existing framework.

A curriculum will only be as effective as the teachers using it and the way it is presented. Any reading curriculum must be presented with an intentional instruction design that:

- ▶ emphasizes the introduction to and use of explicit and systematic strategies
- ▶ follows an instructional sequence:
  - ▷ teacher modeling or direct instruction
  - ▷ guided practice
  - ▷ scaffolding while students apply the newly acquired skill
  - ▷ independent practice
- ▶ is systematic and builds on previously acquired skills
- ▶ contains intentionally aligned materials

Further, any curriculum must be research-based. This means its effectiveness has been proven through studies conducted according to the standards of the field.

Reading specialists might participate in many areas of reading curricular planning. They might serve on curriculum adoption committees or plan and implement formal studies of the effectiveness of curricular changes and additions. In doing so, they should be aware of several criteria:

- ▶ alignment to standards
- ▶ ease and efficiency of use
- ▶ presence of scaffolds

- ▶ level of student engagement
- ▶ opportunities for enrichment/extension
- ▶ balance of teacher-guided and independent practice
- ▶ alignment among multiple curricular materials

Another important consideration is the actual pragmatics of implementation. Any solution must be used to be effective. It does a school little good, for example, to have multiple subscriptions to online phonics intervention programs if they are never used or are used incorrectly.

SAMPLE QUESTION

5) **A textbook sales representative meets with the principal and reading specialist to demonstrate and discuss a new core reading program. What is the MOST important question for the reading specialist to ask?**

A. "How will this program augment our existing reading program?"

B. "Can the program be delivered by a parent or volunteer tutor?"

C. "What research has been done to back up the effectiveness of the program?"

D. "Will students transferring from another school be successful with this program?"

THE LEARNING ENVIRONMENT

Schools and classrooms should be **literacy-rich environments**. This means they provide opportunities for students to develop literacy across the content areas. Literacy-rich environments begin in the early childhood and early elementary classroom. This is where students try different ways to connect reading and writing to their pragmatic use. For example, labeling items in the classroom (e.g., wall, door, computer) can help even very young students make an association between print and meaning. Classroom materials that promote exploration of print, such as a classroom library with a designated reading area and easily accessible literacy centers full of intriguing materials, will interest young children in reading.

Digital resources are becoming a more important part of the reading classroom. Digital e-readers and digital books offer multimodal exposure to various texts for students of all ages. Technology can also make texts accessible to a broader audience. Audio recordings of books are helpful for students who are blind; students with low vision can also benefit from these recordings and from large-print screens, too. Picture dictionary and translation apps help English language learners access a variety of texts. There are even programs that enable young students to author their own books and share them with others.

In addition to a classroom library, students should visit the school library early and frequently. Teachers should help them choose books that match their interests and are of an appropriate complexity.

Most elementary reading classrooms allow for **flexible grouping**. Students are grouped by several criteria (e.g., skill level, learning style, interests). This prevents them from feeling labeled as a "good" or "bad" reader. It also allows for fluidity and movement among groups as skill level improves. Teachers can customize activities for any group of students. For example, students can read **leveled texts** that vary based on text complexity (typically based on Lexile level) or varied word counts.

Even when the entire class is reading the same text, teachers can provide **tiered assignments**. For example, students still practicing decoding explicit information can work with a list of comprehension questions with a depth of knowledge (DOK) level of 1. More proficient students can use a mix of similar questions with a DOK level of 2 or 3 and/or those that require a constructed response. Advanced students might benefit from curriculum **compacting**, whereby they move on to new skills at a faster rate than peers once they show mastery of objectives.

Texts for reading practice should match the reader and purpose. They are categorized as being at the independent level, the instructional level, or the frustration level. The **independent level** includes texts that are easy for students to read (around 95 percent accuracy). These texts can be used for many independent reading activities. **Instructional texts** that are challenging but still manageable (around 90 percent accuracy) are used mainly with teacher guidance. **Frustration level** texts, or those that are quite difficult for the student (less than 90 percent accuracy) should generally be avoided, though some research indicates that they can be effective in paired reading activities with heavy scaffolding from peers or teachers.

SAMPLE QUESTION

6) A reading specialist is working on a new Drop Everything and Read (DEAR) program in a middle school. In meeting with teachers, which is the MOST important strategy for the reading specialist to recommend?

   A.   help students find a book of interest at their independent reading level

   B.   encourage students to read a book with at least a 1300 Lexile level

   C.   ask students oral comprehension questions after the reading period

   D.   focus on helping students develop prosody during the program

COMMUNICATION AND COLLABORATION

COMMUNICATION SKILLS

Reading specialists must be skillful communicators. They should be able to explain goals and progress with students and parents and work on a school-wide team with teachers and administrators. This means they must be viewed as a trusted resource among many groups of people.

Reading specialists should work to empower educators to improve instruction and be continuously reflective practitioners. Unless the reading specialist has a supervisory or managerial role, interactions should be supportive rather than evaluative. Even when a reading specialist is evaluating a program as a whole, they should not assign blame to teachers or staff.

For example, a reading specialist visits a third-grade classroom to see how the school's purchase of a new intervention software is working. During the visit, the reading specialist notices that the teacher is sending students who have completed other work to the computer to work in the software and seems unaware of its purpose in providing targeted interventions for phonics and spelling skill gaps.

Instead of saying, "I would like to speak with you about how to use the new software correctly," the reading specialist can offer support with a comment like, "I have some ideas for how to more seamlessly integrate the new software into the daily routine. Do you have some time to meet to discuss?"

Reading specialists must help to ensure student learning and improve reading outcomes across the school. By working to unify others under a shared vision of success and being clear about objectives and processes, reading specialists will gain their trust. This will allow them to be effective in their various roles as they hold workshops and information sessions for parents and community members, work to build and maintain school-wide literacy efforts, and support teachers and other educators in their delivery of literacy instruction and interventions.

DID YOU KNOW?

A recent report by the Speak Up Research Project, which polls parents from schools across the nation, found that the majority of parents want information sent to them directly via text or email rather than looking for it on the school's website or social media page.

SAMPLE QUESTION

7) **A reading specialist sits in on a conference between an eighth-grade English teacher and the parents of a struggling student. The teacher focuses only on homework not being done, poor attendance, and lack of attention to detail in written work. The teacher leaves the meeting feeling like she was unsuccessful in forming a partnership with the parents. What is the BEST feedback for the reading specialist to give?**

   A.   "In the future, try to focus only on academics, not behavioral concerns."

   B.   "In the future, try to include both positive and constructive negative feedback with parents."

   C.   "Conferences should be focused more on metrics like test scores and grades than general feedback."

   D.   "Conferences should always include the student so that teachers can be fully transparent with their remarks."

WORKING WITH THE COMMUNITY

The reading specialist works as part of a large multidisciplinary team of stakeholders. All stakeholders want improved educational outcomes in the school, which results in a positive contribution to students and community.

One role of the reading specialist is advocacy. **Advocacy** refers to the public support or recommendation for certain causes or policies. Reading specialists might present reports to the school board or other decision-makers regarding curricular or policy changes. They might serve as the school's representative or liaison to literacy-based nonprofit groups.

Reading specialists might also help prepare press releases or marketing materials to highlight a school's reading program. In all these interactions, the reading specialist should be professional and positive and try to represent the school or district in the best possible way.

Improving literacy often requires help from the local community. Forming partnerships beyond the school's walls is essential, especially in schools without appropriate resources. With the support and approval from the school leadership team, the reading specialist might work with various entities to provide services and programming to students, teachers, and parents. Some of these entities include:

▶ the local chamber of commerce, which might have an education committee devoted to school outreach

▶ national nonprofit groups like Reading Is Fundamental and local community-based nonprofit groups

▶ community libraries

▶ supplemental education and tutoring service providers

▶ textbook/ed-tech publishers whose reps often provide training and professional development

▶ volunteer organizations

▶ parent-teacher organizations or other parents' groups

Reading specialists can often get help from these entities. Many schools work with such organizations to provide volunteer tutoring, guided storybook reading, mentorship programs, summer reading programs, and so on. Reading specialists should make sure that these organizations are reputable and, if applicable, are an approved district service provider. They should also make sure that any on-campus volunteers have participated in background checks or badging processes as laid out in the school or district policies.

SAMPLE QUESTION

8) A reading specialist is speaking at a back-to-school night about the state's new "Read by 3" initiative. The specialist should primarily focus the presentation on

    A. quantitative data that shows where the district stands in relation to overall state goals.

    B. qualitative data about the quality of instruction at the school and overall student satisfaction.

    C. ways parents can support the initiative at home.

    D. ways parents can volunteer in the classroom.

CONFLICT RESOLUTION

All workplaces experience differences in opinion. However, to facilitate a shared purpose in increased reading achievement, the reading specialist must be a consensus-builder. When changing instructional practices is an objective, some colleagues may not want to change practices they see as effective. When unanimity is not possible, **consensus**, or general agreement, should be the goal. In a consensus, all members of the group agree that they can live with a decision and will not actively fight against it.

One of the best ways to build consensus is by trying to figure out what a person might need to support an initiative or change. For example, a reading specialist meets with teachers to start a new reading log program. Some teachers do not support the new program, saying, "We never get any parental support for these kinds of things." The reading specialist can then address this issue. Perhaps the reading specialist talks about the support they will provide to help bridge the home-school divide through holding parent information sessions, creating an online portal for parents to report reading minutes, and so on. This support might help overcome the teachers' objections to the new program.

> ### QUICK REVIEW
>
> One of the top reasons people resist change is feeling a loss of autonomy and control. What are some concrete ways a reading specialist can help teachers take ownership of new initiatives?

Reading specialists might find resistance when providing instructional coaching to teachers. As previously mentioned, much of this resistance can be overcome by approaching teachers in a collegial, instead of evaluative, manner. However, when reading specialists do encounter resistance or conflict, prompt and transparent (preferably in-person) communication is important. Still, any discussion aimed at resolving conflict should be held outside the range of students. Further, at no time should an educator belittle another in front of students. This can be detrimental to students by forcing them to "take sides," which might destroy otherwise strong student-teacher relationships.

SAMPLE QUESTION

9) A reading specialist receives a forwarded email from the assistant principal from an angry parent. The parent's daughter, a fourth-grader, has been participating in school-sponsored afterschool tutoring for several months but has made no progress in terms of higher reading grades. The parent has asked the assistant principal to evaluate the afterschool tutoring program, which she believes to be ineffective. How should the reading specialist handle this situation?

  A. respond to the parent directly, assuring her that the program is backed by research

  B. respond to the assistant principal with an assurance that the program is effective and backed by research

  C. meet with the classroom teacher to find out more about the student and determine if additional interventions might be appropriate

  D. remind the assistant principal that grades are solely the responsibility of the classroom teacher and that the tutoring program is the problem

DEVELOPMENTAL PSYCHOLOGY

CHILD GROWTH AND DEVELOPMENT

There are many theories on cognitive and social development that influence instructional practices. Various theorists have contributed to current practices and their impact on student learning. **Cognitive development** refers to the way people think and develop an understanding of the world around them through genetics and other learned influences. The areas of cognitive development include information processing, reasoning, language development, intelligence, and memory.

Social development refers to learning values, knowledge, and skills that allow children to relate to others appropriately and effectively and contribute to family, the community, and school in positive ways. Social development is directly influenced by those who care for and teach the child. It is indirectly influenced through friendships, relationships with other family members, and the culture that surrounds them. As children's social development progresses,

DID YOU KNOW?

Psychologist and behaviorist B.F. Skinner was also a pioneer in educational technology. In 1954, he invented a prototype for what he called the teaching machine. The machine used a system of hole punches and tapes to give students immediate feedback after answering a question, much like today's educational technology platforms.

they begin to respond to influences around them and start building relationships with others.

Many theories about child cognitive and social development fall into one of two broad categories: behaviorism and constructivism. **Behaviorism** concerns observable stimulus-response behaviors. It suggests that all behaviors are learned through interactions with the environment through classical or operant conditioning. Therefore, our mind is a tabula rasa, or blank slate, at birth. In contrast, **constructivism** states that learning is an active process, and knowledge is constructed based on personal experiences. The learner is not a "blank slate" as suggested by behaviorism. Instead the learner uses past experiences and cultural factors to gain knowledge in new situations.

SAMPLE QUESTION

10) A reading specialist observes *Reading Mastery*, a highly scripted teacher-directed method of phonics instruction, being used in a kindergarten classroom. As students respond by saying words or sounds in choral unison, the teacher immediately corrects errors or offers praise for correct responses. Which theoretical foundation is this reading program based on?

A.   behaviorism

B.   constructivism

C.   hierarchy of needs

D.   multiple intelligences

DEVELOPMENTAL DOMAINS

What do children need in order to grow? In the 1950s, Dr. Benjamin Bloom led a group of researchers who studied learning processes. His team identified three domains, or categories, of learning: cognitive (knowledge), social (attitude), and psychomotor (skills). Each domain has its own hierarchy, which means that it is divided into categories, or degrees of complexity, that must be *mastered* before moving to the next level. This is also known as Bloom's theory of mastery learning.

The **cognitive domain** deals with intellectual development. Some of Dr. Bloom's students revised the categories of the cognitive domain in the 1990s. The new categories, in order from simplest to most challenging, are remembering, understanding, applying, analyzing, evaluating, and creating. (Bloom's taxonomy is discussed in more detail later in this section.)

Elizabeth J. Simpson expounded on the physical domain in 1972. The physical domain, also called the **psychomotor domain**, deals with all aspects of motor skill development. Simpson's categories of the physical domain in order of complexity are as follows:

▶   perception (awareness)

▶   set (readiness)

- ▶ guided response (imitation)
- ▶ mechanism (proficiency)
- ▶ complex or overt response (skilled)
- ▶ adaptation and origination (modification and construction)

For example, in the perception domain a child may sense that squiggles on a page form letters and make words. At the set stage, students are interested in learning to write the letters for themselves. During the guided response stage, the student is able to copy or trace letters with teacher support. In the mechanism phase, the student is proficient in writing letters and no longer needs support. During the complex or overt response stage, the student begins to show some talent in fine motor skills. At the adaptation and origination stage, the student can create impressive, unique designs.

The social domain is called the **affective** or **social-emotional domain**. The affective domain includes emotions, motivation, and attitudes. The categories of the social domain are:

- ▶ receiving phenomena (attentive/aware)
- ▶ responding to phenomena (participation)
- ▶ valuing (respect)
- ▶ organization (balance/prioritization)
- ▶ internalizing values (discriminating)

A student in the receiving stage might, for example, learn about a local animal shelter. In the responding to phenomena stage, the child may express the desire to adopt a shelter pet. In the valuing stage, the student may volunteer at the shelter. In the organization stage, the student will encourage others to spay and neuter their animals and to adopt shelter pets. In the internalizing values stage, the student will participate in establishing a no-kill shelter.

The moral domain theory is not part of Bloom's domains of learning. It was developed by psychologist Lawrence Kohlberg based in theories by child development psychologist Jean Piaget. The **moral domain** deals with the acquisition of morals and values. The categories of the moral domain are preconventional morality, conventional morality, and postconventional morality. During **preconventional stages**, the child behaves well because it is in their own best interest. During the **conventional stage**, the child conforms to societal expectations. During the **postconventional stage**, the person is driven by their own ethics and morals, even when it is not popular.

SAMPLE QUESTION

11) How is systematic phonics instruction related to Bloom's theory of mastery learning?

A. It focuses on the most useful sounds and letters first.

B. It introduces CVC words for initial spelling instruction.

C. It requires success with easier sounds before proceeding to more difficult ones.

D. It encourages students to read connected texts that allow them to apply phonics skills.

JEAN PIAGET

Cognitive development in children has been studied in many ways throughout the years. In 1936, the prominent theorist **Jean Piaget** proposed his **theory of cognitive development**. Piaget's theory came from several decades of observing children in their natural environments. He posited that a child's knowledge developed from schemas, or units of knowledge that use past experiences to understand new experiences.

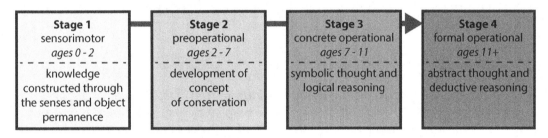

Figure 7.1. Jean Piaget's Stages of Development

According to Piaget, schemas constantly change due to two complementary processes: assimilation and accommodation. Assimilation is taking in new information and relating it to an existing schema, or what the child already knows. Accommodation occurs when schema changes to allow for new knowledge. Piaget states that there is an ongoing attempt to balance accommodation and assimilation to gain equilibration.

The core of Piaget's theory is the idea that cognitive development happens in four stages of increasing sophistication and abstract levels of thought. The stages always happen in the same order and build on learning that occurred in the previous stage.

The **sensorimotor stage** is first, taking place in infancy. During this stage, infants show intelligence through motor activities without using symbols. They have limited knowledge of the world around them; however, their world knowledge is developing through physical interactions and experiences. At around seven months, children develop object permanence, or memory of an object even if it has been removed from their immediate environment. The increase in physical development, or mobility, in this stage allows for the progression of new intellectual abilities. Symbolic language abilities begin to develop at the end of this stage.

The **preoperational stage** takes place from toddlerhood to early childhood. This stage is characterized by the demonstration of intelligence through symbols. Language abilities mature at this stage, and memory and imagination develop rapidly. Thinking, however, is nonlogical, nonreversible, and egocentric.

The **concrete operational stage** takes place from the elementary years to early adolescence. In this stage, children begin to use actions that are logical and rational when thinking and solving problems. They begin to understand permanence and conservation, or the concept that weight, volume, and numbers may remain the same even though appearance changes. In this stage, operational, or reversible thinking, develops, and egocentric thinking is reduced.

The final stage is the **formal operational stage**, which occurs from adolescence through adulthood. During this stage, children become able to independently navigate through problems and situations. They should be able to adapt to different situations by applying learned knowledge. A major cognitive transition occurs in this stage whereby adolescents are better able to think in more advanced, efficient, and complex ways.

SAMPLE QUESTION

12) **A reading specialist observing a kindergarten classroom at circle time notices that the teacher is trying to help students understand humorous irony in the book he is reading. What feedback might the reading specialist give after the class observation?**

   A.   Students gain little from being read to aloud, and reading instruction should be based primarily on phonics drills.

   B.   Students should be grouped by level and reading books at their skill level instead of participating in large group–shared storybook reading.

   C.   Students of this age are typically not able to sit and listen to a story being read and should be encouraged to work at centers most of the day.

   D.   Students of this age have not yet fully developed capabilities in abstract thought sufficient to allow them to detect irony.

LEV VYGOTSKY

Theorist **Lev Vygotsky** introduced the social development theory and the zone of proximal development. This theory states that social development plays a critical role in cognitive development and that there is a **zone of proximal development (ZPD)** that cognitive development depends on. The ZPD is achieved when children are engaged in social behavior with adults or peers. According to Vygotsky, cognitive development is better achieved through interactions or help from peers or an adult than through individual actions.

The ZPD is the distance between a child's actual developmental level, as demonstrated by independent problem-solving, and the potential developmental level, as demonstrated under adult or peer guidance. Children typically follow an adult's or a more capable peer's example and are eventually able to complete certain tasks alone.

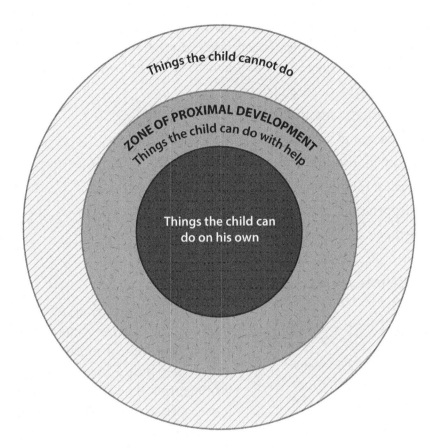

Figure 7.2. The Zone of Proximal Development

Vygotsky's ZPD has been modified and changed over the years and forms the foundation for the concept of scaffolding. **Scaffolding** is when a teacher or more capable peer provides guidance and support to the child in his or her ZPD, as appropriate, and gradually scales back the support when it is no longer necessary.

SAMPLE QUESTION

13) **Which reading instructional strategy draws from the zone of proximal development (ZPD)?**

   A.   neurological impress

   B.   semantic feature analysis

   C.   KWL charting

   D.   semantic impressions

HOWARD GARDNER

A third theorist contributing to the field of early childhood development is **Howard Gardner**. Dr. Gardner is a professor of education at Harvard whose **theory of multiple intelligences** was published in 1983. This theory suggests that the traditional method of testing intelligence, IQ testing, is limited and that there are nine different types of intelligence to characterize the ways children and adults develop skills and solve problems. One's potential is correlated to his or her learning preferences. Dr. Gardner's suggested intelligences are as follows:

- ▶ verbal-linguistic intelligence
- ▶ logical-mathematical intelligence
- ▶ spatial-visual intelligence
- ▶ bodily-kinesthetic intelligence
- ▶ musical intelligence
- ▶ interpersonal intelligence
- ▶ intrapersonal intelligence
- ▶ naturalist intelligence
- ▶ existential intelligence

QUICK REVIEW

Which developmental domains would be addressed within each of Gardner's multiple intelligences?

Gardner states that, although today's schools and culture focus heavily on linguistic and logical-mathematical intelligence, we should focus equally on other intelligences. The theory of multiple intelligences encourages educators to reflect on how schools operate and make changes to ensure that teachers are trained to instruct in a variety of ways to meet the intelligence needs of all children. Using this theory can develop children's strengths and build confidence as well as provide teachers with teaching and learning tools that reach beyond the typical lecture, textbook, and worksheet methods.

SAMPLE QUESTION

14) **A reading specialist asks a seventh-grade student to design and create a hallway bulletin board advertising the school-wide book fair. This student most likely has strengths in which type of intelligence?**

   A.   verbal-linguistic intelligence

   B.   spatial-visual intelligence

   C.   bodily-kinesthetic intelligence

   D.   existential intelligence

JEROME BRUNER

Jerome Bruner is another significant theorist in the field of education. According to Bruner, there are three **modes of representation** in which learners interpret the world: enactive, iconic, and symbolic. These modes are followed in sequence, but they are not age dependent. The modes of representation depend on how familiar the learner is with the subject matter. This means that what is being taught must be appropriate and ready for the learner instead of the learner being ready for the subject matter. In other words, any subject can be taught to any individual at any age, but the material must be modified to the appropriate form and stage for the learner.

Bruner's **enactive stage** posits that knowledge is stored through motor responses. This stage applies not only to children but adults as well. Some tasks completed as adults would be difficult to describe in the iconic (picture) mode or the symbolic (word) form. In the **iconic stage**, knowledge is stored through visual images. Finally, in the **symbolic stage**, knowledge is stored through words, mathematical symbols, or other symbol systems.

SAMPLE QUESTION

15) **A prekindergarten classroom has several books with pictures and minimal text that help students master key concepts like counting. How are these picture books related to Bruner's modes of representation?**

   A.   They help young students explore concepts through iconic representation.

   B.   They help young students still in the enactive stage of representation.

   C.   They encourage young students to begin to make inferences.

   D.   They encourage young students to make a connection between written and spoken language.

ALBERT BANDURA

Another important theorist is Albert Bandura. His **social learning theory** presents the idea that people learn best by observing, imitating, and modeling behaviors, attitudes, and emotional reactions. Bandura's social learning theory includes a social element—the idea that people can learn new information and behaviors simply by observing other people.

There are three core concepts in this theory. First, people can learn by observation through three basic models: a live model, a verbal instructional model, and a symbolic model. A live model is an individual demonstrating or acting out a behavior. The verbal instructional model provides descriptions and explanations of a behavior. The symbolic model is when real or fictional characters portray behaviors in books, movies, television, or online media.

The second core concept is the idea that a person's mental state and motivation can determine whether a behavior is learned or not. Bandura theorizes that not only does external environmental reinforcement contribute to learning, intrinsic reinforcement, or internal reward, does as well.

The final concept of Bandura's theory is the idea that even though a behavior is learned, there may not be a change in behavior. In contrast to behaviorist learning, which states that there is a behavioral change once something new is learned, observational learning states that new information can be learned without behavioral changes.

Bandura's theory combines the cognitive and behavioral learning theories with four requirements for learning: attention, retention, reproduction, and motivation. To learn new information, one must be paying **attention**; any distractors will negatively affect observational learning. **Retention** is the ability to store and retrieve information at a later time. **Reproduction** is performing the observed and learned behavior. The last requirement is **motivation**. One must be motivated to reproduce the observed behavior, either by external or intrinsic motivators.

SAMPLE QUESTION

16) **A reading specialist is presenting the school's new sustained silent reading (SSR) program to faculty. This will take place every afternoon at 1:00 p.m. The reading specialist wants to use ideas from social learning theory. To do this, she should emphasize to teachers that during SSR time they should**

   A.   monitor all students closely to make sure everyone is on task.

   B.   meet with co-teachers to review lesson plans.

   C.   ask comprehension questions to confirm student understanding.

   D.   participate by reading a book or magazine of interest.

ERIK ERIKSON

Theorist **Erik Erikson** contributed to the field of child development with his **theory of psychosocial development**. This theory outlines eight stages from infancy through adulthood. Each stage is characterized by a psychosocial crisis that will have a positive or negative effect on personality development. Erikson suggests that a healthy personality is developed by the successful completion of each stage. An inability to successfully complete a stage may lead to the inability to complete upcoming stages. This may result in an unhealthy personality and sense of self. However, this can be successfully resolved in the future.

Erikson's first stage, **trust versus mistrust**, takes place during a child's first eighteen months. This stage is characterized by an infant's uncertainty about the world. These feelings can be resolved by a primary caregiver who provides stability and consistent, predictable, and reliable care that will help the infant develop a sense of trust and secure feelings, even when threatened. However, if an infant has received inconsistent, unpredictable, or unreliable care, the infant might develop a sense of mistrust and carry the feeling into other relationships, which may lead to anxiety and insecurities.

Erikson's second stage is **autonomy versus shame and doubt**. This stage is characterized by a child's physical development and occurs between the ages of eighteen months and three years. During this stage, children begin to assert their independence and autonomy and discover their many skills and abilities. Erikson believes that parents and caregivers should be patient and allow children to explore their independence by providing support and encouragement. If children are supported and encouraged, they will become confident and secure with their abilities. However, if they are criticized, controlled, or not allowed to exhibit independence, they may have feelings of inadequacy, shame, and doubt, and become dependent on others.

The third stage is **initiative versus guilt**, which occurs between the ages of three and five. In this stage, children continue to assert their independence more frequently while interacting with other children. Children develop interpersonal skills through play by planning and initiating activities or making up games with other children. If these skills are encouraged, a child will feel secure in taking initiative. However, if a child is not allowed to develop these skills, they can develop a sense of guilt—perhaps feeling like a nuisance—and lack self-initiative.

Industry versus inferiority is the fourth stage of the psychosocial development theory. During this stage—between the ages of five and twelve—teachers play an important role since children are now in school. Additionally, friends begin to play a significant role in a child's self-esteem during this time as they seek the approval of their peers. If children are encouraged by parents, teachers, and peers, they begin to develop a strong sense of confidence. If children are not encouraged, they might feel inferior and doubt their abilities.

The fifth stage, **identity versus role confusion**, occurs between the ages of twelve and eighteen. Adolescents in this stage will struggle to figure out who they are and what they believe in. They may try out different friends, styles, and belief systems on their way to figuring out who they are. Those who are successful will develop a strong personal identity. Adolescents who struggle in this stage will have a weak sense of self and lack confidence in their own beliefs.

SAMPLE QUESTION

17) A reading specialist is conducting a research study in her school to measure the effectiveness of teacher praise on levels of oral reading confidence. Which of Erikson's stages are the students in the study most likely in?

   A. trust versus mistrust

   B. autonomy versus shame and doubt

   C. industry versus inferiority

   D. intimacy versus isolation

ABRAHAM MASLOW

Abraham Maslow made significant contributions to the field of child development. Maslow is best known for the **hierarchy of needs**, a motivational theory that consists of five needs: physiological, safety, love, esteem, and self-actualization. He presented the idea that basic human needs are arranged hierarchically. To attain the highest level—self-actualization—one must reasonably meet the growth needs in each stage.

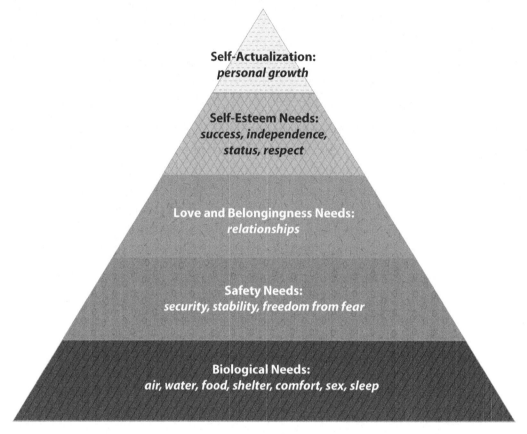

Figure 7.3. Maslow's Hierarchy of Needs

These needs are presented in a hierarchical order and shown in a pyramid, with physiological needs at the bottom and self-actualization at the top. Physiological needs include basic needs such as air, food, drink, shelter, warmth, sex, and sleep. Following physiological needs are safety needs, which include order, law, stability, protection from elements, security, and freedom from fear. Next is love and a feeling of belonging, or friendships, intimacy, trust, receiving and giving affection, and feelings of acceptance or feeling like a part of a group.

Maslow divided esteem needs—which appear after love—into two categories: esteem for oneself and the need for respect from others. Children and adolescents have a greater need for respect and reputation, as these arrive before real self-esteem, or dignity, can develop. The final level is self-actualization, or a feeling of personal growth, self-fulfillment, or reaching maximum personal potential.

Maslow states that everyone has the capability and desire to move up the hierarchy. However, progress can be disrupted by the inability to meet lower-level needs. One's life experiences can influence progression up the hierarchy, and some may even move back and forth between levels, which means everyone will progress in different ways.

SAMPLE QUESTION

18) A reading specialist conducting morning tutorials worries that the physiological needs of a few students are not being met, causing them to lack focus in the morning. Which other professional might the reading specialist consult to help with this problem?

    A.   special education teacher

    B.   school psychologist

    C.   school social worker

    D.   attendance clerk

BENJAMIN BLOOM

Finally, **Benjamin Bloom** made major contributions to classifying educational objectives and the theory of mastery learning or domains of learning. He is best known for developing **Bloom's taxonomy**, a hierarchy of skills that build on each other from simple to complex and concrete to abstract. Bloom's original taxonomy was created in 1956 with the following categories:

▶   knowledge, or simple recall of information

▶   comprehension, or the ability to understand and use information

▶   application, or being able to use abstract thinking in concrete situations

▶   analysis, or the ability to break down an idea or concept into parts and recognize the relationships between ideas or concepts

▶   synthesis, or putting together elements or parts to make a whole

▶   evaluation, or the ability to judge material and the method of its purpose

In 2001, a group of professionals across the fields of education and psychology revised Bloom's original taxonomy to include action words to label the categories and subcategories and describe the process in which learners work through knowledge. These categories are:

▶   remembering—the ability to recognize and recall

▶   understanding—interpreting, exemplifying, classifying, summarizing, inferring, comparing, and explaining

▶   applying—being able to execute or implement

▶   analyzing—being able to differentiate, organize, or attribute

▶ evaluating—checking or critiquing

▶ creating—generating, planning, and producing

Figure 7.3. Bloom's Taxonomy

Incorporating Bloom's taxonomy into current practices has many benefits. One of these is establishing objectives or learning goals so that teachers and children understand the purpose of instruction. Another is that Bloom's taxonomy provides teachers with a framework for organizing objectives. From these objectives teachers can plan and use appropriate instruction, design and implement purposeful and valid assessments, and ensure that instruction and assessments are objective-driven.

SAMPLE QUESTION

19) A reading specialist is reviewing a teacher-created sixth-grade reading assessment that includes the following question:

What can you infer about Dr. Markham based on the passage?
A. He is a kind man.
B. He is an old man.
C. He is unhappy.
D. He is excited.

Which level of Bloom's taxonomy does this assessment item fall under?

A. remember

B. understand

C. apply

D. analyze

MOTIVATION THEORIES

Motivation theory explains the driving forces behind conduct. There are several motivation theories. According to **self-determination theory**, everyone has a perceived locus of causality (PLOC). People with a higher internal PLOC are more likely to feel in control of their circumstances and are motivated by internal rewards, or **intrinsic motivation**. People with an external PLOC feel that outside forces are controlling their behavior and are motivated by external rewards, or **extrinsic motivation**. Helping students understand their PLOC will enable them to feel more in control of their own behavior.

Attribution theory suggests that internal attribution (personality flaws) is assumed when other people make mistakes. Victim-blaming occurs because people tend to view the victim as a predictable stereotype. When someone makes a mistake, they tend to view the cause as external. People usually think of themselves as more complex than they give others credit for being. Blaming others and making excuses destroys relationships. Teachers should be careful about applying internal attributions to students and should help students understand that others are as multifaceted as they are. It is important to recognize when students, parents, and coworkers make limited internal attributions about other students, parents, and coworkers.

Cognitive dissonance theory refers to the uneasiness that is felt when someone has conflicting thoughts. To resolve cognitive dissonance, people will change their behavior, change their thoughts about the behavior, or justify the behavior. Creating cognitive dissonance carries with it the power of persuasion. Recognizing and helping students recognize where the internal conflict is coming from will help resolve it. As an example, Tammy and Tiffany are good friends who have a lot in common. They agree on everything. Tammy loves art and is excited that Tiffany is in her class. After the first week, Tiffany begins complaining that art is "dumb" and "boring." Tammy is confused because either her feeling about art is wrong or her feeling about agreeing with Tiffany about everything is wrong. Tammy will feel uncomfortable until she is able to resolve that inner conflict.

Classic conditioning involves learning a response to stimuli or the environment. If students view a classroom as safe, inviting, and interesting, they are less likely to miss class and more likely to pay attention. **Operant conditioning** involves eliciting a response through rewards or punishment. Intermittent rewards, such as preferred activities, praise, and tangible rewards, are powerful tools for modifying classroom behavior.

SAMPLE QUESTION

20) A reading specialist working with a group of second graders decides that she will use extrinsic motivation to increase interest during reading intervention time. Which is the BEST extrinsic motivator for her to use?

    A.   ask students to write down a goal and then develop steps to work toward it

    B.   encourage students to think of how much more confident they will feel once they are reading fluently

    C.   warn students of the long-term consequences of not reading fluently by third grade

    D.   provide students with specific, targeted praise for meeting or exceeding expectations

REVIEW

Read the question, and then choose the most correct answer.

1

A reading specialist notes that a second-grade student finds a story challenging to read independently but has more success with it during neurological impress. What can be said about this situation?

A.   The story is at the student's independent reading level.

B.   The neurological impress created a zone of proximal development.

C.   The neurological impress helped the student understand symbolic representation.

D.   The story is at the student's frustrational reading level.

2

Which of the following best describes scaffolding?

A.   methods by which students are encouraged to read independently for pleasure

B.   the way teachers plan lessons so that all students can learn from the same curriculum

C.   the method by which students are helped by more capable peers or adults within their zone of proximal development

D.   the way teachers or paraprofessionals provide live translation accommodations to ESOL students

3

Which of the following is an example of Jerome Bruner's iconic mode of representation?

A.   A student reads the word "gardening" by sounding out each letter sound.

B.   A student learns how to swing a baseball bat after explicit instruction.

C.   A student sees a picture of a pizza and says the word "pizza."

D.   A student understands that the plus sign indicates two quantities being joined together.

4

A teacher observes that after one student has begun to call out in class instead of raising his hand, other students are imitating this behavior. Which of the following theories explains this behavior?

A.   Jean Piaget's theory of cognitive development

B.   Jerome Bruner's modes of representation theory

C.   B.F. Skinner's theory of behaviorism

D.   Albert Bandura's social learning theory

5

A reading specialist and principal meet with an educational sales representative, who shows them a new software product. Its graphic displays are impressive, and it looks like it would be highly engaging for elementary school students. However, the specialist knows that the program's approach is not aligned with state standards. What is the BEST recommendation for the specialist to make to the principal?

A.   The software should be purchased, as it will engage and interest students in building literacy.

B.   The software should be modeled for teachers before any decision is made.

C.   The software should not be purchased because it does not align with state standards.

D.   The software should not be purchased because research shows digital reading programs to be ineffective.

6

A teenager who changes groups of friends is MOST LIKELY in which of Erikson's stages of psychosocial development?

A.   autonomy versus shame and doubt

B.   identity versus role confusion

C.   industry versus inferiority

D.   trust versus mistrust

7

A reading specialist is working with a high school English teacher to develop more rigorous assessment items. The goal is to write questions that fall within Benjamin Bloom's second level of understanding. Which of the following assessment items meets this cognitive level goal?

A.   What is the name for writing that tries to persuade others?

B.   Critique the following persuasive essay for its use of rhetorical conventions.

C.   Write a three-sentence summary of the persuasive essay.

D.   Create an outline for a persuasive essay.

8

A reading specialist is providing intensive one-on-one intervention to a third-grade student. Which is the BEST extrinsic motivation to give the student after she has fluently read a challenging text?

A.   Give her a piece of candy for each word read correctly.

B.   Encourage her to think about how good reading the text made her feel.

C.   Provide her with explicit and concrete verbal praise.

D.   Have her read the text once more to invoke a sense of pride.

9

A reading specialist notes that the school has limited communication with parents regarding students' reading progress. Which of the following actions should the reading specialist take to improve the situation?

A. Make a plan to meet with each student's family at least once per grading period.

B. Create templates that teachers can use to quickly send home information to parents via email or in print.

C. Hold a professional development event for teachers that emphasizes the importance of communication with parents.

D. Meet with teachers who lack solid communication skills and plan a training that will give them techniques for active listening.

10

Which of the following would be part of a needs-assessment as a reading specialist plans a reading intervention program at an elementary school?

A. sending out a survey to teachers

B. scheduling parent conferences

C. meeting with textbook publishers

D. holding a professional development event

Answer Key

Sample Questions

1) A. Incorrect. The teacher seems to be moving through the curriculum too quickly and not giving students opportunities for practice and reinforcement.

   B. Correct. The teacher might not know how quickly to move through the material. A meeting to discuss the needs of all students, individualization, and scaffolding is the best plan.

   C. Incorrect. Referral for evaluation of special education services should only be done if there is a reason to believe students need such services. It seems that the first line of defense is more appropriate classroom instruction.

   D. Incorrect. This is not feasible. All classrooms will likely need at least some whole-class reading instruction. The teacher needs to slow the pace of the lessons as a first step.

2) A. Incorrect. Tier 3 interventions are more intense, individualized intervention services.

   B. Incorrect. This is not directly related to providing such services during core instructional time.

   C. Correct. Pull-out intervention services remove a student from core instruction if given during class time. This is important for reading specialists to consider when designing reading programs.

   D. Incorrect. Students will be more or less focused at a given time of day depending on learning style and other factors.

3) A. Incorrect. Allowing choice of topic usually encourages students to make a selection based on personal interests.

   B. Incorrect. Some students might not have these materials at home.

   C. Incorrect. Students need to learn how to use online sources, but providing guidance on evaluation of sources would be appropriate.

   D. Correct. Some students might not have internet access, a computer, or a printer at home. It is better to provide these resources rather than assign homework that not all students are able to complete.

4) A. Incorrect. This creates extra work for the teacher and does not help expand knowledge.

   B. Incorrect. The teachers are better served by seeing what they have learned in an authentic context as being modeled successfully.

   C. Correct. Teachers will be able to see these strategies modeled and may receive confidence to try the strategies in their own classrooms.

D.   Incorrect. While it might be appropriate to provide mentoring, this teacher will likely not have time to review everyone's lesson plans. It is also beyond the teacher's job description.

5)   A.   Incorrect. A core reading program would replace the existing program, not augment it.

B.   Incorrect. A parent or volunteer might use a supplemental/intervention reading program but not a core reading program. The teacher would use that.

C.   **Correct.** It is most important to ask about research proving the program's effectiveness.

D.   Incorrect. This might be a valid question, but it is not as important as asking about the research behind the program.

6)   **A.**   **Correct.** A book that students are able to read independently without frustration will be the most appealing.

B.   Incorrect. This Lexile level will not match the needs of all students, and students should choose texts that match their proficiency.

C.   Incorrect. This obscures the purpose of DEAR, which is to read silently and independently for a sustained period.

D.   Incorrect. Prosody is developed during oral reading, not silent reading.

7)   A.   Incorrect. A school psychologist or counselor may be needed to consult on behavior concerns, but this would still not resolve the communication break with the parents.

B.   **Correct.** The teacher should try to form a positive connection with parents and not focus entirely on negatives.

C.   Incorrect. Focusing conferences on metrics is not a good idea since parents may not be familiar with them. Further, a student is more than grades alone, so conferences should be multifaceted.

D.   Incorrect. Some conferences can include students, but this is not a requirement. Sometimes there are issues that parents want to discuss privately with teachers or vice versa.

8)   A.   Incorrect. This is not the most productive use of time in a room full of parents, who might not fully understand this quantitative data.

B.   Incorrect. This might boost parent confidence in the school, but it is not aligned to the objective, which is to discuss the new Read by 3 initiative.

C.   **Correct.** This is the most efficient and effective use of time. While the reading specialist will likely give background and specifics about the initiative, the bulk of the presentation is best spent focusing on how parents can support the initiative.

D.   Incorrect. This might be *part* of what the reading specialist discusses, but it should not be the primary focus. Some parents will not be able to volunteer in the classroom and might feel there is nothing in the presentation for them if this is its primary focus.

9)   A.   Incorrect. The fact that the program is backed by research will not be reassuring if the parent feels it is not helping her child.

B.   Incorrect. This does not help solve the issue and does not address the parent's concerns.

C.   Correct. Meeting with the teacher will help the reading specialist understand the particular needs of the student and why her grades are not improving. It might then help to determine what other types of interventions or services might be helpful to the student.

D.   Incorrect. While grades are the teacher's domain, this does not address the parent's concerns.

10) **A.   Correct.** Direct instruction relies on the theoretical roots of behaviorist theory. Students receive immediate feedback, which allows them to change their response as needed.

B.   Incorrect. Constructivism is associated with more indirect approaches to reading.

C.   Incorrect. Maslow's hierarchy of needs describe basic human needs not directly related to reading instruction.

D.   Incorrect. Gardner's theory of multiple intelligences posits that humans have multiple types of intelligences in different domains. This does not apply to this scenario, as it is solely focused on verbal/linguistic intelligence.

11) A.   Incorrect. This is true but is unrelated to mastery learning.

B.   Incorrect. This is true of systematic phonics instruction, but it does not relate directly to mastery learning since it does not specify one skill being mastered before moving on to the next one.

C.   Correct. In mastery learning, students must master each skill before proceeding to the next one.

D.   Incorrect. Again, this is true of most systematic phonics instruction but is unrelated to mastery learning.

12) A.   Incorrect. Research shows that shared storybook reading is very effective in developing beginning reading skills.

B.   Incorrect. Most kindergarten students will not be reading books, and grouping students strictly by skill level can be detrimental to self-esteem.

C.   Incorrect. By kindergarten, students should be able to listen to a short age-appropriate book being read loud.

D.   Correct. The teacher should be reminded that students of this age are still in the preoperational stage and are not yet able to understand abstractions like irony.

13) **A.** **Correct.** In neurological impress, a teacher reads the same text as a student almost simultaneously as both point to the words, modeling automaticity and prosody. The teacher is the "more capable" adult that scaffolds student learning in the ZPD.

    B. Incorrect. Semantic feature analysis is a grid system that helps students make connections between texts, vocabulary, or other items.

    C. Incorrect. KWL charting helps students think about what they already know and want to know before reading and what they learned after reading.

    D. Incorrect. Semantic impressions is a strategy in which students use vocabulary words from a story to write their own story and then compare the two versions.

14) A. Incorrect. Verbal-linguistic intelligence involves reading, writing, and speaking.

    B. **Correct.** This student is likely good at art and design, meaning they have spatial-visual intelligence.

    C. Incorrect. Bodily-kinesthetic intelligence refers to physical movements like sports.

    D. Incorrect. Existential intelligence involves thinking philosophically, not designing a bulletin board.

15) **A.** **Correct.** The pictures, or "icons," in the books help students understand concepts through a representation appropriate for their developmental level.

    B. Incorrect. The enactive stage stores knowledge in motor responses like walking, running, and so on.

    C. Incorrect. This may be true, but it is not related to Bruner's theory.

    D. Incorrect. Picture books would only do this if they were read aloud. Further, this is not related to Bruner's theory.

16) A. Incorrect. Monitoring students is important but not related to social learning theory.

    B. Incorrect. SSR is not the time for reviewing lesson plans.

    C. Incorrect. SSR is designed to be less formal and more free reading.

    D. **Correct.** By modeling the desired behavior, per Bandura's social learning theory, teachers can help students engage in the behavior they see.

17) A. Incorrect. Trust versus mistrust takes place during infancy.

    B. Incorrect. Parents are still the most influential figure in this stage. These are children in early childhood who are not yet reading.

    C. **Correct.** School-age children (five to twelve) need encouragement and praise to help them feel successful and not "inferior."

    D. Incorrect. Intimacy versus isolation is a stage in young adulthood in which friends tend to be the most influential figures.

18) A.   Incorrect. The special education teacher likely cannot provide solutions for tired and hungry students.

B.   Incorrect. These students are most likely hungry and sleepy, situations the school psychologist does not specialize in.

C.   Correct. A social worker is the best professional to help students whose basic physiological needs like food and sleep are not being met.

D.   Incorrect. The attendance clerk can likely only provide information on attendance, not possible solutions.

19) A.   Incorrect. Bloom's "remember" or "recall" category only asks students to recall or identify information stated explicitly in the text.

B.   Correct. Making inferences falls under the category of "understand" since students are asked to construct meaning and then draw a conclusion.

C.   Incorrect. "Apply" refers to using a concept in a new or novel context.

D.   Incorrect. "Analyze" refers to breaking something into parts and/or organizing or outlining information.

20) A.   Incorrect. This would require intrinsic motivation, which the students do not seem to have.

B.   Incorrect. This is aimed at intrinsic motivation.

C.   Incorrect. This would probably not motivate students and might alarm them.

D.   Correct. Praise is a simple and reliable form of extrinsic motivation. Young children want teachers to recognize their accomplishments.

REVIEW

1) A. Incorrect. The story is most likely at the student's instructional reading level.

B. **Correct.** The zone of proximal development is the difference between what students can do independently and what they can do with help.

C. Incorrect. A second-grader should already understand that letters are symbols for spoken language.

D. Incorrect. This text is most likely at the student's instructional, not frustrational, reading level.

2) A. Incorrect. Scaffolding involves assistance, not independent work.

B. Incorrect. Learning from the same curriculum involves pyramid planning within the Universal Design for Learning (UDL).

C. **Correct.** Scaffolding allows students to complete tasks and activities they might not be able to complete alone.

D. Incorrect. Translation services are an accommodation, not scaffolding.

3) A. Incorrect. Reading a word by sounding out letter sounds is symbolic representation.

B. Incorrect. Swinging a baseball bat is enactive representation whereby knowledge is stored in motor responses.

C. **Correct.** Knowledge stored in picture form demonstrates iconic mode.

D. Incorrect. Understanding symbols describes the symbolic mode of representation.

4) A. Incorrect. The theory of cognitive development is about children developing in a predictable sequence based on observable knowledge gains.

B. Incorrect. The modes of representation theory relates to matching the mode of representation with the learner's developmental level.

C. Incorrect. The theory of behaviorism is about repeating behaviors that are positively reinforced, and there is no indication that this behavior was reinforced.

D. **Correct.** Social learning theory is the idea that people learn best by observing and imitating the behaviors of others.

5) A. Incorrect. The software may engage students, but all programs must align with state standards.

B. Incorrect. It is good to get teacher input, but if the software is not aligned with standards, it should not be purchased.

C. **Correct.** Curriculum should be aligned with state or national standards and with other parts of the curriculum.

D. Incorrect. Not all digital reading programs are ineffective, but they should be aligned with state standards.

6)   A.   Incorrect. The autonomy versus shame and doubt stage is typically from eighteen months to three years. This is when a child first begins to assert independence and autonomy.

     B.   Correct. In the identity versus role confusion stage, between the ages of twelve and eighteen, children try to figure out who they are and what they believe in, so they may change groups of friends.

     C.   Incorrect. The industry versus inferiority stage is typically between the ages of five and twelve. This is the first time that friends begin to play an important role in self-esteem.

     D.   Incorrect. The trust versus mistrust stage occurs in infancy and involves building trusting relationships with caregivers.

7)   A.   Incorrect. Asking students to name something is simply a recall question.

     B.   Incorrect. Critiquing an essay is at the fifth level of Bloom's taxonomy, which requires learners to evaluate or critique.

     C.   Correct. Summarizing falls within Bloom's second level of understanding.

     D.   Incorrect. Creating an outline is at the sixth level of Bloom's taxonomy.

8)   A.   Incorrect. Candy is an extrinsic motivator but is impractical and not related to the goals of reading.

     B.   Incorrect. Thinking about feelings is an example of intrinsic motivation.

     C.   Correct. Praise is one of the best extrinsic motivators in education.

     D.   Incorrect. Invoking a sense of pride is intrinsic motivation.

9)   A.   Incorrect. The reading specialist probably does not know each student well enough to hold a personal conference. There is likely not enough time to hold conferences with each family every grading period.

     B.   Correct. Templates are an appropriate resource for teachers and will likely help improve communications if the materials are already created and the technique is easy to use.

     C.   Incorrect. In this situation, a professional development event would not provide any concrete or actionable materials or steps.

     D.   Incorrect. Meeting with teachers might be helpful, but communication from the teacher to the parents must come first. Active listening is not the most helpful training as a first step.

10) **A.   Correct.** A survey provides input from teachers and helps determine the needs of the school.

     B.   Incorrect. Parent conferences might be part of an intervention program but not part of the initial needs assessment.

     C.   Incorrect. Meeting with publishers would occur only if an additional curriculum needed to be purchased.

     D.   Incorrect. A professional development event would occur only after the intervention program is decided upon.

Practice Test

Read the question, and then choose the most correct answer.

1

A reading specialist is asked to give a professional development presentation on pre-writing strategies for fifth-grade teachers. Which of the following strategies is she MOST LIKELY to include?

A. COPS mnemonic

B. predict-o-gram

C. semantic impression

D. RAFT method

2

Which of the following components of language involves the study of units of language that communicate meaning?

A. semantic component

B. syntactic component

C. phonological component

D. pragmatic component

3

Which is the MOST important factor to consider when examining a home language survey?

A. succinctness of parent responses

B. the language in which the parent completes the survey

C. the possibility that the parent got a relative to complete the survey

D. the likelihood that a student might need language supports

4

A reading specialist is creating a school-wide intervention program to improve reading performance. What first step should he take?

A.   purchase an evidence-based curriculum

B.   hire a staff of interventionists

C.   conduct a needs assessment

D.   evaluate overall teacher performance

5

Which of the following is an example of an authentic assessment?

A.   After a unit on letter-writing, students are asked to write and send a letter to a person they know.

B.   After a unit on letter-writing, students are given an oral exam on key terms they have learned.

C.   After a unit on making inferences, students take a written multiple-choice test.

D.   After a unit on making inferences, students write an essay about what they have learned.

6

A reading specialist is observing a ninth-grade classroom with several English language learners who need additional vocabulary development practice. Which of the following strategies should the specialist recommend to the teacher?

A.   teaching fix-up strategies

B.   using a language experience approach (LEA)

C.   instruction in common idioms

D.   incidental vocabulary learning

7

While using a QAR strategy, which types of questions do not require students to consider text evidence in their response?

A.   Right There questions

B.   Think and Search questions

C.   Author and You questions

D.   On My Own questions

8

Which of the following statements describes an effective reading curriculum?

A.   It is based on incidental phonics instruction.

B.   It is explicit and systematic.

C.   It contains digital texts.

D.   It is continuous from kindergarten through twelfth grade.

9

Which of the following would make the greatest impact on students' writing abilities?

A.   inviting professional writers to share their experiences with the class

B.   setting aside time each day for sentence diagramming and oral drill

C.   having students write only about topics they care about deeply

D.   allowing time for writing each day or during each class

10

Which of the following is an essential characteristic of effective guided storybook reading?

A.   students seated in a semicircle around the teacher with a specific place on a carpet

B.   a story that is narrated in the first-person point of view from the perspective of the protagonist

C.   a follow-up activity in which students draw a picture based on the climax of the story

D.   an interactive experience in which students are engaged in oral responses

11

Which of the following best describes the research on systematic phonics instruction with English language learners?

A.   less effective than a whole-language approach

B.   effective when combined with vocabulary instruction and automatic word recognition

C.   effective when combined with an emergent phonics curriculum that evolves with student interest

D.   less effective than an embedded phonics approach

12

A standardized assessment instrument that measures reading and language skills is widely used across the nation. Recently, educators have become critical of the assessment results and their ability to screen for possible reading disabilities, noting that many students are being falsely identified. What additional information would be MOST helpful for the educators to gather regarding the norm-referenced assessment to determine its current efficacy?

A.   when the test was last calibrated per a representative norming group

B.   which other schools and districts are using the assessment

C.   how many questions the assessment has at each cognitive level

D.   which other norm-referenced assessments are similar to the test

13

After a third-grade student reads a short story aloud, the teacher asks him the following question: "Where was the story set?"

This type of assessment can BEST be described as a

A.   benchmark assessment.

B.   summative assessment.

C.   informal assessment.

D.   standards-based assessment.

14

Which of the following is necessary for students to succeed in analogy-based phonics?

A.   existing knowledge of basic phonics patterns

B.   memorization of a sight word list

C.   ample access to texts at the independent reading level

D.   explicit instruction in code-switching

15

A teacher wants to help students make and refine predictions as they read. Which activity would BEST meet this goal?

A.   list-group-label

B.   semantic gradients

C.   Peer-Assisted Learning Strategies (PALS)

D.   Directed Reading-Thinking Activity (DR-TA)

16

A high school English teacher gives each student a checklist to compare their research paper against before submitting. Which of the following skills is the teacher helping students to develop?

A.   self-assessment

B.   fix-up strategies

C.   transactional reading

D.   guided writing

17

The distinction between continuant and non-continuant sounds is based on which of the following characteristics?

A.   if the vocal tract is in a fixed configuration as the sound is produced

B.   whether vocal folds do or do not vibrate as a sound is produced

C.   the degree of complexity of a sound when spoken

D.   the number of syllables it takes to fully articulate a sound

18

Phonemes present in a student's native language

A. can be rapidly transferred to a second language.

B. should be forgotten once English language instruction begins.

C. will have no correlation with English phonology.

D. might be pronounced incorrectly once a second language is acquired.

19

After yearly state accountability testing, a reading specialist notes that students scored much lower than the previous year on questions that assess determining meaning of multiple-meaning words in context. What action should the reading specialist take first?

A. Conduct a school-wide assessment to flag students who might benefit from English as a second language instruction.

B. Conduct classroom observations to determine which teachers are not providing adequate vocabulary instruction.

C. Conduct a needs assessment with teachers' input to determine the state of vocabulary instruction and what additional resources or trainings might be needed.

D. Conduct a professional development event focused on teachers whose students scored the lowest on the tests, focusing on ways they can improve test performance.

20

A reading specialist is co-planning a phonics lesson with a special education teacher for a group of students with intellectual disabilities. Which of the following should the educators consider in their planning?

A. ways that students can generalize knowledge

B. methods to increase summarization skills

C. strategies for building knowledge of cognates

D. differences in individual registers and dialects

21

A reading specialist is helping a sixth-grade reading teacher with strategies to integrate reading and grammar instruction. Which of the following strategies should the specialist recommend?

A. combining instruction in pronouns with point of view

B. combining instruction in diagramming sentences with making inferences

C. encouraging students to critique the way authors create a mood through word choice

D. encouraging students to fuse together sentences from a short story to make run-ons

22

A ninth-grade English teacher asks students to submit possible topics for their 2,000-word research papers. One student submits the topic of "television." What is the BEST feedback for the teacher to provide?

A. think about how to narrow the focus

B. develop a pro/con list based on the topic

C. focus on gathering primary sources

D. begin with an outline to guide drafting

23

A young child says the following: "To go dog me!"
Which component of oral language is he still developing?

A. phonological component

B. semantic component

C. syntactic component

D. receptive component

24

A reading specialist notices that the school's assessment instrument for universal screening for reading difficulties is overidentifying male students. Which of the following statements is true of the assessment instrument?

A. It is norm-referenced.

B. It lacks practicality.

C. It lacks consequential validity.

D. It is criterion-referenced.

25

Which of the following comes after the direct instruction portion of a reading lesson in the instructional sequence?

A. guided instruction

B. independent practice

C. leveled texts

D. curriculum compacting

26

A response to intervention (RTI) framework uses assessment data in which of the following ways?

A. to monitor student progress and adjust support

B. to provide annual state accountability data

C. to determine overall teacher effectiveness

D. to provide a model for enrichment planning

27

A fourth-grade student is faced with the following sentence:

She was green with jealousy.

Which of the following word attack strategies is MOST LIKELY to help the student determine what the word "green" means in this sentence?

A. using graphophonic cues

B. using orthographic patterns

C. using context clues

D. using morphemic analysis

28

A science teacher asks the reading specialist to help curate a list of titles for fifth-grade students to read independently about scientific topics. Which of the following should he consider?

A. whether the texts allow students to apply fix-up strategies

B. the degree to which the texts will permit morphemic analysis

C. the overall qualitative and quantitative text complexity

D. whether the texts are complex enough to be read with 50 percent accuracy

29

A preschool student cannot write her name independently, but after drawing a self-portrait, she asks her teacher to write her name as a model so she can copy it onto her drawing. This student is demonstrating which of the following?

A. phonemic awareness

B. procedural knowledge of writing

C. conceptual knowledge of writing

D. cognate awareness

30

A reading specialist is asked to observe a first-year fourth-grade teacher and provide feedback on a lesson. The teacher is working on a unit on adjectives and descriptive writing. She asks students to first describe an object in the room with as many words as possible orally in small groups. Each group then decides on the adjectives they like best and writes a paragraph that describes the object in detail. What feedback might the reading specialist give this teacher?

A. Oral language and written expression should be taught in a distinct, separate unit.

B. Written language should always take precedence over oral language and be undertaken independently.

C. Helping students see the connection between oral and written communication is a well-thought-out strategy.

D. Having students work together to produce written assignments will make grading challenging.

31

A reading specialist asks first-grade students to read words from a Dolch word list. What is the reading specialist screening for?

A.   phonemic awareness

B.   sight word acquisition

C.   rate and fluency

D.   basic phonics skills

32

Samantha is a fourth-grade student with many friends who is liked by her classmates. She is struggling to meet grade-level expectations for reading. Her teacher, who believes in Howard Gardner's theory of multiple intelligences, wants to tell Samantha's parents something positive about her. Which of the following statements should the teacher make?

A.   Samantha has strong verbal-linguistic intelligence.

B.   Samantha has strong spatial-visual intelligence.

C.   Samantha has strong intrapersonal intelligence.

D.   Samantha has strong interpersonal intelligence.

33

A prekindergarten teacher jots down notes as she observes a group of students at a literacy center. Which of the following is the BEST description of this method of assessment?

A.   formal, standardized assessment

B.   formal, unstandardized assessment

C.   informal, standardized assessment

D.   informal, unstandardized assessment

34

A fifth-grade teacher plans a lesson on digital dictionary skills. What type of vocabulary instruction is being provided?

A.   incidental vocabulary learning

B.   word-learning strategies

C.   semantic impressions

D.   semantic features analysis

35

Reading texts used for direct instruction or guided instruction should be at

A.   the student's independent reading level.

B.   the student's frustrational reading level.

C.   the student's instructional reading level.

D.   the target Lexile level for the grade above.

36

A reading specialist wants to give teachers concrete strategies for teaching students metacognition as they read. Which of the following resources should the reading specialist use?

A.   a list of self-reflective questions

B.   an oral fluency assessment rubric

C.   a bundle of leveled readers

D.   a chart of digraphs and vowel teams

37

A reading specialist providing feedback to a fifth-grade teacher suggests that students should read aloud pieces they have written. The reading specialist is MOST LIKELY suggesting this because

A.   students of this age are still developing oral language skills.

B.   the teacher should grade writing only after hearing it read aloud.

C.   this is a simple way for students to publish their work.

D.   oral reading is the optimal time for mechanics instruction.

38

A fourth-grade teacher asks a reading specialist to help her ELL students interact more with peers and build oral language proficiencies. Which of the following activities should the reading specialist suggest?

A.   the Frayer Model

B.   list-group-label

C.   think-pair-share

D.   predict-o-gram

39

What is the BEST definition of "procedural safeguards"?

A.   policies outlining parent and student rights and methods for due process

B.   policies outlining the procedures that a school will follow before suspending a student

C.   modifications made to the classroom environment to ensure safety of all students

D.   a triage of scaffolds to provide accommodations for students with disabilities

40

The authoring cycle is referred to as a recursive process because

A.   writers go through the steps in a strict logical sequence.

B.   writers may have to return to a previously completed part of the process.

C.   multiple modalities are used to create meaning in writing.

D.   proficiencies are developed only very gradually with much sustained effort.

41

A reading specialist wants to show that students in the fourth grade are not meeting national standards for reading and writing to advocate for funding for a new intervention program. Which of the following assessment results is the reading specialist MOST LIKELY to reference?

A.   Differential Ability Scales (DAS-II)

B.   English and reading subtests of the ACT

C.   Peabody Picture Vocabulary Test (PPVT-4)

D.   results from annual state accountability tests

42

A kindergarten teacher says to a student, "We study at the li/brar/y. Where do we study?" This activity is designed to promote which of the following?

A.   phoneme blending

B.   phoneme segmentation

C.   awareness of orthographic pattern

D.   concepts of print

43

A character map would be an appropriate semantic organizer for which of the following types of texts?

A.   a nonfiction passage about snails

B.   a poem about the beauty of nature

C.   a short story about a young girl

D.   an argumentative essay about school uniforms

44

What information do interviews with parents or guardians provide that home language surveys might not?

A.   insight into the language or languages spoken at home

B.   broader information on the child's educational background

C.   quantitative assessment data that can be used for placement decisions

D.   information on the family's immigration status

45

During a conference, a parent asks the reading teacher to explain her daughter's score of seventy-seventh percentile on the Stanford Achievement Test. How should the reading teacher explain the score?

A.   The student answered 77 percent of the questions on the test correctly.

B.   The student outperformed 23 percent of other test takers.

C.   The student outperformed 77 percent of other test takers.

D.   The student performed equal to or outperformed 77 percent of test takers.

46

A high school English class watches and then discusses a video of a TED Talk. They agree that they enjoyed the speaker's message but that his tone seemed too angry, which obscured the message. Which aspect of oral communication did they critique?

A. paralinguistics

B. prosody

C. morphology

D. semantics

47

A reading specialist is starting a new reading intervention program. After conducting screening measures, she finds that a group of students require Tier 2 interventions. Which step should the specialist take before beginning the interventions?

A. conduct a professional development event

B. hire paraprofessionals

C. inform parents

D. purchase a basal reading curriculum

48

Which early literacy activity would be conducted FIRST in terms of developmental sequence?

A. students reading high-frequency sight words from a chart

B. students reciting the sound of each letter in sequence

C. students manipulating words through phoneme substitution

D. students clapping out onset and rime as a word is spoken

49

A student reading a text at around 85 percent accuracy with at least 75 percent comprehension is reading at the

A. independent reading level.

B. instructional reading level.

C. frustrational reading level.

D. career readiness reading level.

50

One advantage of texts in a digital format is that they

A. can be read at a faster rate.

B. may have multimodal elements.

C. are always up to date.

D. are written at a lower level of complexity.

51

A sixth-grade teacher asks a reading specialist how to help ELL students navigate the writing process, particularly the revising and editing phase. Which of the following strategies should the reading specialist recommend?

A.   encourage ELL students to read their work aloud to check for grammatical errors

B.   pair ELL students with peers whose first language is English during writing conferences

C.   allow ELL students to type their essays and use the spell-check feature

D.   provide heavy scaffolding to include the teacher directly identifying errors for the student

52

A reading specialist working in an inclusive classroom has a student diagnosed with autism spectrum disorder (ASD) who uses a picture board for communication. What type of communication does this practice augment?

A.   pragmatic communication

B.   nonverbal communication

C.   receptive oral language

D.   expressive oral language

53

False positives in universal screening measures for reading difficulties are common because most universal screening instruments

A.   lack reliability.

B.   lack validity.

C.   are somewhat impractical.

D.   are quite sensitive.

54

A preschool teacher observes that an infant knows that an object still exists even when it is out of the child's view. This child is MOST LIKELY in which of Piaget's stages of cognitive development?

A.   sensorimotor

B.   preoperational

C.   concrete operational

D.   formal operational

55

A dynamic assessment is distinct from other assessment methods because it allows for

A.   instruction to be embedded into an assessment.

B.   decreased instances of measurement error.

C.   broader stakeholder participation.

D.   assessment without the use of written language.

56

A reading specialist providing Tier 2 interventions to a group of students notices that several of them get stuck on the word "simply," though everyone understands the meaning of the word "simple." What guiding question can the specialist ask to help students decode this word?

A.   Can you name something that is simple?

B.   What word means the opposite of "simple"?

C.   How many syllables does this word have?

D.   What does the -*ly* at the end of a word mean?

57

While observing writing conferences in a middle school classroom, a reading specialist hears a student suggest to a peer that he delete an irrelevant sentence from his essay. The reading specialist would MOST LIKELY praise the student for her suggestion to improve the essay's

A.   tone.

B.   organization.

C.   style.

D.   focus.

58

A reading specialist observes the classroom of a sixth-grade English teacher who uses class discussion on controversial issues as a pre-writing technique to help students form opinions for persuasive essay topics. The reading specialist notices that the discussion gets very heated, and several students appear to have hurt feelings. What feedback might the specialist give the teacher?

A.   Avoid oral discussion of controversial issues, as sixth graders lack the socio-emotional competence to understand diverse perspectives.

B.   Pre-writing activities should be conducted individually and not cooperatively, as diverse perspectives obscure the intended focus.

C.   Set class-wide ground rules about appropriate language and interactions with peers who express diverse or contradictory perspectives.

D.   Focus the discussion on topics that students have no fixed opinion about so that perspectives will be less diverse and discussions less heated.

59

Which of the following published assessment instruments would likely be used as part of a comprehensive evaluation for special education services for a student who may have dyslexia?

A. Goldman-Fristoe-Woodcock Test

B. the coding and mazes subtests of the Wechsler Intelligence Scale for Children

C. Vineland Adaptive Behavior Scale

D. Rapid Automatized Naming Test

60

A reading specialist is planning a program for community members to visit elementary school classrooms to talk about their careers and how they use reading and writing in their jobs. Which organization is MOST appropriate for this purpose?

A. the community library

B. the teacher's union

C. a textbook publisher

D. the chamber of commerce

61

Which of the following statements describes the greatest disadvantage of self-assessment?

A. It does not encourage metacognition.

B. It is only effective with very young children.

C. It provides only one perspective.

D. It prevents ownership of learning.

62

Why do young English language learners need vocabulary development activities alongside synthetic phonics instruction for accurate decoding?

A. Decoding relies on advanced oral language skills and expressive vocabulary.

B. Decoding includes making meaning of a word after it has been sounded out.

C. ELLs may struggle with digraphs not present in their native language.

D. ELLs may struggle with orthographic conventions.

63

In linguistics, the term "place of articulation" refers to which of the following?

A. the loudness or softness of a sound

B. the pitch of a sound

C. the variations of a phoneme

D. the way the mouth makes a sound

64

A seventh-grade teacher wants to activate students' background knowledge before reading a nonfiction passage on space exploration. Which of the following activities BEST meets this goal?

A. asking students to freewrite a story set in outer space with extraterrestrial characters

B. having students construct a Milky Way galaxy out of construction paper and glitter

C. having students think about careers of the future that may be possible because of space exploration

D. asking students to write down three things they know about space exploration

65

A reading specialist is collecting data on foundational literacy skills in a kindergarten classroom. She observes an English language learner complete the following exercise:

Directions: Read the word aloud. Then circle the picture that matches the word.

  BALL

The student sounds out the word correctly as /b/ /a/ /l/ but then circles the picture of the bug. Which of the following conclusions might the reading specialist draw?

A. The kindergarten teacher is not providing systematic phonics instruction.

B. The student has recognized a false cognate.

C. The student may need further vocabulary instruction.

D. The kindergarten teacher is not providing sufficient instruction in phonemic awareness.

66

A reading specialist presents a professional development event about an innovative new strategy for engaging reluctant readers. Several teachers think the new method will be "too much trouble." How should the reading specialist proceed?

A. continue to present different strategies at PD events until one is embraced by teachers

B. offer to model the strategy and help implement it in the classroom

C. provide case studies to encourage teachers to read up on the strategy's efficacy

D. encourage teachers to create their own strategies for engaging reluctant readers

67

Which of the following strategies is most useful for helping students develop coherence and organization in their writing?

A.   freewriting or journaling

B.   DR-TA

C.   RAFT

D.   framed paragraphs

68

In which situation would a reading teacher use an Informal Reading Inventory (IRI)?

A.   to assign students to a particular small reading group

B.   to determine students' progress toward end-of-year objectives

C.   to assess whether students have a specific learning disability related to reading

D.   to screen for developmental delays in speech and language

69

A student with a visual impairment may need specialized targeted instruction in learning to read because

A.   sociological foundations for reading comprehension may be lacking.

B.   linguistic foundations for reading comprehension may be delayed.

C.   cognitive foundations for reading comprehension may differ.

D.   cultural foundations for reading will be underdeveloped.

70

A ninth-grade student has completed a data dump pre-writing exercise with the topic of "autonomous vehicles." What should she do next?

A.   use her word list to prepare an outline

B.   think of synonyms for each of the words

C.   draft her essay using all the words

D.   select the best words from the list

71

A reading specialist is giving a professional development presentation for kindergarten teachers to promote the development of listening and speaking skills. Which of the following should he include in his presentation?

A.   recommendations for holding Lincoln-Douglas–style debates

B.   best practices when teaching oral recitation of prose

C.   ways to get the most out of show-and-tell

D.   strategies for promoting self-regulation

72

A preschool teacher is introducing the letter sounds in a sequence of one per week. He introduces /b/ in the beginning of the year but does not introduce /d/ until several weeks later. Why would he introduce the letter sounds in this sequence?

A. /d/ is a much more challenging sound for the mouth to form than /b/.

B. /b/ is a much more useful sound than /d/ and can be immediately applied.

C. Letter sounds should be introduced in an alternating consonant and vowel pattern.

D. Letter sounds that can be easily mixed up should be spaced apart to avoid confusion.

73

A reading specialist sees an elementary school teacher using instructional techniques that are not evidence-based. What should the specialist do?

A. stop the class and model a more appropriate technique

B. report the teacher to the principal

C. discuss different instructional techniques in the follow-up meeting after class

D. give the teacher several journal articles and hope that they will change instructional methods

74

A high school teacher wants to help students understand themselves better and apply some of what they have learned about themselves to their overall learning goals and education. Which of the following assessment instruments would be MOST useful for the teacher to use?

A. an intelligence test such as the Stanford-Binet Intelligence Scales (SBS)

B. a norm-referenced test such as the Wechsler Individual Achievement Test (WIAT-III)

C. a criterion-referenced test such as the Partnership for the Assessment of Readiness for College and Career Assessment (PARCC)

D. a personality test such as the Myers-Briggs Type Indicator (MBTI)

75

In systematic, explicit synthetic phonics instruction, word patterns should be introduced based on

A. students' interests and abilities.

B. degree of difficulty.

C. students' native language.

D. the order they appear in texts.

76

A teacher brings in a nature magazine, a thesaurus, a novel, and a history textbook. As he holds up each text, he asks students why they might read each. This is MOST LIKELY an anticipatory set for a lesson on which concept?

A.   making inferences

B.   choral reading

C.   setting a purpose

D.   identifying text structure

77

Peer review activities can be an effective part of the writing process when they

A.   occur within a structured framework.

B.   use homogenous grouping.

C.   encourage brutal honesty.

D.   take place without teacher assistance.

78

What is the most common pattern of syntax in spoken English?

A.   verb + subject + object

B.   preposition + verb + subject

C.   subject + verb + object

D.   object + preposition + verb

79

Which of the following BEST illustrates an effective use of curriculum compacting?

A.   A student selects their own topic for a research paper.

B.   A student moves through the first two chapters of the textbook more quickly than peers.

C.   A student skips the first two chapters of the textbook because the student has mastered these skills.

D.   A student researches a solution to a global problem and presents the results to the class.

80

Which of the following literacy-based classroom activities will also aid students in social development?

A.   choral reading

B.   writing conferences

C.   the Frayer Model

D.   Elkonin boxes

81

Educators working in inclusive classrooms that contain ELLs should focus

A. only on English language proficiency (ELP) standards.

B. only on content area standards.

C. primarily on IEP goals.

D. on both ELP and content area standards.

82

Which of the following activities BEST assesses knowledge of letter-sound correspondence for kindergarten students?

A. timing students as they recite the alphabet

B. timing students as they read from a sight word list

C. checking off known phonemes from a chart

D. checking off known letter names from a chart

83

A first-grade teacher using a phonics through spelling approach would MOST LIKELY encourage students to use which of the following strategies?

A. segmentation

B. deletion

C. blending

D. substitution

84

Which activity would a reading specialist recommend to a second-grade teacher to help students summarize texts?

A. written retellings

B. language experience approach (LEA)

C. QAR strategy

D. SQ3R strategy

85

Which of the following statements BEST explains why reading specialists should attend professional development events to increase their own learning?

A. They must stay informed about new research and methodology.

B. They must be superior to classroom teachers and display more knowledge and expertise.

C. They should network with other professionals to increase their future employment opportunities.

D. They should spend as much time as possible in the field and outside of the school building.

86

A reading specialist sees the following list on an elementary classroom board:

Long A	Short A
paper	apple
danger	catwalk
grape	scan

Which of the following spelling activities is the class MOST LIKELY engaged in?

A.   cover-copy-compare

B.   segmentation

C.   word sorts

D.   word families

87

A reading specialist is working with prekindergarten teachers to integrate a new music and songs curriculum into the classroom. Some teachers question the need for such activities. What can the reading specialist say to help the teachers understand the utility of the program?

A.   Such activities can help students develop vocabulary, oral language skills, and phonemic awareness.

B.   Such activities can help students develop letter-sound correspondence, orthographic patterns, and oral language skills.

C.   Students who do not excel in other parts of the curriculum may enjoy singing songs, which might build their confidence.

D.   Students need to be bombarded with auditory stimuli in order to make meaning of the world around them.

88

A librarian and a reading specialist are working together to order new books for a K–3 school library. Which of the following books should they select?

A.   books with Lexile ranges below 500 to reach all readers

B.   books with the highest ratings on Amazon

C.   books representing broad cultures and ethnicities

D.   books with elaborate illustrations to engage all readers

89

A classroom using an embedded phonics approach would likely include which of the following?

A.   phonics worksheets

B.   connected texts

C.   spelling lists

D.   vocabulary workbooks

90

A third-grade student is always first to finish his independent reading work, but he consistently misses many comprehension questions at a DOK level of 2 or 3. Which of the following strategies should his teacher recommend?

A.   making better use of graphophonic cues

B.   using a dictionary when needed

C.   reading texts at the instructional level

D.   slowing down the reading rate

91

Shared or interactive writing activities draw upon the theoretical framework of which theorist?

A.   B.F. Skinner

B.   Abraham Maslow

C.   Lev Vygotsky

D.   Jean Piaget

92

A reading specialist is making a list of scaffolds to help middle school reading teachers to follow the Universal Design for Learning (UDL) in their classrooms with ELLs. Which of the following scaffolds is the BEST one to include on the list?

A.   pull-out instruction on cognate awareness

B.   a supplemental curriculum designed for ELLs

C.   excusing ELL students from collaborative learning activities

D.   allowing students to use a picture dictionary or electronic translator

93

An educator conducting an assessment wants to know if a student has mastered the concept of conservation. Which technique is the teacher MOST LIKELY to use?

A.   showing a child a stuffed animal, leaving the room with the stuffed animal, returning to the room without the stuffed animal, and then asking the child if the stuffed animal still exists

B.   having the child's mother enter the room and then leave the room and ask the child if the mother still exists even though she is out of the room

C.   showing a child two pieces of pizza that are the same size but one has been cut in half, then asking the child which piece represents more

D.   showing a child two piles of blocks—one has ten blocks and one has five blocks of the same size—then asking the child which pile has more

94

A prekindergarten teacher uses a checklist to record the date students have mastered certain developmental milestones. This is an example of using assessment to

A.   design interventions.

B.   screen for possible delays.

C.   determine program placement.

D.   evaluate mastery of objectives.

95

A sixth-grade English teacher is reading through student journals. Though the journals are given a grade based on completion, what else should the teacher consider to help guide future instruction?

A.   gaps in student knowledge of punctuation and mechanics

B.   possible presence of undiagnosed disabilities

C.   need for targeted handwriting instruction

D.   any code-switching or use of a specific dialect or register

96

A prekindergarten teacher wants to expose students to a variety of sources of environmental print. Which of the following materials would be MOST effective?

A.   leveled readers

B.   signs and labels

C.   Elkonin boxes

D.   letter-sound charts

97

A reading specialist gives a talk to parents and community members about the importance of reading and speaking to children who are preverbal. Why might the reading specialist give such a talk?

A.   Most parents believe little interaction is necessary during the period in which their child is not speaking.

B.   Children with strong linguistic foundations will have stronger comprehension of texts as they become readers.

C.   When young children grow up without enough stimulation, they are less likely to enjoy reading.

D.   Some parents focus more on the transactional reading relationship instead of its oral language component.

98

Which of the following is a requirement for learning, according to Albert Bandura?

A.   motivation

B.   stimulus

C.   reward

D.   movement

99

Which member of the multidisciplinary team is MOST LIKELY to provide interventions to students to improve oral language skills?

A.   special education teacher

B.   reading specialist

C.   educational diagnostician

D.   speech language pathologist

100

A reading specialist observing a fourth-grade classroom notices that one group of students keeps scoring less than 50 percent on each spelling test. What recommendation might the reading specialist make to the classroom teacher?

A.   switch to an incidental approach to spelling

B.   switch to a developmental approach to spelling

C.   focus on spelling words at the independent spelling level

D.   focus on spelling words at the frustrational reading level

Answer Key

1)

A.   Incorrect. The COPS mnemonic would be part of a discussion of editing, not pre-writing.

B.   Incorrect. A predict-o-gram is a reading comprehension/vocabulary building exercise in which students predict how a set of words will be used in a text.

C.   Incorrect. Semantic impression is a vocabulary exercise in which students write their own story based on words from a text.

D.   Correct. The RAFT method has students ask what the role of the writer will be, who the audience will be, what format will be used, and what topic will be presented.

2)

A.   Correct. The semantic component of language involves meaning of words and morphemes, or word parts.

B.   Incorrect. The syntactic component refers to stringing words into sentences.

C.   Incorrect. The phonological component refers to the sounds of language.

D.   Incorrect. The pragmatic component refers to the way language is used for a specific purpose.

3)

A.   Incorrect. Parents not comfortable communicating in English may write succinct responses.

B.   Incorrect. Just because a parent is not fluent does not mean his or her child is not fluent.

C.   Incorrect. Having a relative help with the survey is common and acceptable if the survey is not in the parents' native language.

D.   Correct. Determining if the student needs language supports is the goal of the home language survey.

4)

A.   Incorrect. The necessity of a new or additional curriculum cannot be determined until after a needs assessment.

B. Incorrect. Interventionists cannot be hired until it is determined when, how, and where such interventions will take place.

C. **Correct.** A needs assessment is the first step that will drive the next steps.

D. Incorrect. Teacher performance is usually evaluated by principals or other administrators, not reading specialists.

5)

A. **Correct.** Writing and sending a letter after a unit on letter-writing is an authentic assessment because it assesses student knowledge in a relevant and real-world way.

B. Incorrect. This is an oral versus written assessment and does not involve applying what has been learned in a real-world context.

C. Incorrect. A multiple-choice test is a standard summative assessment.

D. Incorrect. Writing an essay is also a standard summative assessment, though it focuses on recall versus application.

6)

A. Incorrect. Fix-up strategies help while reading when comprehension breaks down, but they are not aimed at vocabulary development.

B. Incorrect. The language experience approach (LEA) is an integrated reading and writing approach, but it is not specifically directed at vocabulary development.

C. **Correct.** Explicit vocabulary instruction, such as lessons on common idioms, will aid ELLs the most.

D. Incorrect. English language learners need explicit vocabulary instruction. Incidental vocabulary instruction cannot be solely relied upon.

7)

A. Incorrect. Right There questions require students to identify explicit information in the text.

B. Incorrect. Think and Search questions require students to synthesize information from multiple parts of the text.

C. Incorrect. Author and You questions require students to make inferences, predictions, and conclusions based on the text.

D. **Correct.** On My Own questions are based on background knowledge or opinions, not just evidence from the text.

8)

A. Incorrect. Incidental phonics instruction is not as effective as explicit phonics instruction.

B. **Correct.** Any effective reading curriculum is explicit and systematic, meaning it is direct, unambiguous, and follows a clear and logical order.

C. Incorrect. Digital texts are useful, but they are not an essential part of an effective reading curriculum.

D. Incorrect. Continuity is helpful, but usually continuity from K–3 or K–6 is the most essential. A high school curriculum will be different, as there are different skills involved.

9)

A. Incorrect. Writers sharing experiences with the class might be interesting and would help students understand the writing process, but it is not the most impactful activity.

B. Incorrect. Grammar drill in isolation is ineffective.

C. Incorrect. Writing only about topics they care about might be more enjoyable for students, but it is unrealistic that they will be able to do this throughout their academic careers.

D. Correct. Writing as much as possible is one of the best ways to improve writing ability.

10)

A. Incorrect. Children seated on the floor is a common but not essential component, especially if there are only one or two children.

B. Incorrect. The point of view of the story does not matter.

C. Incorrect. Drawing pictures is an interesting extension activity, but it is not an effective guided reading experience.

D. Correct. Guided storybook reading can help students develop oral language skills as they craft responses.

11)

A. Incorrect. Phonics is more effective than a whole-language approach in almost all cases.

B. Correct. Vocabulary instruction and automatic word recognition are effective strategies for ELLs.

C. Incorrect. Students need to learn phonics in a systematic way, not in a way that matches their interests.

D. Incorrect. Systematic phonics is needed with ELLs. It is unlikely that they will learn phonics incidentally through an embedded approach.

12)

A. Correct. The norms established by the test makers may not be current.

B. Incorrect. Other schools and districts may also be getting many false positives.

C. Incorrect. The number of questions is not related to false identification.

D. Incorrect. Finding other, similar norm-referenced assessments might help if the instrument is ineffective, but this doesn't help further investigate this particular instrument.

13)

A. Incorrect. A benchmark assessment measures progress toward meeting final objectives.

B. Incorrect. A summative assessment is given at the end of a unit of study.

C. Correct. An oral comprehension check is an informal assessment measure.

D. Incorrect. A standards-based assessment measures performance against predetermined criteria.

14)

  A.   **Correct.** In analogy-based phonics, students apply knowledge of existing patterns, such as word families, to unknown words.

  B.   Incorrect. Sight word memorization is part of increasing automaticity, but it is not directly related to analogy-based phonics.

  C.   Incorrect. All students need access to a variety of texts.

  D.   Incorrect. Code-switching occurs when students switch between two languages or dialects. It is not related to analogy-based phonics.

15)

  A.   Incorrect. List-group-label is a vocabulary learning strategy.

  B.   Incorrect. Semantic gradients is also a vocabulary learning activity.

  C.   Incorrect. PALS refers to students partnering with classmates to aid in comprehension.

  D.   **Correct.** In DR-TA, students make predictions and then read up to a predefined point. They then refine their predictions based on text evidence.

16)

  A.   **Correct.** Students are being encouraged to reflect on their writing and self-assess it based on established criteria.

  B.   Incorrect. Fix-up strategies are used when comprehension breaks down while reading.

  C.   Incorrect. Transactional reading is a theory that readers bring their own background to a text as part of making meaning of it.

  D.   Incorrect. Guided writing involves educators or other "experts" helping students compose a piece of writing.

17)

  A.   **Correct.** Continuant sounds include vowels, fricatives, and nasals. They are spoken through a fixed configuration of the vocal tract. Non-continuant sounds include diphthongs, semivowels, stop sounds, and affricatives. They are produced as the vocal tract changes over the pronunciation of the sound.

  B.   Incorrect. Vocal fold vibration describes a voiced or unvoiced sound.

  C.   Incorrect. Degree of complexity has to do with categorizing sounds but is not related to continuant and non-continuant sounds.

  D.   Incorrect. Syllabication is different from continuant and non-continuant sounds.

18)

  A.   **Correct.** Many languages have similar sounds, and knowledge of sounds can be transferred rapidly if similar.

  B.   Incorrect. Students should not be encouraged to forget their native language under any circumstances.

  C.   Incorrect. Many languages, particularly those that originate from Latin, have similar phonemes.

  D.   Incorrect. Students will still speak their first or native language with fluency, even after becoming fluent in a second language.

19)

A. Incorrect. ESL instruction might be needed for some students, but this should be assessed at enrollment, not after annual tests.

B. Incorrect. The problem seems school-wide and not limited to specific classrooms. It is better to approach the problem from an entire-school perspective.

C. Correct. A needs assessment is the logical first step. The school may need a supplementary vocabulary curriculum or more teacher training.

D. Incorrect. Any professional development event should be focused on improving student learning, not improving test scores in isolation.

20)

A. Correct. Students with intellectual disabilities benefit from instructional techniques that help them generalize knowledge and apply it in context.

B. Incorrect. If students are studying phonics, they are probably not ready to write summaries.

C. Incorrect. There is no indication that the students are also ELLs, so cognate instruction would not be helpful.

D. Incorrect. Considering the differences in students' registers and dialects is important but is not the main goal of this plan.

21)

A. Correct. Combining instruction in pronouns with point of view is a logical way to integrate these two concepts; they are extensions of each other.

B. Incorrect. Diagramming sentences is no longer a best practice, and it is not related to making inferences.

C. Incorrect. Word choice is distinct from grammar.

D. Incorrect. Students should not be encouraged to purposefully construct incorrect sentences.

22)

A. Correct. "Television" is too broad a topic for a 2,000-word research paper, so the best feedback is to think about how to narrow the focus.

B. Incorrect. A pro/con list is a good brainstorming activity, but this will likely not lead to a narrowed focus.

C. Incorrect. The topic is too broad, which will make locating specific sources a challenge.

D. Incorrect. An outline should not be created until a topic is narrowed.

23)

A. Incorrect. He seems to be using sounds to form words. The phonological component of language refers to the sounds of language.

B. Incorrect. He seems to have some understanding of words and their meaning. The semantic component of language involves meaning of words and morphemes, or word parts.

C.   **Correct.** He is still developing the ability to string words together into sentences that convey meaning. The syntactic component of language refers to stringing words into sentences.

D.   Incorrect. He is speaking, not listening (receptive oral language). This is expressive communication.

24)

A.   Incorrect. The assessment is not comparing students against a norming group or other standard.

B.   Incorrect. The assessment is not impractical. It is overidentifying a certain student segment.

C.   **Correct.** Consequential validity refers to the degree to which an assessment avoids inequity in identification.

D.   Incorrect. The assessment is not criterion-referenced.

25)

A.   **Correct.** After direct instruction, a well-thought-out lesson should include guided instruction whereby students can apply what they have learned.

B.   Incorrect. Independent practice should occur only at the end of the lesson, after guided instruction.

C.   Incorrect. Leveled texts can be used as any part of the instructional sequence. This term describes matching the text to the reader.

D.   Incorrect. Curriculum compacting refers to advanced learners moving more quickly through the curriculum by skipping parts they have already mastered.

26)

A.   **Correct.** Assessments are used frequently in an RTI framework to monitor progress and adjust tiered supports.

B.   Incorrect. End-of-year standards-based assessments are used to provide annual state accountability data.

C.   Incorrect. Teacher effectiveness is measured based on numerous factors, not just assessment data.

D.   Incorrect. Assessment data can help identify students who might benefit from enrichment, but enrichment is not part of the RTI framework.

27)

A.   Incorrect. The student can likely sound out the word easily.

B.   Incorrect. The student can likely sound out the word and will not need to identify spelling patterns.

C.   **Correct.** If the student knows what "jealousy" means, then this context can help determine what "green" means in this sentence.

D.   Incorrect. "Green" is a relatively easy word to decode that most fourth graders should be able to read. It has no affixes, so morphemic analysis is not helpful.

28)

A.   Incorrect. Texts at the independent reading level should be relatively easy for students to read. Selection should not be based on whether texts can cause comprehension breakdowns.

B.   Incorrect. These texts are for science study, not for examining the structure of words.

C.   Correct. The specialist would want to consider such things as Lexile level, length, and vocabulary, as well as qualitative features such as overall knowledge demands.

D.   Incorrect. This describes texts at the frustrational reading level, which should not be used for independent reading.

29)

A.   Incorrect. The student is not demonstrating an understanding of the sounds or phonemes in words.

B.   Incorrect. The student is not demonstrating how to form the letters of her name independently.

C.   Correct. The student is demonstrating an understanding that the letters of her name will label the picture. This is an understanding of the concept of writing in that it is used to communicate meaning.

D.   Incorrect. Cognates are words that have similar forms in two languages. This is helpful for ELL students, but this scenario does not represent an awareness of cognates.

30)

A.   Incorrect. While oral language can be taught separately, it is not necessary to focus on this skill in isolation.

B.   Incorrect. It is important that students get some independent writing practice, but it is not necessary in every assignment. Further, written language should not always take precedence over oral language.

C.   Correct. This positive feedback on the teacher's plan is appropriate and might help to boost the first-year teacher's confidence.

D.   Incorrect. This is not necessarily true. The teacher can plan how to assess the project using a number of effective methods.

31)

A.   Incorrect. Dolch lists are sight word lists that students should have memorized.

B.   Correct. The reading specialist is determining students' degree of sight word acquisition.

C.   Incorrect. Rate and fluency are skills that could be better assessed through reading a connected text.

D.   Incorrect. Dolch words are sight words that should be instantly recognized, not sounded out.

32)

A.   Incorrect. Samantha would likely be strong in reading if verbal-linguistic intelligence were one of her strengths.

   B.   Incorrect. Spatial-visual intelligence might make Samantha a good artist but not necessarily good with social interactions.

   C.   Incorrect. Strong intrapersonal intelligence means Samantha understands herself well but not necessarily others.

   D.   **Correct.** Samantha gets along well with classmates, indicating that she has strong interpersonal intelligence.

33)

   D.   **Correct.** Observational records are an informal assessment method and are not standardized. Standardized assessments are generally multiple-choice published instruments.

34)

   A.   Incorrect. Incidental vocabulary learning involves students learning vocabulary in the context of authentic activities such as reading texts.

   B.   **Correct.** Being skilled at using a dictionary helps students to learn new words as they encounter them.

   C.   Incorrect. Semantic impressions is a vocabulary learning strategy, but it is not related to dictionary skills.

   D.   Incorrect. Semantic features analysis is a vocabulary learning strategy that helps students think more deeply about vocabulary words.

35)

   A.   Incorrect. Texts at the independent reading level would be too simple.

   B.   Incorrect. Texts at the frustrational reading level would be too difficult.

   C.   **Correct.** Texts at the instructional reading level should be used for most direct instruction and guided instruction. These texts are challenging but still manageable.

   D.   Incorrect. Lexile ranges might differ by student, so texts should be individualized as much as possible.

36)

   A.   **Correct.** A list of self-reflective questions like "Do I understand?" or "How much do I understand?" could help students with metacognition as they read.

   B.   Incorrect. This rubric would help teachers assess oral fluency, not teach metacognition.

   C.   Incorrect. Leveled readers are not directly related to metacognition.

   D.   Incorrect. A chart of digraphs and vowel teams would be more useful for phonics instruction.

37)

   A.   Incorrect. Some students are still developing oral language skills. But reading a self-authored piece of writing does not target development of these skills unless prosody is emphasized.

   B.   Incorrect. Student writing can be graded effectively in its written form.

   C.   **Correct.** Publishing is the last stage in the writing process.

D.   Incorrect. Mechanics instruction would interrupt students and the audience's enjoyment of the piece being read.

38)

A.   Incorrect. The Frayer Model is a semantic organizer that helps with vocabulary acquisition.

B.   Incorrect. List-group-label is also a vocabulary-building activity.

C.   Correct. Think-pair-share will help students communicate with classmates after first thinking about a topic and then sharing their thoughts with a peer.

D.   Incorrect. Predict-o-gram is also a vocabulary-building activity in which students predict how words will be used in a text.

39)

A.   Correct. This is part of IDEA. Parents must receive written notice of these safeguards.

B.   Incorrect. A school should have such a policy in a handbook and should hold a manifestation meeting before suspending a student.

C.   Incorrect. Some classrooms may require such modifications to meet the needs of all students, but this is not the definition of "procedural safeguards."

D.   Incorrect. Teachers should provide accommodations as outlined in the IEP, but this is not what is meant by procedural safeguards.

40)

A.   Incorrect. Writers do go through logical steps, but this is not what is meant by the recursive writing process.

B.   Correct. In the revision process, for example, writers might have to return to the pre-writing or drafting stages.

C.   Incorrect. Writing can be multimodal if it uses sound or graphic elements, but this is not what is meant by the recursive writing process.

D.   Incorrect. It is true that quality writing takes time, but this is not what is meant by the recursive writing process.

41)

A.   Incorrect. The DAS is an intelligence test. It does not measure reading and writing performance against a set standard.

B.   Incorrect. The ACT is not developmentally appropriate for students in fourth grade.

C.   Incorrect. The PPVT assesses vocabulary, not reading and writing.

D.   Correct. Results from state accountability tests can be compared with set standards.

42)

A.   Correct. Phoneme blending exercises ask students to make words out of sounds.

B.   Incorrect. Phoneme segmentation has students breaking a word down into its component phonemes.

C.   Incorrect. An oral exercise like this would not help students determine or recognize orthographic pattern.

D.   Incorrect. An oral exercise would not promote concepts of print.

43)

A.   Incorrect. Character maps show actions, feelings, appearance, and dialogue. This is unlikely to apply to snails.

B.   Incorrect. Nature is not a character.

C.   Correct. The character map can help readers organize thoughts on how the girl looks, acts, feels, and speaks.

D.   Incorrect. A character map describes the actions, feelings, appearance, and dialogue of a person. It is not argumentative.

44)

A.   Incorrect. Home language surveys also provide information about home language.

B.   Correct. Parent or guardian interviews can provide a fuller picture of a child's educational background, including gaps in schooling or other situations that may have resulted from the family's relocation.

C.   Incorrect. Some assessment instruments do provide quantitative data, but a parent interview provides qualitative, not quantitative, data.

D.   Incorrect. Parents are unlikely to give information about immigration status, and it is irrelevant to a student's need for language supports.

45)

A.   Incorrect. This is not the way percentile on norm-referenced tests are expressed.

B.   Incorrect. If this were true, the student would have scored in the twenty-third percentile.

C.   Incorrect. The student outperformed *or performed equal to* 77 percent of test takers.

D.   Correct. This is how percentile is measured on norm-referenced tests such as the Stanford Achievement Test.

46)

A.   Correct. Paralinguistics refers to the parts of speaking outside of the words themselves, such as tone, loudness, inflection, and pitch.

B.   Incorrect. Prosody refers to reading something with appropriate expression.

C.   Incorrect. Morphology refers to the study of the forms of words.

D.   Incorrect. Semantics refers to the meaning of words.

47)

A.   Incorrect. A PD event might be helpful, but it is not necessary prior to conducting Tier 2 interventions with students.

B.   Incorrect. Tier 2 interventions can be conducted by interventionists or teachers, not necessarily paraprofessionals.

C. **Correct.** Parent communication is an essential component of an RTI framework. Parents should be informed if their children are identified as being at-risk and in need of interventions, so they can support efforts.

D. Incorrect. The basal curriculum is the core reading curriculum already used in the classroom. This is not a curriculum used for intervention.

48)

A. Incorrect. Sight word recognition typically comes after phonemic awareness.

B. Incorrect. Reciting the sound of each letter in sequence is an early literacy skill, but phonemic awareness comes first.

C. Incorrect. Phoneme substitution does promote phonemic awareness, but it is more advanced than identifying onset and rime.

D. **Correct.** This is a very basic and simple activity to promote beginning phonemic awareness. Students can clap out /d/ /og/.

49)

A. Incorrect. Texts at the independent level can be read with 99 percent accuracy and at least 90 percent comprehension.

B. **Correct.** Texts at the instructional level should be used for teacher-guided instruction.

C. Incorrect. Frustrational-level texts can be read at less than 85 percent accuracy with less than 50 percent comprehension.

D. Incorrect. PARCC has established Lexile guidelines by grade, but they are not based on individual students.

50)

A. Incorrect. This is not necessarily true. It may take longer to access and scroll through some digital texts.

B. **Correct.** One advantage of digital texts is that they might contain audio and video that help communicate across different modes.

C. Incorrect. Not all digital texts are kept up to date.

D. Incorrect. Level of complexity is not a characteristic of digital texts.

51)

A. Incorrect. ELL students are unlikely to pick up on grammar and usage errors simply through reading aloud.

B. **Correct.** Having ELLs review their work with a peer whose first language is English is an effective way to use homogenous grouping and actively involve ELLs in the revision process.

C. Incorrect. All students should have access to native-speaking peers before submitting a final draft. Using a spell-checker does not allow for active engagement.

D. Incorrect. The goal is to involve the student in the process; scaffolding only involves the teacher. It also robs the student of the opportunity to work with peers and be an active participant in the writing process.

52)

A.   Incorrect. The picture board does not augment pragmatic communication; it *is* pragmatic communication.

B.   Incorrect. The picture board is a method of nonverbal communication. It is not augmenting nonverbal communication.

C.   Incorrect. Receptive oral language is listening.

D.   Correct. The picture board augments expressive oral language (speaking) and allows the student to use expressive communication with others.

53)

A.   Incorrect. Screening instruments that lack reliability should not be used.

B.   Incorrect. Screening instruments that lack validity should not be used.

C.   Incorrect. Most screening instruments are highly practical and easy to use.

D.   Correct. Because the goal of universal screening is identifying ALL students who might be at risk and might benefit from interventions, there are often high rates of false positives.

54)

A.   Correct. During the sensorimotor stage, at around seven months of age, children develop object permanence.

B.   Incorrect. The preoperational stage involves the use of symbols and egocentrism.

C.   Incorrect. The concrete operational stage is characterized by rational problem-solving.

D.   Incorrect. The formal operational stage is from adolescence through adulthood. It is characterized by more advanced, efficient, and complex thinking.

55)

A.   Correct. In a dynamic assessment, the zone of proximal development is used, and students are taught something or scaffolded by the examiner and then assessed again.

B.   Incorrect. Measurement error is present in all types of assessment, especially those that rely on the way an examiner behaves or interacts with the examinee.

C.   Incorrect. A dynamic assessment only includes the examinee and the examiner, not stakeholders.

D.   Incorrect. An assessment such as the Peabody Picture Vocabulary Test does not use written language. However, this is not a defining characteristic of a dynamic assessment.

56)

A.   Incorrect. The students already understand what "simple" means.

B.   Incorrect. Students know what "simple" means, so this is not helpful.

C.   Incorrect. The number of syllables is not relevant to decoding the word.

D.   Correct. If students activate their structural cuing system, they can make the connection that *-ly* describes how something is being done, because it is an adverb.

57)

A.   Incorrect. Tone refers to the attitude the writer has toward the subject and audience.

B.   Incorrect. Organization refers to the logical order of details within a text.

C.   Incorrect. Style refers to the overall approach to a piece as demonstrated by word choice and other rhetorical devices.

D.   Correct. This student is helping her peer ensure his writing remains true to its overall point or focus.

58)

A.   Incorrect. Sixth graders should have the socio-emotional competence to understand and respect diverse perspectives and interact courteously with classmates.

B.   Incorrect. Pre-writing activities can be effective when conducted individually and cooperatively.

C.   Correct. Rules such as "always focus comments on the argument, not the person," and "use the most respectful language possible when expressing disagreement" can help students conduct these discussions more effectively with fewer hurt feelings.

D.   Incorrect. Lively discussions are not necessarily negative and can give students the opportunity to practice oral language skills.

59)

A.   Incorrect. The Goldman-Fristoe-Woodcock Test assesses auditory discrimination.

B.   Incorrect. The Wechsler test assesses motor skills.

C.   Incorrect. The Vineland Adaptive Behavior Scale assesses behavior.

D.   Correct. Rapid naming is linked to fluency and can indicate the possibility of certain learning disabilities like dyslexia.

60)

A.   Incorrect. The library most likely employs people in limited fields like library science.

B.   Incorrect. A teacher's union will have few contacts outside of education professions.

C.   Incorrect. Textbook publishing does not present a broad perspective and people with different careers.

D.   Correct. The local chamber of commerce is likely to have contacts with a broad range of working professionals.

61)

A.   Incorrect. Self-assessment does encourage metacognition because it asks students to examine their own learning and mastery of material.

B.   Incorrect. Self-assessment, if outlined thoroughly beforehand, can be effective among students of varying ages.

C.   Correct. A self-assessment provides only the student's perspective, not multiple perspectives.

D.   Incorrect. Self-assessment does promote ownership of learning, and students assess their own learning at the end of a project or unit.

62)

A.   Incorrect. Basic decoding relies on having enough oral skills to make meaning of words, not on advanced oral language skills and expressive vocabulary.

B.   **Correct.** To truly decode, a student must know the meaning of the word after sounding it out. ELLs may need exposure to basic English vocabulary to help in this process.

C.   Incorrect. Though ELLs may struggle with unfamiliar digraphs, vocabulary development will not necessarily be helpful.

D.   Incorrect. Spelling conventions are not related to problems in decoding based on deficiencies in vocabulary knowledge.

63)

A.   Incorrect. Loudness or softness describes volume.

B.   Incorrect. Pitch is not part of articulation.

C.   Incorrect. Variations of phonemes are allophones.

D.   **Correct.** Place of articulation refers to where the sound originates in the mouth and how the mouth moves to make a certain sound.

64)

A.   Incorrect. Freewriting can be an interesting and creative writing activity, but it does not help students to activate actual background knowledge that may be beneficial before reading a nonfiction passage.

B.   Incorrect. An art project such as this would not activate background knowledge and is probably not developmentally appropriate for seventh-grade students.

C.   Incorrect. Having students think about space exploration careers might be a good extension activity after reading the passage, but it does not help activate background knowledge.

D.   **Correct.** Having students write down what they know about the topic will help them retrieve background information about space exploration to set them up for more successful comprehension of the passage.

65)

A.   Incorrect. The student was able to sound out the word, which means the teacher is probably providing systematic phonics instruction.

B.   Incorrect. A false cognate has a similar spelling in two languages but different meanings.

C.   **Correct.** The student was able to sound out the word, but not fully decode it for meaning since the student did not correlate the sounds with the meaning of "ball."

D.   Incorrect. The student was able to sound out the word, so the student seems to have adequate phonemic awareness for the exercise.

66)

A.   Incorrect. This would be time-consuming and might not result in a successful outcome.

B.   **Correct.** Modeling the strategy helps overcome teacher concern about it being "too much trouble."

C.   Incorrect. Asking teachers to research the strategy on their own without support would be a burden on them.

D.   Incorrect. It is good for teachers to come up with their own strategies, but not at the expense of trying an innovative strategy that has proven effective.

67)

A. Incorrect. Journaling is writing without an explicit focus on coherence and organization.

B. Incorrect. DR-TA stands for directed reading-thinking activity and is a reading comprehension exercise.

C. Incorrect. RAFT helps students plan for writing by thinking about their role, audience, format, and topic. It is not specifically targeted to coherence and organization.

D. Correct. Using framed paragraphs, students fill in scripted blanks in a paragraph with a focus on organization and coherence.

68)

A. Correct. An Informal Reading Inventory (IRI) helps determine a student's independent, frustrational, and instructional reading levels, making it a useful tool for grouping.

B. Incorrect. A benchmark assessment would be most useful to determine end-of-year objectives.

C. Incorrect. An IRI is not a thorough enough instrument to determine the presence of a specific learning disability. A team evaluating a student would likely use many different methods of assessment.

D. Incorrect. An IRI is not specifically focused on speech and language.

69)

A. Incorrect. A vision impairment is not part of sociological foundations.

B. Incorrect. Linguistic foundations refer primarily to oral language skills, which are not the most strongly impacted by vision impairments.

C. Correct. Part of the psychological or cognitive foundations for reading rest in the way the eyes work with the brain to process information. In a student with a vision impairment, this process may differ since the student may read via haptics.

D. Incorrect. Cultural foundations for reading comprehension are not related to vision impairments.

70)

A. Incorrect. The list needs to be refined before an outline is made.

B. Incorrect. Coming up with synonyms for the words might be an interesting vocabulary exercise, but it is not the next step after the data dump.

C. Incorrect. The goal of a data dump is to list ALL words even remotely related to a topic, so some may not be appropriate for the essay.

D. Correct. After a data dump, students can refine their list by circling the most closely associated words or crossing out unrelated words.

71)

A. Incorrect. Kindergarteners are unlikely to participate in such structured debates.

B. Incorrect. Kindergarteners are unlikely to be orally reciting prose.

C. Correct. Show-and-tell can help young students develop both listening and speaking skills.

D.   Incorrect. Promoting self-regulation is an appropriate professional development topic, but it is not related to the development of speaking skills.

72)

A.   Incorrect. Both /d/ and /b/ are similarly formed by the mouth.

B.   Incorrect. Both /d/ and /b/ have similar utility.

C.   Incorrect. There is no rule on alternating consonant and vowel sounds.

D.   Correct. The /d/ and /b/ sounds are very similar. To avoid confusion, it is best to introduce them spaced apart.

73)

A.   Incorrect. Interrupting the class to model a strategy would likely make the teacher feel disrespected. The classroom teacher should be allowed to retain control of the classroom.

B.   Incorrect. The reading specialist has a responsibility to take action and mentor the teacher as best as possible.

C.   Correct. Discussing the issue after class is the most tactful and effective solution.

D.   Incorrect. This type of indirect approach might not cause the teacher to reconsider their methodology.

74)

A.   Incorrect. An intelligence test might discourage some students who do not perform well.

B.   Incorrect. The WIAT-III tests academic achievement and would not necessarily help students better understand themselves.

C.   Incorrect. PARCC also tests academic achievement and mastery of specific learning objectives.

D.   Correct. A personality test would help students learn about themselves: the way they react to situations, how they interact with others, and so on.

75)

A.   Incorrect. Student abilities will increase as they are introduced to more complex patterns.

B.   Correct. Part of systematic phonics instruction is introducing word patterns in a purposeful sequence based on degree of difficulty.

C.   Incorrect. While students can transfer existing phonics knowledge from their native language, this does not typically determine the order in which word patterns are introduced.

D.   Incorrect. The order of word patterns in texts is related more to an incidental phonics approach or an embedded phonics approach.

76)

A.   Incorrect. Students are not making inferences because the purpose for each is quite clear.

B.   Incorrect. Choral reading involves the class reading aloud together and is designed to improve fluency.

C. **Correct.** Setting a purpose helps students think about the purpose they will have for reading different types of texts.

D. Incorrect. The students are not examining the way each text is organized. They are thinking about why a person might read each.

77)

A. **Correct.** Peer review activities should occur within a carefully structured framework so that students have explicit and targeted tasks.

B. Incorrect. Peer review activities can be successful with a variety of grouping strategies.

C. Incorrect. This is not appropriate. Some students may not know how to be brutally honest without hurting other students' feelings.

D. Incorrect. Teachers should carefully monitor peer review activities and help students stay on track, offering guidance and feedback as appropriate.

78)

A. Incorrect. A verb + subject + object pattern would be "Bake I a cake."

B. Incorrect. A preposition + verb + subject pattern would be "For you bake I (a cake)."

C. **Correct.** The subject + verb + object pattern is "I bake a cake."

D. Incorrect. An object + preposition + verb pattern makes no sense.

79)

A. Incorrect. A student selecting a topic is an example of choice, not curriculum compacting.

B. Incorrect. A student moving through materials quickly is an example of acceleration.

C. **Correct.** Curriculum compacting allows for advanced students to move on to new material more quickly than peers if they have demonstrated mastery of skills.

D. Incorrect. This describes project-based learning.

80)

A. Incorrect. Choral reading involves no social interaction, as students are reading synchronously.

B. **Correct.** Writing conferences help students learn to give constructive feedback and be aware of others' feelings.

C. Incorrect. The Frayer Model is a graphic organizer to promote vocabulary development.

D. Incorrect. Elkonin boxes help students identify phonemes in words.

81)

A. Incorrect. Students need to build proficiencies in content area standards as well as ELP standards.

B. Incorrect. Students need to master English language proficiency standards and content area standards.

C. Incorrect. Unless eligible for both language learning support and special education services, ELLs will not have an IEP.

D.   **Correct.** Educators should focus on both content-specific standards and helping students develop English language proficiency.

82)

A.   Incorrect. Timing students reciting the alphabet assesses only knowledge of letter names.

B.   Incorrect. Timing students reading from a sight word list assesses automaticity/sight word recognition.

C.   **Correct.** Students can use a letter-sound chart to check off each phoneme, or letter sound, they know.

D.   Incorrect. Checking off letter names assesses only knowledge of letter names, not knowledge of letter sounds.

83)

A.   **Correct.** A phonics through spelling approach encourages students to segment words into their individual phonemes and then write each.

B.   Incorrect. Students would not delete phonemes in a phonics through spelling approach.

C.   Incorrect. Blending is used when decoding words while reading, not necessarily while spelling.

D.   Incorrect. Students would not be substituting phonemes to spell words in a phonics through spelling approach.

84)

A.   **Correct.** Written retellings have young students write a few sentences about what they have read.

B.   Incorrect. The language experience approach (LEA) involves the class creating and reading a story based on a shared experience.

C.   Incorrect. QAR strategy helps students determine what type of question is being asked.

D.   Incorrect. SQ3R strategy is an overall reading comprehension strategy (survey, question, read, recite, review).

85)

A.   **Correct.** Keeping current on the newest techniques and research is the best way for reading specialists to increase their learning.

B.   Incorrect. The reading specialist should be a valuable resource for reading instruction, but the goal is not to be superior to teachers or more knowledgeable than them.

C.   Incorrect. Networking is an advantage of in-person events only, and some PD events are asynchronous or web-based.

D.   Incorrect. The reading specialist should spend most of their time in classrooms observing and assisting teachers.

86)

A.   Incorrect. There is no indication that students are writing the words from memory and then checking them.

B.   Incorrect. The words are not segmented based on phonemes or syllables or any other segment.

C.   Correct. Word sorts are a way for students to sort spelling words into categories based on orthographic patterns.

D.   Incorrect. Word families are words that all have similar structures, like "peach," "reach," and "each."

87)

A.   Correct. Singing songs is a great way to build vocabulary, oral language, and phonemic skills in young children.

B.   Incorrect. Singing songs will mainly help develop oral language skills, not orthographic skills or letter-sound correspondence.

C.   Incorrect. One cannot know that students who are weak in other areas may excel at singing songs.

D.   Incorrect. It is important to provide many opportunities for students to listen and respond, but they do not need to be "bombarded with auditory stimuli."

88)

A.   Incorrect. A Lexile range below 500 leaves out more advanced readers who might want more challenging texts.

B.   Incorrect. Amazon ratings do not necessarily mean the title is appropriate, though ratings from a more education-oriented source (such as the *School Library Journal*) might be referenced.

C.   Correct. It is important that reading materials represent broad cultures and ethnicities.

D.   Incorrect. By third grade, students will be reading more diverse texts, some of which might not include "elaborate illustrations."

89)

A.   Incorrect. An embedded phonics approach uses authentic reading experiences, not worksheets.

B.   Correct. An embedded phonics approach uses connected texts and teaches phonics explicitly only as needed.

C.   Incorrect. Spelling lists are not related to an embedded phonics approach.

D.   Incorrect. Vocabulary worksheets are not related to embedded phonics.

90)

A.   Incorrect. Decoding does not seem to be the issue; he just needs to slow his pace to better analyze what he is reading.

B.   Incorrect. The issue does not seem to be related to vocabulary.

C.   Incorrect. It does not seem like the text is too easy or hard for the student; he just needs to read it more slowly.

D.   Correct. Slowing the reading rate is a helpful fix-up strategy when comprehension breaks down, and it can increase comprehension of challenging parts of a text.

91)

A. Incorrect. Skinner was a proponent of behaviorism, or a learned response to environmental stimulus.

B. Incorrect. Maslow's work focuses on the hierarchy of human needs.

C. Correct. Vygotsky's zone of proximal development is the space in which a learner can accomplish something with the help of someone more skilled. This is similar to interactive writing, in which a teacher or "expert" aids in the process.

D. Incorrect. Piaget's work was more focused on developmental stages, not scaffolding of learning by a more capable individual.

92)

A. Incorrect. Pull-out instruction does not allow for all students to learn from the same curriculum and thus does not follow UDL.

B. Incorrect. A curriculum designed only for ELLs does not follow UDL principles.

C. Incorrect. Dismissing ELLs from group activities would isolate them and does not follow UDL principles.

D. Correct. A picture dictionary or electronic translator would allow ELLs to participate fully in activities by helping them with vocabulary.

93)

A. Incorrect. This activity would assess object permanence.

B. Incorrect. This activity would also assess object permanence and would possibly upset the child.

C. Correct. If the child says, "They are the same," then the child has mastered the concept of conservation.

D. Incorrect. This activity assesses math skills and counting ability, not conservation.

94)

A. Incorrect. The teacher is not designing interventions based on the assessment data.

B. Correct. Screening for possible delays is a way to assess developmental milestones.

C. Incorrect. The data is not being used to determine which class or group the students should be placed in.

D. Incorrect. Developmental milestones are not the same as learning objectives.

95)

A. Correct. Knowing student skill gaps will help the teacher target instruction.

B. Incorrect. Undiagnosed disabilities will not likely be evident in students' journals.

C. Incorrect. Sixth grade typically does not involve handwriting instruction.

D. Incorrect. In an informal writing assignment like journaling, it might be appropriate for students to code-switch or use a dialect or register.

96)

A. Incorrect. Students do not encounter leveled readers in their environment. Pre-K students will probably not be using leveled readers.

B.   **Correct.** Signs and labels in the classroom are good sources of environmental print that can help students develop print awareness.

C.   Incorrect. Elkonin boxes are not environmental print. They are an intentional exercise to promote phonemic awareness.

D.   Incorrect. Letter-sound charts are explicit instructional material, not environmental print.

97)

A.   Incorrect. Most parents know that they must interact with their child.

B.   **Correct.** Students with a strong linguistic foundation, including oral language development, will be stronger readers.

C.   Incorrect. There are many factors that can contribute to reading difficulties, and lack of stimulation is not necessarily a common issue.

D.   Incorrect. Most parents do not study educational theory and are unaware of transactional reading theory.

98)

A.   **Correct.** Bandura's social learning theory posits that learners must have attention, retention, reproduction, and motivation in order to learn something.

B.   Incorrect. Stimulus is related to pure behaviorist theory.

C.   Incorrect. When a learner is given a reward or punishment based on response to a stimulus, this is part of pure behaviorist theory.

D.   Incorrect. It is not necessary for a learner to physically move, according to Albert Bandura.

99)

A.   Incorrect. The speech language pathologist, not the special education teacher, generally provides interventions to students to improve oral language skills.

B.   Incorrect. The reading specialist may work with students to improve oral language skills to an extent, but the speech language pathologist specializes in these interventions.

C.   Incorrect. The educational diagnostician is most qualified to diagnose learning disabilities, not necessarily give oral language interventions.

D.   **Correct.** Many students who need interventions to improve oral language skills get these services from a speech language pathologist.

100)

A.   Incorrect. An incidental spelling approach would be ineffective.

B.   **Correct.** With a developmental approach, the teacher could tailor spelling instruction and assessment to each student's current level.

C.   Incorrect. Spelling words are typically pulled from a student's instructional, not independent, spelling level.

D.   Incorrect. Students will be unable to decode spelling words at the frustrational level.

To take your second TExES Reading

Specialist practice test, follow this link:

www.cirrustestprep.com/texes-reading-online-resources.

Made in the USA
Coppell, TX
22 December 2022

90577245R00149